W9-DIM-753

WITHDRAWN

*Lonnie R. Helton, EdD*
*Mieko Kotake Smith, PhD*

# Mental Health Practice with Children and Youth
## *A Strengths and Well-Being Model*

*Pre-publication*
*REVIEWS,*
*COMMENTARIES,*
*EVALUATIONS . . .*

"Lonnie R. Helton and Mieko Kotake Smith have written a book that will be of considerable interest and importance to all who work with children. Designed to provide guidance to human services professionals working with children and their families, the text presents a strengths perspective, defining children's capacities and capabilities rather than their deficits. The authors have crafted strategies for mental health care workers as well as teachers, social workers, day care caregivers, parents, and others who invest time and energy in caring for the young.

The authors provide detailed case examples throughout the text, and weave these examples with explanatory material that provides a context for understanding critically important experiences and life events that can have devastating or rewarding effects on children's lives.

Perhaps the most significant contribution that this important book will bring to the field is the perspective the authors provide on the period of adolescence. They provide the most detailed examination of risk factors that I have observed in any account of this period, and they also offer a thorough account of the cultural and societal context for adolescent development.

I strongly recommend this book for use as a reference, textbook, or timely and relevant sourcebook for anyone seeking to understand how adults can help build institutions that support and nourish the immense capacities of all children and youth. The authors have written an enormously readable text that blends research, case examples, and highly useful action steps."

**Kathryn Borman, PhD**
*Associate Director, David Anchin Center,*
*Professor of Anthropology,*
*University of South Florida*

*More pre-publication*
*REVIEWS, COMMENTARIES, EVALUATIONS . . .*

"This book is a long-awaited text on the strengths perspective in working with children. The shift to a developmental and strengths perspective has been motivated by many realities of practice, including the need to move away from a pathology-based approach. This book brings together thinking from a strengths and well-being approach with that of work with children, in a comprehensive and practical way.

The book covers important issues ranging from theoretical considerations to practice approaches and child therapies. The inclusion of case studies and stories about children in each chapter offers the reader immediate application and therefore enhanced understanding of the text.

The authors include discussions about children's development in various cultural and ethnic contexts, discussing the empowerment of children in a global context, thus providing broad, worldwide applicability. A new way of responding to the mental health needs of children had to be found. It is for this reason that this text, particularly for work with children, is so welcomed. I look forward to assigning it to our students."

**Linda Smith, MSocSc**
*Registered Social Worker*
*and Lecturer, School of Human*
*and Community Development,*
*University of the Witwatersrand,*
*South Africa*

The Haworth Social Work Practice Press
An Imprint of The Haworth Press, Inc.
New York • London • Oxford

# Mental Health Practice with Children and Youth

## *A Strengths and Well-Being Model*

## THE HAWORTH SOCIAL WORK PRACTICE PRESS
### Social Work Practice in Action
### Marvin D. Feit
### Editor in Chief

*Human Behavior in the Social Environment: Interweaving the Inner and Outer World* by Esther Udang

*Family Health Social Work Practice: A Knowledge and Skills Casebook* edited by Francis K. O. Yuen, Gregory J. Skibinski, and John T. Pardeck

*African-American Social Workers and Social Policy* edited by Tricia B. Bent-Goodley

*The Social Work Student's Research Handbook* by Dominique Moyse Steinberg

*Mental Health Practice for Children and Youth: A Strengths and Well-Being Model* by Lonnie R. Helton and Mieko Kotake Smith

# Mental Health Practice with Children and Youth
## *A Strengths and Well-Being Model*

Lonnie R. Helton, EdD
Mieko Kotake Smith, PhD

THSWPP

The Haworth Social Work Practice Press
An Imprint of The Haworth Press, Inc.
New York • London • Oxford

Published by

The Haworth Social Work Practice Press, an imprint of The Haworth Press, Inc., 10 Alice Street, Binghamton, NY 13904-1580.

Cover design by Marylouise E. Doyle.

**Library of Congress Cataloging-in-Publication Data**

Helton, Lonnie R.
    Mental health practice with children and youth : a strengths and well-being model / Lonnie R. Helton, Mieko Kotake Smith.
        p.   cm.
    Includes bibliographical references and index.
    ISBN 0-7890-1574-9 (case)—ISBN 0-7890-1575-7 (soft)
    1. Child mental health services. 2. Teenagers—Mental health services. 3. Child psychology. 4. Adolescent psychology. I. Smith, Mieko Kotake. II. Title.
RJ499.H524 2004
362.2'083—dc22

                                                                                                    2003021017

I would like to dedicate this book to my late partner and best friend, Mr. Robert O. Evans Jr., whose strength, support, and love saw me through the initial stages of this project and continue to motivate me.—L. R. Helton

I dedicate this book to my husband, Mr. James A. Smith, whose strength, courage, and love have inspired me to realize my own strengths.—M. K. Smith

# ABOUT THE AUTHORS

**Lonnie R. Helton, EdD,** is Associate Professor of Social Work in the School of Social Work at Cleveland State University, where he teaches human behavior in the social environment and social work practice at both the BSW and MSW levels. He has taught child welfare practice and social work with children classes and has worked as a clinical consultant/trainer in treatment foster care and juvenile court settings. Before joining academia, he worked for 17 years as a clinical social worker in interdisciplinary programs serving children and families in the fields of community mental health, inpatient pediatrics, inpatient psychiatry, and developmental abilities.

Dr. Helton has written many articles, two book chapters, and coauthored the textbook *Social Work Practice with Children: A Diversity Model.* He serves on several community committees and advisory boards, and is a member of the National Association of Social Workers, the Academy of Certified Social Workers, and the Association for Advancement of Social Work with Groups. He does consulting and training as a certified child welfare trainer in Ohio, and continues to do training and work that addresses a holistic, culturally competent assessment and practice with children.

**Mieko Kotake Smith, PhD,** is Professor of Social Work in the School of Social Work at Cleveland State University. She has worked at community-based mental health agencies as Director of Adult Care and Director of Research and Training. She has also provided planning and evaluation consultation to county children and family service agencies. She has published several articles in mental health journals, including the *Psychosocial Rehabilitation Journal,* and chapters in two books on multicultural education. In 1998 she published a monograph, *Adolescents with Severe Emotional and Behavioral Disabilities: Transition to Adulthood,* based on a three-year study of middle school and high school students in special education classes.

Dr. Smith is currently completing a family strengthening project in which families of children with severe emotional disturbance participated to learn nurturing ways to parent their children. She is finishing a three-year research study of vocational rehabilitation of adults with severe psychiatric disabilities. The Community Living Skills Scale (CLSS) she developed 15 years ago is still used to evaluate mental health services for adults. Dr. Smith was President of the Ohio Program Evaluator's Group and Chairperson of the Women Celebrating Bicentennial in the Cleveland area. Currently she serves on the Cuyahoga County Community Mental Health Board of Governors.

# CONTENTS

# Acknowledgments

We would like to express our deepest appreciation to many people who have guided us through our professional development and while we were completing this book. We thank the following persons:

**L. R. Helton:** I would like to thank my friends and family, and especially my colleagues in the Department of Social Work who were there for me and helped me to find my own resilience in dealing with the loss of my loved ones in recent months. I thank my academic and professional mentors over the years, especially Dr. Kathryn M. Borman, Professor Joanne I. Bell, Dr. Maggie Jackson, and the late Cecilia J. Dwyer, all of whom inspired me by their commitment to improving the quality of life and well-being of all children.

**M. K. Smith:** I express my thanks for the support and guidance that many colleagues and friends provided me. They include all my colleagues in the Department of Social Work who extended unlimited encouragement and loving support, especially during the recent medical crisis, and all of my children who married me as their father married me. These children of a stepfamily have shown me that children achieve an optimal level of adaptation if their environment recognizes and supports their strengths.

We thank our graduate assistants, including Beverly Moore and Dennis Graham, for their library research and proofreading of the original manuscript, and Kimberly Baga, for her assistance in revising, formatting, and editing the final manuscript.

# Chapter 1

# The Strengths and Resilience of Children

> There is no greater insight into the future than recognizing when we save our children, we save ourselves.
>
> Margaret Mead

Child welfare and other human service professionals have traditionally viewed children in terms of their problems and liabilities rather than from a perspective that focuses on their strengths. Children have every right to be engaged, evaluated, and offered assistance in a manner that will enable them to become aware of and maximize their potential. The perspective presented here is an effort to accentuate the strengths and competencies of children that lead them to be resilient. Despite incredible hardship, many children are not only able to overcome these barriers but also achieve successful development and a quality of life comparable to those who have not faced such difficulties.

In this book, the authors refer generally to children as any individual from birth up to the age of twenty-one. However, when adolescents are being referred to as such, they will be called adolescents, and will include children ages twelve through twenty.

## THE STRENGTHS PERSPECTIVE

The strengths perspective emphasizes children's assets, capabilities, and attributes, as well as their adaptive abilities. Children's capabilities often are perceived marginally, if at all, when they are placed in foster care or residential settings. Historically, this viewpoint is consistent with the problem-focused nature of intervention with children, which centers upon dependency, family dysfunction, and abuse and neglect. Andrews and Ben-Arieh (1999) state that the body of knowledge about children's problems and threats to their survival far surpasses known information about children's strengths, satisfaction, and realization of opportunities. Furthermore, they offer two critical factors that must be considered in developing quality-of-life factors: (1) focus on the child as the unit of observation and (2) consider the child's perspective (Andrews and Ben-Arieh, 1999, p. 109). Moreover, Cummins (1996) reviewed twenty-seven well-being studies and identified seven domains of well-being: material well-being; health; safety; productive activity (e.g., employment, work, and schooling); place in the community (e.g., socioeconomic status, community involvement, self-esteem, and empowerment); intimacy; and emotional well-being (e.g., mental health, morale, and spiritual well-being).

Moreover, since the 1960s researchers interested in social indicators and quality-of-life measurement have addressed the well-being of children and youth in an effort to assist child advocacy groups, policymakers, other child and family researchers, the media, and service providers. This body of research has been especially useful since programming for children and adolescents has moved from institutionalization to family- and community-focused services. This research explores the condition of children, the monitoring and tracking of child outcomes, and the setting of goals (Land, Lamb, and Mustillo, 2001).

The strengths perspective suggests that children possess promising qualities for healthy development and should not be seen as victims of circumstance. The strengths perspective leads to intervention emphasizing individuals' capacities, talents, competencies, visions, and hopes (Saleebey, 1996). Kaplan and Girard (1994) state that people are more likely to change when their strengths are supported. Other undergirding tenets of the strengths perspective include empowerment, resilience, and membership. DeJong and Miller (1995) state that the assumptions underlying the strengths perspective are grounded in the belief that social workers must increasingly respect and utilize clients' ways of viewing themselves and their worlds in the process of intervention. Rapp (1998) suggests that the strengths perspective helps to elucidate and bring forth the hope that individuals have for success in their lives. Interventions founded on strengths will assist persons in building their willpower so that they can become engaged in step-by-step plans for achieving their goals. Saleebey (2002) believes that a number of practice trends in the helping professions subscribe to the strengths perspective and include developmental resilience, healing and wellness, solution-focused therapy, assets-based community development, and narrative and story. In such practice models children are encouraged to take pride in their positive traits and accomplishments. For example, children in a new foster home or school must be helped to maximize their strong personal assets, and adults must be forever mindful to reinforce children's resilience in coping within harsh environmental conditions.

Children's service workers and counselors are increasingly changing traditional assessment protocols and have begun to focus more on the child's and family's strengths. This process has proven to be a major shift in thinking about and planning for children with multiple needs and challenges. However, many workers feel compelled to address at-risk aspects of children in their assessment. Graybeal (2001) notes that social workers are mandated to complete structured assessment forms that inevitably lead to problem lists, pathology, and psychiatric diagnoses; agency forms are more likely than not dictated by agency policy and insurance (e.g., managed care) guidelines. Thus, children are often uprooted from their family environment and placed in what would appear to be a safe and appropriate setting before a thorough evaluation may be completed. However, the placement that is best suited for the child might actually hinge on a comprehensive assessment of such variables as unique learning styles and exceptional talents which might be best addressed in particular settings. The person-in-environment (PIE) assessment, developed by Karls and Wandrei (1994), shows much promise for evaluating children and youth placed as it assesses their issues within a broader framework of social problems and challenges.

Saleebey (1996) points out that practice which integrates a strengths perspective invariably takes into account the client's cultural and personal stories, narratives, and even folklore. This approach is a natural direction for children, who generally respond openly to stories and share their own life experiences through storytelling. For example, some African-American clients bring many strengths and assets to the counseling process that have resulted from their struggle against racism and discrimination (Westbrooks and Stark, 2001). Many children also respond to bibliotherapy (the therapeutic use of books) and joint storytelling with the therapist to share more openly their thoughts, feelings, and expectations.

In addition, the strengths perspective addresses the diversity of children's living environments, which may range from single-parent families to trigenerational kinship arrangements. Step- and blended families, which have been frequently scrutinized in the past for not meeting children's needs, are now recognized for their strong and nurturing qualities. Joint custody and shared living arrangements have afforded divorced parents opportunities to be with their children throughout their growth and development into adulthood. With a strengths perspective, children's counselors help children expand their self-awareness and enhance self-esteem by jointly coconstructing positive stories about family and peer relationships.

Human service professionals are frequently impressed that many children from deprived and abusive backgrounds develop into healthy individuals. Something in their personality enables them to cope against the odds and overcome extreme obstacles. This is the core of resiliency. According to Benard (1997), children who are resilient tend to view life more positively, are able to laugh at themselves, and find alternative ways of looking at things. And this resilience would seem to stem from the natural openness and responsiveness that are indigenous to being a child. Moreover, Benard (1997) describes resilient children as possessing the following characteristics: social competence, problem-solving skills, autonomy, and a sense of purpose and future. Saleebey (2002) emphasizes the presumption that all individuals have untapped reserves of capacity, energy, courage, fortitude, and integrity, as well as other assets. The strengths perspective perceives the client as the true expert on his or her situation, which often places the professional in the role of a facilitator or consultant (Sheafor, Horejsi, and Horejsi, 2000). Weick et al. (1989) affirm that although the professional acknowledges limitations, a conscious effort is made to accentuate gains aleady made, and they go on to state, "the question is not what kind of life one has had, but what kind of life one wants" (p. 353). With children, helping professionals must listen carefully to the child's language, self-perception, and feelings about his or her future in every counseling session and team planning conference.

Along this line, Petr (1998) states that children have little power in the world and maintains that adults are the authority figures over children in both families and social agencies. He refers to a concept known as *adultcentrism,* which is founded on the idea of shaping or molding children to fit adult prototypes and patterns of socialization. Stage theorists such as Freud, Erikson, and Piaget view children as incomplete persons who are on their way to becoming adults. Petr (1998) notes that if all goes well, children move through these stages and become well-socialized, acculturated adults. Children are viewed from this mind-set as being dependent, amoral, egocentric, illiterate, irrational, emotionally unstable, unproductive, and present oriented. On the contrary, adults are perceived as independent, moral, sociocentric, literate, rational, emotionally stable, productive, and future oriented. Petr (1998) also proposes four principles to combat adult-centrism in delivering services to children:

> (1) Take time to learn and value children as children; (2) Routinely conduct individual interviews with children; (3) Involve child as fully as possible in decisions that affect the child's life; (4) Support changes in social work research and education. (p. 21)

This intervention model will go far in empowering children to have a role and a say in what happens to them within the context of children's services.

The literature on the resilience of children is growing rapidly, and it has begun to question and inevitably conjecture whether children are born with certain characteristics that lead to resilience or whether they may be taught skills of resilience. Resiliency has been alluded to as the factors and processes that bring about successful adjustment and adaptation in the face of challenging and threatening circumstances (Garmenzy and Mastern, 1991; Werner, 1993). Resilient children seem to transcend severely neglectful and abusive environments to become successful adults. Resilience, it would seem, stems from both personal characteristics and environmental conditions. The personal capabilities of resilient children include but are not limited to strong intellectual ability, a positive attitude toward others, physical attractiveness, enthusiasm, and an internal locus of control (Downs et al., 2000). Moreover, resiliency in children is attributed to external factors such as the support and expressed interest of individuals outside of the abusive family and the parents' expectations of academic achievement and provision of at least a sporadically stable home environment (Smith and Carlson, 1997).

Research indicates that fathers play a critical role in helping adolescents become resilient (Zimmerman, Salem, and Notaro, 2000). In a Midwestern study of 850 ninth-grade adolescents over a three-year period, Zimmerman, Salem, and Notaro (2000) examined three measures of problem behavior: polydrug use, delinquency, and violent behavior. The ethnic and racial breakdown of the subjects follow: 80 percent African American, 17 percent white, and 3 percent mixed (white and African American). Father involvement was determined by scales measuring the average amount of time spent together, social support, and school support. Findings suggest that the involvement of fathers plays a vital role in helping adolescents eschew problem behavior. The researchers noted as well that the findings were the same when only African Americans were included.

## THE STRENGTHS OF CHILDREN

The strengths of children, essential for their healthy development and successful transition to adulthood, can be understood relative to challenges they face. Without those challenges, the strengths of children might not be evident. The emerging resiliency literature has made significant contributions to understanding a broad range of conditions from poverty to such personal characteristics as temperament and cognitive functioning, social relationships, and community resources contributing to healthy adaptation in the face of adversity (Windle, 1999). Resiliency is the essence of strength.

Studies have found that resiliency is associated with various outcomes among children. Those outcomes include academic performance (Noam, Pucci, and Foster, 1999; Walsh and Betz, 1990; Murry and Brody, 1999), drug and alcohol addiction (Noam, Pucci, and Foster, 1999), self-esteem or sense of self-worth (Markstrom, Marshall, and Tryon, 2000; Turner, 2000), physical health (Markstrom, Marshall, and Tryon, 2000), coping and adaptation (McCubbin et al., 1998; Cowen et al., 1990; Norman, 2000), psychopathology (Masten, Best, and Garmezy, 1990), and antisocial behavior (Garmezy, 1985).

## DEFINING RESILIENCY

Researchers offer several definitions of resiliency. Markstrom, Marshall, and Tryon, (2000) define resiliency as "an adaptive, stress resistant personal quality that allows an individual to thrive despite unfortunate life experiences" (p. 693). According to Norman (2000), it is simply "the ability to bounce back from, or to successfully adapt to, adverse conditions" (p. 3). Another definition provided by Noam, Pucci, and Foster (1999) is "the ability to overcome adverse circumstances and thrive amidst an array of challenges, rather than any specific behaviors, which allow them to successfully navigate the complex environments many confront every day and to make productive realistic life choices" (p. 61). These definitions focus on one's competence in making productive choices when one is surrounded by adverse conditions. Thus, resiliency works as a personal resource for navigating the environmental elements to produce positive outcomes. If one lacks resiliency, one has few resources to call on for overcoming such adverse elements as the divorce of one's parents or pressure from peers. In other words, one musters one's resilience to move forward despite the surrounding adversity.

Luthar and Cushing (1999) present risk and competence as the two key constructs that are pivotal components embedded in the construct of resiliency. For example, African-American racial status would be more strongly associated with resiliency than would white racial status. As a minority status poses greater risk due to stress caused by prejudice and discrimination, an African-American child with greater resiliency would be more competent in successfully surviving such risk (Markstrom, Marshall, and Tryon, 2000).

Poverty presents a great risk for children. A child growing up in a poor community faces a greater number of negative factors, including lack of physical safety, poor nutrition, lack of early exposure to healthy leisure activities, and extensive exposure to violence. To cope with these negative elements, a great deal of personal resources is required. The child with greater competency will survive these forces better than a child with less competency. Through successful experience in coping with each negative factor, one accumulates such competency, thus getting ready to meet another challenge. This readiness for another challenge is resiliency.

## DEVELOPMENT OF RESILIENCY

Although most psychologists agree that some children are born with more resiliency than others, Noam, Pucci, and Foster (1999) challenge the notion of "invincible" high-risk children who are not affected by a great deal of adversity. They note previous studies of the existence of at least one adult "who believes in them" as an essential factor in many youth who have succeeded despite great adversity (Cicchetti, 1984; Garmezy, 1981; Higgins, 1994). Noam, Pucci, and Foster (1999) further state that, under the umbrella of support for and trust in them, children benefit from stress and risk that encourage the evolution of resilience, providing them with "their growing ability to give new meaning to old events, self-reflection and exploration of new behaviors" (p. 60). Therefore, resiliency is a fluid property. Only in the face of adversity does resiliency surface as one's strength to overcome difficulties in one's environment. Wolin and Wolin (1993) identified seven resiliencies that emerge to help an individual cope with adversity: insight, independence, relationships, initiative, creativity, humor, and morality. Common risks associated with parental conflicts and divorce include depression and mistrust in others. Children surrounded by a combination of these risk factors must draw strengths from their resiliency and support from others to grow up as healthy adults. Children with greater resiliency can navigate multiple difficulties to yield positive behavior. Supports provided by others in the process are *protective factors.*

Researchers in child welfare have found that resiliency is positively associated with support from family and peers (Markstrom, Marshall, and Foster, 2000; Norman, 2000; Murry and Brody, 1999; McCabe, Clark, and Bernett, 1999; Dembo et al., 1985; Stevens, 1984; VanHasselt et al., 1993; Garmezy, 1985). It is critical that a child perceives support provided by the family during the very early ages. A bond established between a mother and her child immediately after the birth of the child must be reinforced in order for the child to perceive it. Grandparents or other extended family members may also provide such support, establishing a strong bond with the child. Once the child senses or acknowledges this so-called *unconditional* support, the child will feel safe to explore new opportunities. Even if the child does not succeed in new experiences, the child feels safe in the presence of support, thus accumulating tools to use for future challenges.

## CONCEPTUAL MODEL OF RESILIENCY

A major challenge in studying resiliency lies in a lack of agreement on a conceptual framework. Windle (1999) attributes the difficulty to a wide range of characteristics of risk status, including socioeconomic indicators, neighborhood crime statistics, family discord, parental deviance, child maltreatment, family history of alcoholism, substance abuse, mental illness, or childhood psychiatric status or health status. Windle suggests that the adoption and utilization of a uniform framework may enhance integration of findings and advancement of knowledge in the field. Windle (1999) cites the significant contribution of Luthar and Cushing (1999) in this light, as these authors have identified issues related to the use of single versus multi-item stress indexes.

Advancing the idea of a framework that includes multiple resiliency constructs, Kumpfer (1999) discusses six major predictors of resiliency:

1. Stressors or challenges that activate the resilience process in the individual or organizational unit (e.g., family, group, and community)
2. The external environmental context, including the balance and interaction of salient risk and protective factors in the individual child's external environment (i.e., family, community, culture, school, and peer group)
3. Person-environment interactional processes, including transactional processes between the child and his or her environment
4. Internal self characteristics, including internal individual spiritual, cognitive, social/behavioral, physical, and emotional/affective competencies
5. Resilience processes, including short-term or long-term residence or stress processes
6. Positive outcomes or successful life adaptation in specific developmental tasks

Kumpfer provides a model of these six predictors. This model provides a concrete way to organize the complex and dynamic process of facilitating adaptation in a difficult environmental context. Figure 1.1 with slight modification to Kumpfer's model provides students with a tool to study the process of resiliency.

In this conceptual model, we assume that resiliency is accumulated as one produces positive outcomes (adaptation) in the environment where risk factors meet protective factors. When risk factors are greater than protective factors, maladaptation results. Home, school, and community are the major environmental contexts in which children meet both risk and protective factors for the resiliency process. For older children, the context of peer groups expands its presence. Each child brings internal resiliency to encounter risk and protective factors in these environmental contexts. Internal resiliency may be cognitive, emotional, physical, behavioral, and in some cases spiritual in nature.

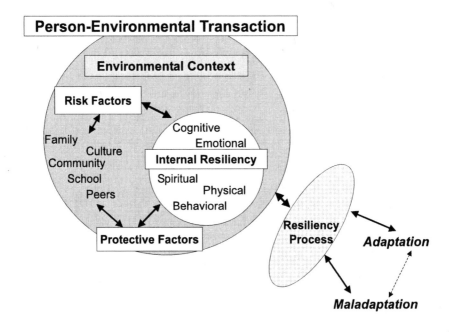

FIGURE 1.1. Conceptual Model of Resiliency (*Source:* Adapted from Kumpfer, 1999.)

## PERSON-ENVIRONMENTAL TRANSACTION FOR THE DEVELOPMENT OF RESILIENCY

Individuals are born with different levels of internal resiliency. This internal resiliency is composed of psychological and physiological strengths that each child has inherited from both parents. The internal resiliency is a reservoir of inner strengths in such various dimensions as the cognitive, emotional, physical, behavioral, and spiritual, which begin to work when the child experiences various interactions in the environment. The child's interactions occur within the contexts of family, peers, school, community, and society. Those contexts of interaction may become protective factors or risk factors for the child.

For example, a boy who has been born to parents with little economic means experiences negative interactions with family members when his parents are unable to provide expensive shoes for him to wear to school. If the child possesses a great degree of inner psychological strength that has been fostered by loving parents, he may endure possible embarrassment among his peers. If the child is exposed to peers at school who tempt him to steal a nice pair of shoes from another child's locker, this child needs a lot of strength to fight back and avoid such temptation. He may have to draw on his spiritual strengths developed through religion classes to fight the temptation. As the child repeats positive behaviors in such a difficult environment, he develops self-confidence in handling another temptation. Thus the child's resiliency leads to adaptation.

On the other hand, the child will give in to the temptation if his reservoir of strengths is not enough to fight back the temptation. So the child may join his peers in engaging in antisocial activities. Thus, the child's resiliency process leads to maladaptation. Of course, one's social interactions in the environment are much more complex than the case of the child without an expensive pair of shoes. But the family, peers, school, and other institutions continuously present protective factors as well as risk factors. For a child to develop a large reservoir of strengths, the child requires consistent protection and support from the immediate environment.

## *Home and Resiliency*

Development of resiliency begins at birth. It has been found that positive emotional and social development among newborn babies results in a greater attachment to their mothers (Belsky and Fearon, 2002; Belsky, Spritz, and Crnic, 1996; Freitag et al., 1996). The bond developed between a baby and its parents, if sustained, becomes a protective factor in the resiliency process. For example, many studies (Dembo et al., 1985; Stevens, 1984; VanHasselt et al., 1993; McCabe, Clark, and Bernett, 1999) found that among high-risk African-American adolescents, family support—the sustained bond between adolescents and adults—is associated with high scholastic self-concept, low levels of antisocial behavior, and low use of alcohol and drugs. In a study of African-American families in foreign environments, McCubbin and others (1998) found that African-American families who spent a significant amount of quality time together showed a high degree of resiliency and adaptation, even when faced with the stress related to discrimination and racism.

Smith (1998) found in a study of youths—one group with severe emotional or behavioral disability and their counterparts without disability—that nondisabled youth discussed recreational activities, sex, and their own problems with their family members significantly more often than those with a disability did. The most recent Center for Substance Abuse Prevention's cross-site evaluation of high-risk youth of racial demonstration program  (U.S. Department of Health and Human Services, 2002), found that family bonding, among other factors, is associated with substance abuse among the target youth who are all racial minorities.

These are just a few examples of the abundant empirical evidence that the sustained bond between a child and family members is a protective factor in the resiliency process, promoting adaptation.

## *School and Resiliency*

A positive school experience promotes protective factors in children and adolescents. In a long-term study of women who had been institutionalized in childhood, Rutter and Quinton (1984) showed how a good school experience can compensate for a home environment considered to be high risk. The girls who showed the capacity to plan (a protective factor) were more likely to have good school experiences. Rutter (1987) attributed the development of the better capacity to plan to the experience of pleasure, success, and accomplishment at school, promoting a sense of their own worth and their ability to control what happened to them. Scholars addressing positive educational experiences (Benard, 1995; Roeser, Eccles, and Sameroff, 1998) agree that caring relationships in the educational process are critical determining factors for resiliency building outside of families. For example, Roeser, Eccles, and Sameroff (1998) found students who viewed their teachers as supportive both academically and emotionally were less likely to experience alienation from school, thus fostering a sense that they have a place in society.

Henderson and Milstein (1996) recommend six keys for promoting resilience in students:

1. Developing prosocial bonding
2. Setting clear, consistent boundaries
3. Teaching life skills
4. Providing caring and support
5. Setting and communicating high expectations
6. Providing meaningful participation

Pikes, Burrell, and Holliday (1998) advocate resilience-building experience for students, recommending certain activities in writing, social studies, reading, mathematics, and science that foster the five traits introduced by Wang, Haertel, and Walberg (1995). These traits are feeling successful, valued, needed, empowered, and hopeful. Many studies point to the importance of high expectations for academic success for students. Benard (1995) found that the combination of high expectations and support helps students believe in themselves and their future, developing the critical resilience traits of self-esteem, self-efficacy, autonomy, and optimism. In the same study by the Center for Substance Abuse Prevention (U.S. Department of Health and Human Services, 2002), the researchers found that school connectedness is a combination of school bonding and the self-efficacy factor, and that this single measure of real connectedness to the school is associated with a recognition of the ability to achieve.

Thus, it is critical that students perceive high expectations and support of teachers to foster school connectedness. School connectedness and school success together are associated with youth choosing peers who do not use substances and choosing not to use substance themselves (U.S. Department of Health and Human Services, 2002). Another new finding of this study is that the internal protective orientation drops toward greater risk around age twelve, bottoming out at age fifteen. The study suggests that family and school connectedness should be foci in prevention interventions for adolescents. One alarming finding is that family and school connectedness with internal protective orientation has a weaker association for adolescent boys than for adolescent girls.

### *Community and Resiliency*

Wandersman and Nation (1998) brought the concept of resiliency into studies of urban neighborhoods full of poverty, noise, and crowding. They cited Garbarino (1995) and Connell and Aber (1995) to underscore resiliency associated with neighborhood factors. Churches, Boys & Girls Clubs, and other institutions provide positive role models for children. Garbarino and Kostelny (1992) noted the protective effect of good social networks in preventing child abuse, and Sampson, Raudenbush, and Earls (1997) observed the relationship between neighborhood characteristics and violence. In a distressed housing complex in New York, for example, an intervention that enabled residents to purchase some abandoned buildings and convert them into residences effectively produced resilient individuals and families who, in turn, changed the nature of the neighborhood.

We cannot underestimate values of neighborhood-based organizations that often provide sanctuaries to residents and at-risk youth, enhancing a personal resource and creating a bridge to a hopeful future for them. McLaughlin, Irby, and Langman (1994) documented a case of collective young people referred to as "Hopefuls," all of whom were poor and had lost a friend or relative to violence in the city, yet did not get involved with drugs, violence, crime, or early pregnancies. The researchers concluded that the Hopefuls escaped useless death by violence and chose a responsible future through participation in an organization that provided the values, the support, the safety, and the skills they needed for believing in their own future. The organization was led by program leaders who saw the young persons' potential, held high expectations for them, and concentrated on their strengths. The U.S. Department of Health and Human Services study (2002) found that the community protection environment provides increasing protection for the older youth as compared to family and schools, suggesting that community assets are more critical for older children in fostering their strengths. Harris (1998) indicated that peers, school, and environment, particularly socioeconomic status, have the greatest influence on personality development, stating, "A child is better off living in a troubled family in a good neighborhood than living in a good family in a troubled neighborhood" (p. 60).

Other community efforts to pay attention to are mentoring programs. Rhodes (1994) focused on "natural" mentors rather than volunteers in community programs. These natural mentors may be teachers, neighbors, extended kin, or ministers. Whoever it is, the mentor provides emotional support and safety for a young person, communicating the belief that the young person will succeed despite adversities in the immediate environment. Davidson and his colleagues (1990) stressed the importance of training for mentors if they are not natural mentors, citing a successful mentoring program in which college students were trained and supervised to be mentors to adjudicated delinquents. Results indicated a reduction of recidivism by 34 percent and saving more than $5,000 in criminal justice costs and more than $7,000 in victim costs per youth.

## CONCLUSION

The strengths and well-being of children must be addressed in every facet of child care, service delivery, and programming. In an adultcentric world, professionals should continually be aware of children's needs and competencies and ensure that they have a voice in what happens to them. Resilience can come from many factors related to family, school, and community life, yet each child will respond differently to these environments based on his or her overall fortitude and personality structure. Professionals throughout the child care professions must carefully assess each child in accordance with his or her unique history, adaptive skills, coping behaviors, and motivation to succeed, often against incredible odds. In the twenty-first century, children are expected to have more rights than in previous generations and to be able to contribute to a world that not only acknowledges their basic needs but also values their right to a strong sense of well-being.

## STRENGTHS STORY: HENRY LESTER

Henry Lester was born into a family of five children living on a farm in the southern United States. The fourth of five children, Henry, along with his siblings, had to work hard on the farm every day to help his parents. Neither of his parents had graduated from high school. There was a definite division of labor, and each child took his or her chores seriously. The family was poor and lived in a small house, which the father had built but never fully completed. The older children were responsible for feeding the animals, milking the cows, and gathering the eggs, and Henry was responsible for carrying water from the spring to the house. Indoor plumbing was not something the family could afford, so Henry had to fetch at least four buckets of water a day. Henry was diligent about his chore but sometimes encountered certain obstacles that made this routine task more complicated. He had to cross dense woods that also served as the neighbor's pig lot; sometimes a mother hog with small piglets would chase him or he would worry about a mad dog rumored to be loose in the community. And at the spring there were large water moccasin snakes, stretched out on wooden boards placed above the water. Still, the family depended on the water and he could not let them down. He was afraid of the snakes and would sometimes poke them with a stick to get them to move into or away from the water.

He loved to read storybooks, especially about horses. Sometimes, Henry would lose track of time while reading, and dusk would arrive. His father had a certain way of glancing at him to let him know that it was time to get the water. He then had to enter the woods and make his way to the spring as he did every day. Twice a year his aunt and uncle would take him to the city for a visit and they had indoor plumbing. Henry lived for those times away from the farm although he missed his family.

Henry experienced a difficult childhood due to illness in the family, including his own. From the time he was a baby, Henry would "black out," which was thought to be a seizure disorder. These episodes happened several times before he was ten years old and once when he was a teenager. His parents would usually revive him at home, but once had to call for an emergency vehicle to rush him to the hospital. There were no real emergency vehicles in the country, so one of the local undertakers used his hearse for emergencies. Henry was terrified when he awoke after a seizure and was lying on a stretcher in a hearse, with the siren blaring. He then realized that his mother was sitting up front with the driver and was relieved. Henry was a sickly child and, as a result, often received special attention from his parents, for which he was teased by his siblings.

When Henry was seven years old, his father, a carpenter and bricklayer, stepped on a rusty nail and did not go to the doctor because the family had very limited insurance coverage. He acquired tetanus from the wound and was in the hospital for weeks in another state, which eroded the family's savings and led to their mortgaging of the farm. Henry's father barely survived this serious illness, and the doctors said it was a miracle. Since Henry's father could not work for a long time, the family's finances were totally depleted. Mrs. Lester had to go to work as a cook at Henry's elementary school. She rode the school bus each day with the children as she had no other transportation. Henry's aunt and uncle often gave the family money and would bring clothing and food for them on a regular basis.

Henry and his siblings picked beans, sold walnuts, and did odd jobs on neighboring farms to help the family out, but they still lost the farm. Henry sadly stood by the fence and watched as the family sold their last cow. By the time Henry was fourteen, two of his older siblings had dropped out of school and left home, and his oldest brother had joined the Navy. While Henry's older brother was stationed in the Navy in Tokyo, he would send money and sometimes presents for the family. Henry remembers wearing his red velvet jacket, with a map of Japan embroidered on the back, to school. He had never had a coat so beautiful and all the children were in awe.

Still, Henry's parents and his aunt and uncle praised his schoolwork and referred to him as "the smart one." The family struggled as Mr. Lester had difficulty finding work and suffered many residual medical problems caused by the tetanus. To complicate life further, Henry's mother also became ill with a mysterious illness that none of the local doctors could diagnose. She had huge boils all over her body that were extremely painful. While their father worked at night, Henry and his younger brother would put ointment on their mother's sores and cry in secret, for their mother had been told that she was likely to die. Finally, she was taken by Henry's aunt and uncle to a doctor in the city who diagnosed an allergic reaction to penicillin. With treatment she made a full recovery.

After losing the farm, the family moved to the city to find work, and Henry was able to get a part-time job as a grocery bagger. He worked hard throughout high school and never gave up on his goal of getting a good education. He stayed up late to do his homework, and he graduated near the top of his high school class. He was sometimes laughed at and called a bookworm by children in the neighborhood. However, he was admitted on scholarship to a work-study college in another state, where he worked in the library, his favorite place on campus. His parents could not afford to buy him a suit for college, but his aunt and uncle bought him one and drove him to the campus. Henry later realized that this hard work gave him much of the strength and motivation necessary to make it. His parents and family were always there for him, even when the family was unsure of how they themselves would survive. He was the only child in his family to achieve a college degree and also went on to complete graduate studies.

## *QUESTIONS FOR DISCUSSION*

1. What is meant by resilience? Name the three areas of a child's life that affect the development of resilience.
2. How do protective and risk factors contribute to one's development of resilience?
3. Look at the resiliency model in Figure 1.1 and apply it to an individual in your life.
4. How does a strengths perspective differ from the assessment model based on problems?

## REFERENCES

Andrews, A. B. and Ben-Arieh, A. (1999). Measuring and monitoring children's well-being across the world. *Social Work* 44(2): 105-115.
Belsky, J. and Fearon, R. M. P. (2002). Infant-mother attachment security, contextual risk, and early development: A moderational analysis. *Development and Psychopathology* 14(2): 293-310.
Belsky, J., Spritz, B., and Crnic, K. (1996). Infant attachment security and affective-cognitive information processing at age 3. *Psychological Science* 72(2): 111-114.

Benard, B. (1997). Fostering resiliency in children and youth: Promoting protective factors in school. In Saleebey, D. (Ed.), *The strengths perspective in social work practice,* Second edition (pp. 167-182). New York: Longman.

Cicchetti, D. (Ed.) (1984). *Developmental psychopathology.* Chicago, IL: University of Chicago Press.

Connell, J. P. and Aber, J. L. (1995). How do urban communities affect youth? Using social science research to inform the design and evaluation of comprehensive community initiatives. In Connell, J. P., Kubish, A. P., Schorr, L. B., and Weiss, C. H. (Eds.), *New approaches to evaluating community initiatives.* Volume 1, *Concepts, methods, and context.* Available at <www.aspeninstitute.org/Programt1. asp?bid=1273>. Washington, DC: Aspen Institute.

Cowen, E. L., Wyman, P. A., Work, W. C., and Parker, G. R. (1990). The Rochester Child Resilience Project: Overview and summary of first-year findings. *Development and Psychopathology* 2(2): 193-212.

Cummins, R. A. (1996). The domains of life satisfaction: An attempt to order chaos. *Social Indicators Research* 38: 303-328.

Davidson, W. S. II, Redner, R., Amdur, R. L., and Mitchell, C. M. (1990). *Alternative treatments for troubled youth: The case of diversion from the justice system.* New York: Plenum Press.

DeJong, P. and Miller, S. D. (1995). How to interview for client strengths. *Social Work* 40(6): 729-736.

Dembo, R., Grandon, G., Taylor, R. W., La Voie, W., and Schmeidler, J. (1985). The influence of family relationships on marijuana use among a sample of inner-city youths. *Deviant Behavior* 6: 267-286.

Downs, S. W., Moore, E. M., McFadden, E. J., and Costin, L. B. (2000). *Child welfare and family services: Policies and practice,* Sixth edition. Boston, MA: Allyn and Bacon.

Freitag, M. K., Belsky, J., Grossman, K., Grossman, K. E., and Scheuerer-Englisch, H. (1996). Continuity in parent-child relationships from infancy to middle childhood and relations with friendship competence. *Child Development* 67(4): 1437-1454.

Garbarino, J. (1995*). Raising children in a socially toxic environment.* San Francisco: Jossey-Bass.

Garbarino, J. and Kostelny, I. (1992). Child maltreatment as a community problem. *Child Abuse and Neglect* 16: 455-464.

Garmezy, N. (1981). Children under stress: Perspectives on antecedents and correlates of vulnerability and resistance to psychopathology. In Rabin, A. I., Annoff, J., Barclay, A. M., and Zuckers, R. A. (Eds.), *Further exploration in personality* (pp. 196-270). New York: Wiley.

Garmezy, N. (1985). Stress-resistant children: The search for protective factors. In Stemvenson, J. E. (Ed.), *Recent research in developmental psychopathology* (pp. 213-233). Oxford: Pergamon.

Garmenzy, N. and Mastern, A. S. (1991). The protective role of competence indicators in children at risk. In Cummings, E. M., Green, A. L., and Karraker, K. H. (Eds.), *Life span development psychology* (pp. 151-174). Hillsdale, NJ: Lawrence Erlbaum Associates.

Graybeal, C. (2001). Strengths-based social work assessment: Transforming the dominant paradigm. *Families in Society* 82(3): 233-242.

Harris, J. (1998). *The nurture assumption: Why children turn out the way they do.* New York: Free Press.

Henderson, N. and Milstein, M. (1996). *Resiliency in schools: Making it happen for students and educators.* Thousand Oaks, CA: Corwin Press.

Higgins, G. (1994). *Resilient adults: Overcoming a cruel past.* San Francisco: Jossey-Bass.

Kaplan, L. and Girard, J. (1994). *Strengthening high-risk families.* New York: Lexington Books.

Karls, J. and Wandrei, K. (Eds.) (1994). PIE manual: Person-in-environment system: The PIE classification system for social functioning problems. Washington, DC: NASW Press.

Kumpfer, K. (1999). Factors and processes contributing to resilience: The resilience framework. In Glantz, M. D. and Johnson, J. (Eds.), *Resilience and development: Positive life adaptations* (pp. 179-224). New York: Plenum Press.

Land, C. L., Lamb, V. L., and Mustillo, S. K. (2001). Child and youth well-being in the United States, 1975-1998: Some findings from a new index. *Social Indicators Research* 56(3): 241.

Luthar, S. S. and Cushing, G. (1999). Measurement issues in the empirical study of resilience: An overview. In Glantz, M. D. and Johnson, J. (Eds.), *Resilience and development: Positive life adaptations* (pp. 129-160). New York: Plenum Press.

Markstrom, C. A., Marshall, S. K., and Tryon, R. J. (2000). Resiliency, social support, and coping in rural low-income Appalachian adolescents from two racial groups. *Journal of Adolescence* 23: 693-703.

Masten, A. S., Best, K. M., and Garmezy, N. (1990). Resilience and development: Contributions from the study of children who overcome adversity. *Development and Psychopathology* 2(4): 425-444.

McCabe, K. M., Clark, R., and Bernett, D. (1999). Family protective factors among urban African-American youth. *Journal of Clinical Child Psychology* 28(2): 137-150.

McCubbin, H. I., Futrell, J. A., Thompson, E. A., and Thompson, A. I. (1998), Resilient families in an ethnic and cultural context. In McCubbin, H. I. and Thompson, E. A. (Eds.), *Resiliency in African-American families* (pp. 329-351). Thousand Oaks, CA: Sage Publications.

McLaughlin, M., Irby, M., and Langman, J. (1994). *Urban sanctuaries: Neighborhood organizations in the lives and futures of inner-city youth.* San Francisco: Jossey-Bass.

Murry, V. M. and Brody, G. (1999). Self-regulation and self-worth of black children reared in economically stressed, rural, single mother-headed families. *Journal of Family Issues* 20(4): 458-484.

Noam, G. G., Pucci, K., and Foster, E. (1999). Development, resilience, and school success in youth: The prevention practitioner and the Harvard RALLY program. In Cicchetti, D. and Toth, S. (Eds.), *Developmental psychopathology: Approaches to prevention and intervention* (pp. 150-202). Rochester: University of Rochester Press.

Norman, E. (2000). Introduction: The strengths prospective and resiliency enhancement of natural partnership. In Norman, E. (Ed.), *Resilience enhancement: Putting the strengths perspective into social work practice* (pp. 1-16). New York: Columbia University Press.

Petr, C. G. (1998). *Social work practice children and their families: Pragmatic foundations.* New York: Oxford University Press.

Pikes, T., Burrell, B., and Holliday, C. (1998). Using academic strategies to build resilience. *Reaching Today's Youth, The Community Circle of Caring Journal* 2(3): 44-47.

Rapp, C. A. (1998). *The strengths model: Case management with people suffering from a severe and persistent mental illness.* New York: Oxford University Press.

Rhodes, J. E. (1994). Older and wiser: Mentoring relationships in childhood and adolescence. *Journal of Primary Prevention* 14(3): 187-196.

Roeser, R. W., Eccles, J. S., and Sameroff, A. J. (1998). Academic and emotional functioning in early adolescence: Longitudinal relations, patterns, and prediction by experience in middle school. *Development and Psychopathology* 10: 321-352.

Rutter, M. (1987). Psychosocial resilience and protective mechanisms. *American Journal of Orthopsychiatry* 57(3): 316-331.

Rutter, M. and Quinton, D. (1984). Long-term follow-up of women institutionalized in childhood: Factors promoting good functioning in adult life. *British Journal of Developmental Psychology* 18: 225-234.

Saleebey, D. (1996). The strengths perspective in social work practice: Extensions and cautions. *Social Work* 41(3): 296-305.

Saleebey, D. (2002). Introduction: Power in the people. In Saleebey, D. (Ed.), *The strengths perspective in social work practice*, Second edition (pp. 3-19). New York: Longman.

Sampson, R. J., Raudenbush, S. W., and Earls, F. (1997). Neighborhoods and violent crime: A multilevel study of collective efficacy. *Science* 277: 918-924.

Sheafor, B. W., Horejsi, C. R., and Horejsi, G. A. (2000). *Techniques and guidelines for social work practice*, Fifth edition. Boston, MA: Allyn and Bacon.

Smith, C. and Carlson, B. E. (1997). Stress, coping, and resilience in children and youth. *Social Service Review* (June): 231-256.

Smith, M. K. (1998). *Adolescents with severe emotional and behavioral disabilities: Transition to adulthood.* Lewiston, NY: Edwin Mellen Press.

Stevens, J. H. (1984). Black grandmothers' and black adolescent mothers' knowledge about parenting. *Developmental Psychology* 21: 1017-1025.

Turner, S. (2000). Recognizing and enhancing natural resiliency in boys and girls. In Norman, E. (Ed.), *Resiliency enhancements: Putting the strengths perspective into social work practice* (pp. 29-39). New York: Columbia University Press.

U.S. Department of Health and Human Services (2002). *Point of prevention: The national cross-site evaluation of high-risk programs.* Washington, DC: U.S. Government Printing Office.

VanHasselt, V. B., Herson, M., Null, J., Ammerman, R. T., Bukstein, O. G., McGillivray, J., and Hunter, A. (1993). Drug abuse prevention for high-risk African-American children and their families: A review and model program. *Addictive Behavior* 18: 213-234.

Walsh, W. B. and Betz, N. E. (1990). *Tests and assesment,* Second edition. Englewood Cliffs, NJ: Prentice-Hall.

Wandersman, A. and Nation, M. (1998). Urban neighborhoods and mental health: Psychological contributions to understanding toxicity, resilience, and interventions. *American Psychologist* 53(6): 647-656.

Wang, M. C., Haertel, G. D., and Walberg, H. J. (1995). The effectiveness of collaborative school-linked services. In Rigsby, L. C., Maynard, C., and Wang. M. (Eds.), *School-community connections: Exploring issues for research and practice* (pp. 283-310). Oxford: Elsevier Science Publishing Co.

Weick, A., Rapp, C., Sullivan, W., and Kisthardt, W. (1989). A strengths perspective for social work practice. *Social Work* 34(July): 350-354.

Werner, E. E. (1993). Risk, resilience, and recovery: Perspectives from the Kauai Longitudinal Study. *Development and Psychopathology* 5: 503-515.

Westbrooks, K. L. and Starks, S. H. (2001). Strengths perspective inherent in cultural empowerment: A tool for assessment with African-American individuals and families. In Fong, R. and Furuto, S. (Eds.), *Culturally competent practice: Skills, interventions, and evaluations* (pp. 101-118). Boston, MA: Allyn and Bacon.

Windle, M. (1999). Critical conceptual and measurement issues in the study of resilience. In Glantz, M. D. and Johnson, J. (Eds.), *Resilience and development: Positive life adaptations* (pp. 161-176). New York: Plenum Press.

Wolin, S. J. and Wolin, S. (1993). *The resilient self.* New York: Villard Books.

Zimmerman, M. A., Salem, D. A., and Notaro, P. C. (2000). Make room for daddy II: The positive effects of fathers' role in adolescence. In Taylor, R. D. and Wang, M. C. (Eds.), *Resilience across contexts: Family, work, culture, and community* (pp. 233-253). Mahwah, NJ: Lawrence Erlbaum Associates, Publishers.

# Chapter 2

# The Care of Children in American Society: Historical Events and Trends

Children are likely to live up to what you believe in them.

Lady Bird Johnson

The twentieth century has been referred to as the century of the child because so many advancements have enhanced the quality of life for children. The twenty-first century holds so much promise for children to have an even better quality of life and to build on their strengths and competencies. Despite amazing hardships and setbacks many children are able to maintain a sense of well-being and hope. Children who grow up in abusive families, children who endure multiple out-of-home placements, and children who face multiple obstacles because of physical or developmental disabilities all prove to us every day that they are contributing members of our society who deserve to have their wants and needs fully addressed.

## EARLY PERCEPTIONS AND TREATMENT OF CHILDREN

Professionals today must be aware that political thinking points to our listening carefully to what children say and taking their opinions seriously (Carroll, 2002). National and international laws declare the rights of children be heard and their wishes be considered on behalf of decision making that will affect their lives. The United Nations Convention on the Rights of the Child (1989) called for the views and input of children to be considered in important decision making (Taylor, 2000). Moreover, in Britain, the Children Act 1989 makes it mandatory for children's opinions to be considered when plans are being made concerning their welfare (Carroll, 2002).

However, it is imperative that we look at the way children have been treated over the centuries to gain a perspective on the dilemmas that they have faced—many of which children, family, and child welfare staff still must address today. The understanding and treatment of children has evolved over time, as children were originally treated as adults, with no differentiation being made for dependency or age. Also, children were considered to be property of the parents, or chattel, if they survived birth and infancy at all (Rose and Fatout, 2003). In early Roman times, the father decided whether the child would live; female children and children with disabilities were commonly killed or sold into slavery. The child who survived did not become a member of the Roman family until the eighth day after birth (Hewitt and Forness, 1984). These practices were performed in other early cultures as a form of social control and to guarantee that those who were fit and productive would share in and earn more resources for the family and the community.

Children who were orphaned were traditionally cared for by their extended families or members of their tribe or community. In both Judaism and Christianity, the care of dependent children was mandated by law. Orphanages and homes for dependent children began at the end of the second century A.D. Parents in the Middle Ages lost many of their children to famine and disease so some researchers have speculated that many parents were reluctant to become too attached to them (Rose and Fatout, 2003). The feudal system in England established the concept of ownership, so that children, especially the poor ones, were at the mercy of their families. Children were considered to be adults, expected to earn their own keep, as soon as they were big enough to work alongside their parents to help sustain the family (Rose and Fatout, 2003). Many children became separated from their families due to illegitimacy, disease, death, and abandonment, thus having to fend for themselves in a threatening world.

Child placement for profit began in England in 1562 and lasted over 300 years (Cohen, 2000). In 1601, the Elizabethan Poor Laws recognized the necessity for families to care for themselves and their children. Those who were not able to maintain their families were placed in poorhouses, along with their children. Poor, troubled, and orphaned children were placed in almshouses where they were often beaten and lived in terrible conditions (Rose and Fatout, 2003). But the Poor Laws did call for children to be viewed as a separate group, and under the system of indenture many poor, abandoned, and illegitimate children were placed by local governing trustees with various artisans to learn a craft or trade. In 1642, Virginia enacted one of many colonial laws which stated that orphans whose estate was not large enough to support them would be apprenticed until age twenty-one to learn a trade (Cohen, 2000). The indenture arrangement ensured that a standard system of care existed for dependent children, and that they would receive appropriate training to become self-sufficient members of society (Downs et al., 2000). The first public child care facility was opened in 1790 in Charleston, South Carolina, to address the care and education of both children whose parents were indigent and those incapable of maintaining them at home (Abbott, 1938).

## NINETEENTH-CENTURY EFFORTS FOR CHANGE

Still, up until the middle nineteenth century there was little recognition given to childhood as a special time for growth and development, with children being viewed as little adults, but of course without the rights. In 1838, British author Charles Dickens published *Oliver Twist* in book form, the largely autobiographical story about a young boy who goes from the poorhouse into an apprenticeship. The popularity of this book spread to the United States as Dickens began to speak out openly and write specific pamphlets against child maltreatment for distribution (Tower, 1993). In the Census of 1870, more than 700,000 children between the ages of ten and fifteen were involved in gainful employment, one-sixth of them working in industries (Cohen, 2000).

Nevertheless, in the late nineteenth century, children's rights received increasing attention due to three major forces. First, the number of children in society decreased, meaning there were more adults to work and also take care of the children. Second, the disciplines of psychology and human learning began to expand the understanding of childhood as a special life stage. Third, there was an increasing concern for the rights of all persons in society, as well as a concern for the need to reform situations that oppressed people (Compton, 1980).

These concerns led to the development of *parens patriae,* a mind-set that calls upon society to intervene so that governmental or professional authorities may provide the necessary child care and sustenance that cannot be provided by uninformed, neglectful, and exploitative parents. This transfer of responsibilities, of course, brought about the development of administrative, judicial, and professional techniques of investigation, decision making, supervision, and care of children (Bremmer, 1970).

During the industrial revolution in the United States, children fell victim to factory owners who would involve them in backbreaking labor lasting sixteen to eighteen hours and under poor working conditions. Migration from rural to urban areas and increasing immigration made life even more difficult for children and families who were struggling to achieve a better quality of life. Families lived in crowded tenements and children wandered the streets, selling papers, peddling flowers, and shining shoes for survival. Child labor laws were nonexistent, and little attention was given to children's need for protection, education, and guidance (Rose and Fatout, 2003).

In 1853, Charles Loring Brace created the New York Children's Aid Society, which advocated for child protection by society and begged for people to pay attention to the increasing misery of immigrants and others who were being disenfranchised by urbanization and industrialization. Poor, neglected, and dependent children, often immigrant children, were sent outside New York City on "orphan trains" and placed on farms to work, as far away as the Midwest. As in earlier times, the children's rights were not considered as they were wrenched away from familiar surroundings and placed far away from the life they had known in the city. For many of these children, their lives improved and they found permanent homes. However, many remained homeless and wandering, not knowing where to locate their next meal.

However, in the latter half of the nineteenth century, children and youth services grew as society began to pay attention to the plight of children, especially their inability to protect and defend themselves against adults and to save themselves from crime. This period in history has been referred to as "the era of child-saving activities" (Rose and Fatout, 2003). A landmark case in 1874 forged the way for child protection in the United States, the case of Mary Ellen Wilson. This ten-year-old child was beaten with a leather strap by her foster parents, and a neighbor could hear her persistent screams. Consequently, the neighbor woman contacted Etta Wheeler, a church worker, who in desperation called Henry Bergh, the founder and director of the American Society for the Prevention of Cruelty to Animals. He launched a lawsuit that resulted in the removal of Mary Ellen from her home and her transfer to a children's home. As a result, the Society for the Prevention of Cruelty to Children was founded in December 1874 (Tower, 1993).

## TWENTIETH-CENTURY INNOVATIONS

After the turn of the twentieth century, some poor parents were provided with material assistance, or *outdoor relief,* which allowed for vulnerable children to stay in their own homes. Nevertheless, because of punitive attitudes toward the poor, such children and their parents were more likely to be sent to almshouses. Almshouses were thought to be such deplorable and degrading places for children that they yielded to orphanages and institutional care, which were thought to be more humane ways of caring for children (Downs et al., 2000). Despite efforts to find homes for children and ensure a better quality of life, there were still more than 750,000 orphans living in the United States in 1920 (Rose and Fatout, 2003).

### Policies and Child Advocacy

A major precedent was established with the passage of the Social Security Act in 1935 as child protection then became a public responsibility. Organizations, such as local Societies for the Prevention of Cruelty to Children and other voluntary agencies, were afforded a more diminished role in addressing child abuse and neglect. As the field of protective services grew in child welfare agencies, the understanding and investigation of physical abuse was expanded. The diagnoses of fractured long bones, brain injuries such as subdural hematomas, and battered child syndrome profiles hastened the drafting of model child abuse legislation in the 1960s (Wolfe, 1999). Between 1963 and 1965, forty-seven states passed child abuse reporting laws (Conrad and Schneider, 1992).

Although child abuse was first described as a social problem in the late nineteenth century, it took professionals and laypeople over ninety years to acknowledge on a grand scale the need for public education, research, and intervention for abused and neglected children (Winton and Mara, 2001). In the United States approximately 50 percent of all child maltreatment cases involve neglect, and about half of child maltreatment fatalities involve child neglect. Moreover, a high percentage of these neglect cases occur in families where the parents are abusing alcohol or other drugs (Sheafor and Horejsi, 2003). Today, all fifty states have laws which require that suspected child abuse and neglect must be reported. Moreover, social workers are attuned more than ever to the importance of using child-centered roles for assessment, clinical support, mediation, brokering, advocacy, and education in helping children and families in child abuse proceedings in court (Anderson et al., 2002).

### Permanency Planning

In the 1970s child welfare practice saw the advent of the permanency planning movement, largely because there were over 520,000 children in out-of-home placements by 1977 (Downs et al., 2000). Permanency planning can be defined as a set of guidelines for maintaining children in families long enough for them to experience sustained, nurturing parents and caretakers, and continuity of relationships that will offer support over their lifetime. More careful consideration was given to whether children should move from foster care to adoption, and clearer standards for termination of parental rights were established. Moreover, child welfare officials across the country began to focus more on case review and case planning in an all-out effort to find permanent homes for children. Thus, placing children in stable, nurturing, and permanent homes over the long term became the central goal of the child welfare system.

Similarly, child welfare professionals concluded that many children were stuck in the foster care pipeline who perhaps should never have entered in the system, had their natural families received comprehensive preventative and educational services. Two landmark pieces of legislation addressed this issue of preserving families and reducing the ranks of children in foster care. These were the Indian Child Welfare Act of 1978 and the Adoption Assistance and Child Welfare Act of 1980 (Downs et al., 2000). This legislation added federal backing to state incentives to keep children in their own homes whenever possible.

The Indian Child Welfare Act (Public Law 608) was passed to reduce the number of American Indian children being placed in non-Indian foster and adoptive homes. This landmark legislation came after many years of advocacy by Native American groups who maintained that such cross-cultural placements robbed Indian children of cultural traditions and identity (Downs et al., 2000). This legislation set a precedent for protecting the cultural values and self-determination of a minority group within American society at large. Congress established a protocol for the placement of Indian children, which began with the Indian tribe's preferences, with extended family and homes approved by the tribe. Most important, state courts were mandated to notify the respective Indian tribe when an Indian child became involved in a custody suit and to give the Indian tribunal court the option to try the case. To enhance child welfare programming, the U.S. government provided money for child welfare and family service programs to enhance services to the American Indian communities (Downs et al., 2000).

Family presentation, unlike many previous child welfare mandates, moved away from the stereotypic view of the pathological family in crisis. Instead, family preservation introduced a holistic, ecological view of the family, which recognized the family's problems as being further exacerbated by such societal and community ills as unemployment and unaffordable child care (Noble, Perkins, and Fatout, 2000). This approach was actually a precursor of the strengths approach to working with families and children, for child welfare programs had begun to look more realistically at the family's limitations and assets within a much broader sociocultural perspective.

By 1984, the number of foster children declined to 275,000 as a result of consistent and focused efforts by child welfare officials to make permanency planning and family preservation programs successful (Downs et al., 2000). However, by 1991, the number of children in care had risen to 429,000, despite these innovative changes to ensure permanency planning and family preservation. The legislation alone could not withstand multiple crises within American society and the American family, such as the crack cocaine epidemic, increased unemployment, economic recession, corporate downsizing, a rising homeless population, and the increase of HIV/AIDS, especially among women with children (Downs et al., 2000).

## CHILD WELFARE PRACTICE

### Trends in Foster Care

As the need for more foster homes expanded, the number of available foster families decreased, and more and more children with exceptional needs were placed within the foster care system. There were pressing needs for foster families to care for children with outstanding physical and behavioral problems, such as attention deficit-hyperactivity disorder, oppositional defiant disorder, and conduct disorder. Many other children were born addicted to crack cocaine, heroin, or other hard drugs, and others were born with fetal alcohol syndrome. Treatment or therapeutic foster care was developed to meet the increasing need for specialized foster care. This intensive system of care was established to provide holistic and intensive services to children who otherwise might be referred for residential care. Therapeutic or treatment foster care provides enhanced training for foster parents on such topics as attachment disorder, child abuse and neglect, grieving, and understanding children who witness violence. Moreover, these homes accept fewer children—some accepted sibling groups to maintain family support—and were monitored daily by phone or home visits by case managers. A growing number of such programs were developed by family service and mental health agencies and offered services via a contractual or per diem arrangement with child welfare agencies. Treatment foster care programs offer daily monitoring of the home environment by phone call or home visit, with each worker being on call to provide emergency assistance or crisis intervention for the families in their caseload.

Child welfare professionals note that foster care has been and continues to be an integral child welfare service, but by design it was always intended to be a temporary service. The Adoption Assistance and Child Welfare Act of 1980 (Public Law 96-272) was designed to limit the number of children placed in foster care and ensure a systematic return to their own families (Wells and Guo, 1999). Several studies have shown that children who are African American, disabled or health impaired (McMurtry and Lie, 1992; Courtney, 1995), Hispanic, neglected, had a higher number of visits with their mothers, or had a higher number of moves during placement (Davis, Landsverk, and Newton, 1997) were less likely to be unified with their families. In their study of children placed in foster care in Cleveland, Ohio, Wells and Guo (1999) found that older children reentered foster care more rapidly than did younger children. For example, infants stayed a median of 17.4 months in foster care compared to eleven months for children age one to twelve years. This research also found that reunified children whose last placement was a group home reentered foster care at a faster rate than did children whose last placement was a kinship home.

### Trends in Kinship Care

In the 1990s, the child welfare system began to look more carefully at kinship care as a preferred placement over nonrelative foster homes. More and more states are realizing the strengths inherent in the placement of children with grandparents, great-grandparents, aunts, uncles, or other close relatives. The 1990 U.S. Census indicated that some 1.1 million American households involved grandchildren living with grandparents (U.S. Bureau of Census, 1990). Kinship care is focused on helping children to remain in familiar environments, continue meaningful relationships with significant others, and maintain a sense of family and cultural identity. It is estimated that over 50 percent of the children placed in Los Angeles are in some form of kinship care (Cohen, 2000). Such placements are arranged by the court system so that the nuclear or extended family members who take the child into their home have legal custody and in many cases receive financial payments, just as any other foster parent would. Although some children might be exposed to ongoing family dysfunction and interference by the child's natural parents, the benefits of family nurturance and continuity of care usually outweigh the risks, especially when close child welfare monitoring is in place.

The kinship care trend has been especially supportive of culturally competent models of practice. An excessive number of children in placement are African American, so kinship care is especially thought to be more appropriate for these children due to the close kinship ties and community networks of African-American culture. Grandparents are the usual kinship caregivers, but the role of the African-

American father in the lives of children within the welfare system is also being explored. O'Donnell (1999) completed a study of seventy-four African-American fathers and described the extent to which these men participated in services on the behalf of their children placed in kinship care. The data indicated that few fathers were involved in case assessment, case planning, and service delivery. Whitley and colleagues (1999) reported on a program in Atlanta, Georgia, called Project Healthy Grandparents that was established in 1995 to determine the effectiveness of an interdisciplinary, community-based program in enhancing the social, psychological, physical, and economic well-being of low-income African-American grandparents so as to prevent child neglect. This project, established at Georgia State University, studied grandparents as heads of household while the parents of the involved children lived elsewhere. The program served fifty grandparents at any given time and attempted to alleviate stresses related to ongoing child care. The project coordinators realized that many grandparents stepped into this crucial child care role during a time of crisis, with little time for planning and deliberate decision making. The mean age of the grandparents was fifty-seven years, and 64 percent of the grandparents were either unemployed or retired. Eighty-two percent of the grandparents were not married and reported that they were raising their grandchildren alone (Whitley et al., 1999).

Case management services in the Project Healthy Grandparents program lasted one year and involved monthly home-based visits by social workers and nurses. Third-year law students provided legal consultation and assistance under supervision, discussing custody arrangements and other legal issues. They were assisted to prioritize their needs, goals, and strengths so that a range of personal, familial, and community resources could be mobilized. They were given an active role in developing care plans and were also well represented on the program's advisory committee. A strengths-based model was used to provide monthly parenting and support group programs, so that participants could express their concerns and share mutual problems with others undergoing similar circumstances. Many of the grandparents in Project Healthy Grandparents reported increases in self-confidence, feelings of empowerment, and a sense of readiness for problem solving.

The kinship care trend continues into the twenty-first century with some child welfare departments opening divisions of kinship care, where entire units of workers intervene exclusively with children placed in kinship care homes. For instance, such a program has been opened as part of the county children's services in a large city in northeastern Ohio. Workers who serve grandparents caring for these children provide ongoing case management services to assist with accessing resources and dealing with problem situations. Many child welfare agencies are developing similar programs to accommodate this fast-growing trend in child welfare and to tailor the services to the needs of families providing kinship care.

With the passage of the Adoption and Safe Families Act of 1997 (Public Law 105-89), foster care was carefully reevaluated and existing state laws, policies, and procedures were remarkably altered. Although long viewed as a transitional service for children, many children were staying in the system much longer than necessary, and their placement did not lead to reunification with natural parents or other relatives. It has been estimated that one-third of the estimated 500,000 children in foster care will never return to their birth parents and that minority children, who constitute 60 percent of the total, will spend twice as long waiting for permanent homes as other foster children (Downs et al., 2000). This new law made provisions regarding the safety of children and specified that the health and safety of the child must be given priority in deciding upon removal from or reunification with the natural family. The so-called reasonable efforts to keep children with their families were deemphasized, as spelled out earlier in PL 272. Petitions for parental rights were to be issued in a number of circumstances: when another child had been murdered by the parent, when an infant had been abandoned, and when a child has been seriously injured, resulting in a felony conviction (Downs et al., 2000).

The Adoption and Safe Families Act also mandated that states file for termination of parental rights if a child remained in foster care fifteen of the previous twenty-two months, unless the child was being cared for by a relative. Also, the legislation reduced the length of time a child may remain in foster care without a permanency hearing from eighteen to twelve months (Wells and Guo, 1999). Other exceptions included documentation of a compelling reason why termination of parental rights would not serve the child's best interest, or the agency's not being able to provide the family with adequate services to ensure the safe return of the child. The Adoption and Safe Families Act also emphasized the importance of kinship care and established a U.S. Advisory Board for Kinship Care to monitor the provision of kinship care in child welfare practice (Downs et al., 2000).

The passage of the Personal Responsibility and Work Opportunity Reconciliation Act of 1996 (Public Law 104-193) brought about drastic welfare reform and was aimed at helping poor families get off Aid to Families with Dependent Children and become more self-sufficient. Professionals in the child care professions fear that the long-range effects of this legislation will have a negative impact on poor families involved in the public welfare system (National Center for Children in Poverty, 1997). Wells and Gou (1999) stated that possible negative consequences might include decreases in total family income; increases in reports of child abuse and neglect; increases in children entering foster care and the child welfare system; slower rates of children being returned home; and faster rates at which reunified children reenter care.

## CONCLUSION

Most professionals today would admit that society has made remarkable strides in the care of children over the centuries. Children have moved from enslavement and being considered "little adults" to having rights that must be protected at all cost. Federal legislation to protect the rights of children at home, in school, and in the community have enhanced the quality of life of all children. From the mid-nineteenth century on, children have slowly gained a status in society that addresses their need to be protected and nurtured to adulthood and independence. Twentieth-century child abuse legislation, innovations in child welfare practice, and special education laws are only a few of the ways that children's rights have been protected.

We have moved from policies of separating children from abusive parents to helping families establish more effective strategies for communication and problem solving. Permanency planning and family preservation have solidified efforts of child welfare professionals to keep children out of foster care while aiding their parents to enhance parenting skills and prevent the escalation of problems that lead to child abuse and domestic violence. In courtrooms today, children, even babies, have a guardian *ad litem* appointed by the court to address their needs as a child, often in placement, divorce, or custody hearings.

Still, we have a long way to go as the United States attempts to adjust to family welfare laws that have restricted resources to many poor children in a society that calls for equal opportunity and social justice for all citizens, including children. Moreover, the United States lags in providing access to health care and still has a high infant mortality rate, regardless of its top rankings in health care technology. In an increasingly multicultural and multilingual society, social workers and other human service professionals must empower disenfranchised families and children and utilize culturally competent strategies for meeting their needs.

## *STRENGTHS STORY: CYNTHIA HARPER*

Cynthia Harper was born to a family of four just outside of Detroit, Michigan, where she also grew up. Cynthia, the Harpers' oldest child, was born with spina bifida. She was a tiny baby who had multiple operations immediately after birth, and the doctors told her parents she might not live beyond six months due to her multiple medical problems. She had severe hydrocephalus and multiple infections related to the spinal operations necessary to keep her alive. She had orthopedic problems caused by her shortened and malformed legs, and as a young child she had to use a wheelchair most of the time. Bowel and bladder operations were performed so that body wastes could be eliminated via bags attached to her abdomen. During childhood, Cynthia loved school and always made straight As. She was fascinated by science and loved to work on her science fair project each year. She won an award almost every time. Her inability to engage in playground sports seemed insignificant when others considered her astute skills as a chess and bridge player.

Still, Cynthia missed school often due to her hospitalizations for multiple neurosurgical and orthopedic procedures. Nevertheless, she had homeschool teachers who helped her keep up with her schoolwork in the hospital and at home while she was recuperating from surgery. Cynthia had many friends at school who never failed to call or visit her when she was sick. Both her family and her teachers were amazed at how well Cynthia adapted to all the changes and uncertainty in her life. The hospital doctors and nurses could not believe her compliance regardless of how painful a procedure might be. She always had a smile on her face, even when she had to be hospitalized and separated from her family countless times. At home, she volunteered to look after the younger siblings when her parents went out, as she was the oldest child. In the fifth grade she decided she wanted to be a scientist so that she could do research to help other children. Cynthia tried hard to walk every day and her efforts paid off. As an early teenager, she was able to use braces to get around and eventually was able to walk without assistance.

Cynthia started reading about her condition and other medical conditions, and she amazed the medical staff with her interests, knowledge, and questions. Upon completing high school as the valedictorian, she went away to college and majored in chemistry. From there she went on to complete a master's and doctor of philosophy in chemistry. Today, she is a biochemist with a major research corporation. Cynthia attributes her success to her own strong will and determination, as well as the remarkable encouragement provided to her by her parents, teachers, and health care providers, which helped to keep her strong. Moreover, she believes that her work as a teacher, author, and researcher has helped many children with disabilities to believe in themselves and make their dreams come true through hard work and endurance. She remains close to her family and is proud that she was able not only to help her retired parents build a new home but also finance her younger brother's college education.

## QUESTIONS FOR DISCUSSION

1. Discuss some of the trends in caring for children that have occurred during the past century in the United States.
2. Discuss how family preservation can best serve the needs of a child who requires out-of-home placement.
3. Discuss several ways in which therapeutic or treatment foster care is tailored to meet the needs of a child with multiple emotional and behavioral disorders.
4. Discuss the trend of kinship care as a foster care option and consider both strengths and limitations of this approach in caring for children who require out-of-home placement.

# REFERENCES

Abbott, G. (1938). *The child and the state,* 2 volumes. Chicago, IL: University of Chicago Press.

Anderson, L. E., Weston, E. A., Doueck, H. J., and Krause, D. J. (2002). The child-centered social worker and the sexually abused child: Pathway to healing. *Social Work* 47(4): 368-378.

Bremmer, R. H. (Ed.) (1970). *Children and youth in America: A documentary history,* Volume 1. Cambridge, MA: Harvard University Press.

Carroll, J. (2002). Play therapy: Children's views. *Child and Family Social Work Journal* 7: 177-187.

Cohen, N. A. (2000). *Child welfare: A multicultural focus,* Second edition. Boston, MA: Allyn and Bacon.

Compton, B. R. (1980). *Introduction to social welfare and social work.* Homewood, IL: Dorsey Press.

Conrad, P. and Schneider, J. W. (1992). *Deviance and medicalization: From badness to sickness.* Philadelphia, PA: Temple University Press.

Courtney, M. (1995). Reentry to foster care of children returned to their families. *Social Service Review* 69: 228-241.

Davis, I., Landsverk, J., and Newton, R. (1997). Duration of foster care for children reunified within the first year of care. In Berrick, J., Barth, R., and Gilberet, N. (Eds.), *Child welfare research review* (pp. 272-293). New York: Columbia University Press.

Downs, S. W., Moore, E. M., McFadden, E. J., and Costin, L. B. (2000). *Child welfare and family services: Policies and practice,* Sixth edition. Boston, MA: Allyn and Bacon.

Hewitt, F. M. and Forness, S. R. (1984). *The education of exceptional learners,* Third edition. Boston, MA: Allyn and Bacon.

McMurtry, S. and Lie, G. (1992). Differential exit rate of minority children in foster care. *Social Work Research and Abstracts* 28(1): 42-48.

National Center for Children in Poverty (1997). *Children and welfare reform.* Issue Briefs 2 and 3. School of Public Health, Columbia University, New York.

Noble, D. N., Perkins, K., and Fatout, M. (2000). On being a strength coach: Child welfare and the strengths model. *Child and Adolescent Social Work Journal* 17(2): 141-153.

O'Donnell, J. (1999). Involvement of African-American fathers in kinship foster care services. *Social Work* 44(5): 428-441.

Rose, S. R. and Fatout, M. F. (2003). *Social work practice with children and adolescents.* Boston, MA: Allyn and Bacon.

Sheafor, B. W. and Horejsi, C. R. (2003). *Techniques and guidelines for social work practice,* Sixth edition. Boston, MA: Allyn and Bacon.

Taylor, A. S. (2000). The UN Convention on the Rights of the Child: Giving children a voice. In Bergin, A. and Lindsey, G. (Eds.), *Researching children's perspectives* (pp. 21-33). Buckingham, UK: Open University Press.

Tower, C. C. (1993). *Understanding child abuse and neglect.* Boston, MA: Allyn and Bacon.

U.S. Bureau of Census (1990). *Current population reports: Marital status and living arrangements.* Series P-20, No. 450. Washington, DC: U.S. Government Printing Office.

Wells, K. and Guo, S. (1999). Reunification and reentry of foster children. *Children and Youth Services Review* 21(4): 273-294.

Whitley, D. M., White, K. R., Kelley, S. J., and Yorke, B. (1999). Strengths-based case management: The application to grandparents raising grandchildren. *Families in Society* 80(2): 110-119.

Winton, M. A. and Mara, B. A. (2001). *Child abuse and neglect: Multidisciplinary approaches.* Boston, MA: Allyn and Bacon.

Wolfe, D. A. (1999). *Child abuse: Implications for child development and psychopathology,* Second edition. Thousand Oaks, CA: Sage Publications.

# Chapter 3

# Children and Family Relationships

Other things may change us, but we start and end with family.

Anthony Brandt

The family continues to be the basic arena for socialization of children and continues to be extremely significant in a child's sense of security, well-being, and self-esteem. Despite traditional beliefs that a two-parent, biological family is the ideal family structure for bringing up children, most would agree that children from all types of families are happy and grow up to be responsible citizens and strong parents themselves. Most professionals would agree that there is no one recipe or formula for family success. In 1990, Beavers and Hampson released the results of their twenty-five-year study on family competence, which suggested that families may be competent regardless of lifestyle or family configuration. They described their model of family competence as follows:

> All families show consistently high degrees of capable negotiation, clarity of individual expression, respect for individual choices, ambivalence, and affiliative attitudes toward one another. Each member appears competent, acknowledged, and assured; the resultant product is a group of individuals who are spontaneous, enjoy each other, and are allowed clear and direct expression of feelings, attitudes, and beliefs. (pp. 30-31)

This description of family competence would enable children to have a voice and be considered as full members of the family, always feeling that they could express their opinions. This style of family communication was described by Satir, Stachowiak, and Taschman (1990) as allowing for the sending of congruent messages in which one's thoughts, feelings, and behaviors are consistent. Thus, the fam-

39

ily member, whether child or adult, will feel more supported or validated, providing immediate gratification and feelings of enhanced self-image. Parents can model congruent communication in many different ways in order to engender positive feelings and resilience in their children at home, at school, and in the community.

Children experience many different family types and structures which reflect the diversity of U.S. culture and family dynamics. Children born into biological families may grow up with both parents, but there is a greater than 50 percent chance that their parents will divorce at some point in their lives. Children in single-parent families, whether because of divorce or death of a parent, often have to adapt to more stringent rules to maintain family continuity, assuming more responsibility and expanded family roles. Children in blended families must adjust to new ways of coping and interacting with a stepparent and often a new set of siblings, as the family unit is reframed and reconstituted. In trigenerational families, children have the benefit of interacting with and being parented by both parents and grandparents, which often enriches family closeness and traditions. In gay and lesbian families, children may have to adjust to different roles played by the natural father or mother and a life partner, as well as discrimination related to homophobia. Adopted children experience the additional challenge of being adopted, as well as the other issues just mentioned. Children adopted may, at first, have difficulty relating to siblings born to the adoptive parents, and may at some point become part of a unified adoptive family network (Helton and Jackson, 1997). Children who are placed in foster care may remain there until adulthood, experiencing numerous transitions in foster home placement and caregiving, or may, at last, be adopted. Still other children may remain in residential child care settings during all or part of their childhood, where house parents and other staff serve as surrogate family members.

## CHILDREN IN BIOLOGICAL FAMILIES

Children born to natural parents generally experience much stability throughout their childhood, including consistent discipline, nurturing, and a sense of trust. Erikson (1963) noted that a sense of trust is first instilled within the family and becomes integral to successful adaptation during later developmental stages. All children need encouragement, affection, love, and consistency in their lives. Although many assume such experiences are available only in biological or natural families, this is not the case. These families today may be overwrought with problems that lead to family dysfunction. Such major problems as substance abuse, domestic violence, child abuse, unemployment, and homelessness erode family life and may lead to family dissolution. Many two-parent families experience difficulty arranging child care since most parents work outside the home and often have different schedules, which means leaving the children home alone or with only one parent.

These children may develop a division of labor to accomplish household tasks while their parent or parents are at work, becoming quite proficient in carrying out essential duties to keep the home running smoothly. Youth taking on household chores such as vacuuming, washing dishes, doing laundry, and caring for younger children is commonplace in the modern American family. The older children may take charge of the younger children and delegate various tasks to be performed. Conversely, in families with a physically ill or developmentally disabled member, a younger child may assume the role of caretaker in what would appear to be a role reversal. Sometimes this role reversal can be difficult for the child with disabilities as he or she may feel that his or her rightful position as an older child has been altered, and the younger child may resent not getting as much attention from the parents as the sibling with disabilities does. The child without disabilities may be expected to assume more household chores to assist the parents who may spend inordinate amounts of time handling the affected child's medical care and educational programming.

In interracial biological families issues may emerge regarding the child's racial and ethnic identity. Children may be confused by being identified as African American, and may sense that they will fit in more easily by assuming the racial and cultural identity of the majority. The family is logically the most appropriate place for discussions of racial identity. Sometimes parents will begin to explain to preschool-aged children about their interracial heritage, and child care professionals may use children's stories (e.g., bibliotherapy) or dolls to describe such differences as skin color and hair texture. However, other parents may wait until the child begins to ask questions about his or her racial heritage or perhaps begins to experience identity issues that may later become problematic if not addressed. Consider the situation of David in the following case scenario:

David, age five, was born to an African-American father, Jeffrey Holt, and a Caucasian mother, Mildred Sellers Holt. Mrs. Holt, a teacher, is ten years younger than Mr. Holt, who was previously married and divorced from another Caucasian woman, with whom he had three children. Mr. and Mrs. Holt have been married for seven years, and David has regular contact with his half siblings from his father's previous marriage. David has light brown skin, green eyes, and soft, curly black hair like his mother. Mr. Holt has dark brown skin, brown eyes, and wears his hair in a short Afro style. The family lives in an ethnically mixed community of Caucasians, African Americans, Asian Americans, and Arab Americans, and everyone gets along well with no emphasis being given to skin color or race in daily activities in the neighborhood.

However, David recently came home from a weekend visit with his widowed grandmother, Margaret Sellers, and started telling the children in the neighborhood that he was white. His mother happened to be sitting on the porch knitting when she heard David share this information. After he came in from playing, she sat him down at the kitchen table and told him that he was not white and that he was not African American. Then she carefully described that he was both Caucasian like Mommy, and African American like Daddy. Still, David insisted that he was white and began to get irritated. At that point, Mrs. Holt said, "Okay, I want you to do something for me. Will you promise?" David veered his gaze away from his mother and was anxious about her proposal, but he agreed to go along with his mother's suggestion. Mrs. Holt said that she would like David to take a bath that evening with his father and she would sit with them in the bathroom while they bathed, to discuss skin color. She then called her husband at work and explained the issue troubling David. He said the bath was a good idea and would allow the family to discuss David's view of himself and also provide a forum for questions and answers.

That evening, after their usual story time, the Holts took David into the bathroom so that he could bathe with his father. Mrs. Holt sat very close by so that they could all discuss the differences in their skin color and racial features. The parents explained to David that his skin and hair color reflected his looking like both of them and explained how special that made him, to be part of two cultures, Caucasian and African American, "fifty-fifty." He seemed to understand and went to bed with a smile on his face. Meanwhile, Mrs. Holt called her mother and spoke with her about the importance of helping David to understand and cope with his biracial heritage. The discussion went well and the grandmother seemed to understand how important these identity issues were for David. The next day, David brought two of his playmates over for ice cream and they were sitting together on the front steps playing with their Transformers toys. Mrs. Holt heard David proudly boast that he was not white, or African American. He said, "I am fifty-fifty." The kids then went on talking and laughing as usual. Through his parents' support, David had come to a better understanding of his true racial and ethnic identity.

## *CHILDREN IN SINGLE-PARENT FAMILIES*

Children in single-parent families have to face the daily challenge of managing in life with only one parent. Considering the high divorce rate in the United States, children quickly learn that their having only one parent at home does not make them unique. Still, many of the duties of the household may be shared by the children to assist their working parent. The percentage of single mothers who work outside the home is estimated at 61 percent; this figure climbs to 70 percent when mothers of children under age eighteen are included (Zastrow and Kirst-Ashman, 2001). Single fathers are more and more common due to their commitment to raising their children after a divorce. In many cases, the father is the more suitable parent due to the mother's insufficient physical or emotional capacity for child care. This is especially true for families in which the mother is addicted to drugs or is the perpetrator of abuse. Many single parents may feel compelled to develop more rules for governing family functioning to ensure the safety and well-being of their children when they are at work or away from the home (Helton and Jackson, 1997). Children in single-parent families may need to take on even more responsibilities for chores such as washing dishes, caring for younger children, and cleaning the house in order for the family to meet its everyday needs.

Children in single-parent families represent a large portion of children in American society due to the high rate of divorce. Children in divorced families experience multiple stressors related to poor parental communication, conflict over visitation, coparenting duties, and time spent alone. Many children of divorce have to assume additional duties at home to help their custodial parent and may resent this additional burden placed upon their leisure time with peers. This is often the case with teenagers who, while struggling for more independence and autonomy, find themselves caring for younger siblings. Others may feel guilty for not doing enough to help their parent maintain the family home. These children may become caught in a catch-22 situation due to their parents' expectation that they develop dual loyalties, which may include the expectation that they will report on the other parent, especially regarding their romantic and financial status.

Single parents who are widowed, whether by natural death or accident, first need to help their children work through their grief by discussing guilt, fears, and depression. Many children have an amazing capacity to understand how such loss will affect them and their role in the family; others need constant nurturing and support. Open communication is extremely important and may include family conferences at mealtimes or a family discussion or "story time" before bed. Some families enjoy reading fairy tales or nursery rhymes, but many enjoy telling about the events of their day or engaging in joint storytelling, which involves each person selecting a topic and/or adding their views to the story.

Christine, age thirty-one, is a single parent who divorced when her sons, Steve and John Jr., were two and five. Their father, John, was having an affair with a co-worker when Christine was pregnant with Steve. He continued to see other women as the marriage deteriorated. Christine had a hard time accepting the divorce although she did receive child support payments for her sons. John Jr. was born with a congenital heart defect and partial blindness, for which she was blamed by the father. She sought counseling and was able to increase her self-esteem by learning to write poetry and play the guitar. She eventually began setting her songs to music and singing them. She encouraged her sons to write out their feelings, which they would discuss in family meetings.

Christine went back to school to work on a travel agent degree, and her confidence as a parent and individual increased tremendously. She took the children on camping trips, went fishing with them, and planned joint family picnics and holiday celebrations with her friend, Sandra. Christine became involved in a local church where she was hired part-time as the secretary, and she also made money by cleaning the houses of fellow churchgoers. She enrolled John Jr. in a school for visually impaired children and became a staunch advocate to ensure that his specialized services were adherent to federal special education legislation. The sons became closer as they entered into late childhood, and Steve often took care of his older brother while his mother did housework. Steve and his mother even participated in a voluntary school lecture series wherein they discussed what it was like to have a family member with disabilities.

## CHILDREN IN BLENDED FAMILIES

Blended families are so common today that they are becoming part of the mainstream American lifestyle. It is estimated that more than 33 percent of all children in the United States live in a blended family before age eighteen (American Psychological Association, 1995). These children experience separation as part of their childhood with divorced, remarried, or single parents. Blended families are known commonly as *stepfamilies.* In these families, children live with one parent who is biological and one who is not. Barbara Perlmutter of Stepfamily Consultation and Counseling reports that more than half of Americans today have been, are now, or will be in one or more stepfamily situations in their lives (Perlmutter and Miki, 2001). She also reports that by the year 2010 it is estimated that there will be more stepfamilies than nuclear families.

There is a myth that stepfamilies or blended families function as well as nuclear families with two parents and children. On the contrary, it is estimated that more than 60 percent of what we call blended families fail (Sims, 2002). Although research has found that children of stepfamilies face a higher risk of emotional and behavioral problems (Featherstone, Cundick, and Jensen, 1992), it has also been estimated that such risk can be mitigated by an intimate relationship providing a buffer against the risk (Palosaari and Aro, 1995). One couple reports a long, painful learning curve and complex relationships between the new stepparent and an ex-spouse, as well as with the children within the family system (Sims, 2002).

Children in blended families face multiple challenges as they transition from ways of being in one family system to a new family unit, where the new lifestyle will be different from the one they knew before. Changes in parental expectations, modes of communication, and family structure can make life almost unbearable for some children. Despite the risks, most children have adjusted to living in a single-parent home within two or three years following their parents' divorce (Dacey and Travers, 1999). However, children are resilient and generally adjust once again after their parents remarry and have an amazing tendency to respond positively to economic, affectional, and social changes brought about by their integration into a new family system.

Until the 1970s, the blended family still evoked thinking about the "wicked stepmother" image or a stepfather who remained largely disengaged from the family. These myths were somewhat challenged by movies and television shows that attempted to present a more unified and positive family unit engendered by two families coming together. One may recall such classic television shows as *Eight Is Enough* and

*The Brady Bunch,* which addressed the merging and conflictual issues just after the marriage, and addressed the development of the families as they became more cohesive, negotiating differences while still maintaining the integrity of the values held in their previous families. Family meetings were held on each show to further family communication and to give each child an opportunity to express his or her feelings about being part of a reconstituted family. These shows, still popular in syndication, reflected the increasing divorce and remarriage rates in the United States, as well as the growing acceptance to the "yours, mine, and ours" philosophy of the blended family. Families were shown as joint decision makers and compromisers. Where family routines and rules were concerned, the shows highlighted the significance of developing new family rituals to reflect the diversity of interests among family members.

Members of blended families are challenged by all the changes but most are motivated to address their differences in a way that will lead to a new level of family togetherness. Families will inevitably discuss the family rules, roles, relationships, and rituals that characterized their previous family constellations and will create new family dynamics that are more consistent with the lifestyle of their new family system (Helton and Jackson, 1997). Professionals may be surprised that the children are the ones to take the lead in developing these new family ways of relating to one another, accomplishing family tasks, and developing norms that will be satisfactory to all family members. For example, Jenny, age seven, whose never-married mother married a widower with three children, ages five, nine, and eleven, suggested that the family ride their bikes on Wednesday evenings at the local park, since the parents worked late on the other days of the week. This activity soon became a family ritual and was enjoyed by all family members because it provided an opportunity for increased communication and relaxation as a family. Children want to feel loved, nurtured, and protected in their new blended family so they often will respond to their stepparent and new sibling cohorts in ways that will pull the family together and enhance their feelings of family ties.

Because children of divorce are likely to be dealing with feelings of rejection, disappointment, and guilt concerning their parents' divorce, they will need time to work through some of those feelings. This may be even more difficult if the parent with custody has criticized or demeaned the other parent in front of the children. Children may believe that since their parent could not save their previous family from breaking up, why should they try hard to build a new family unit? Because most children visit the noncustodial parent on a regular basis, this conflict among their natural parent, stepparent, and stepsiblings is likely to exacerbate after each visit. Lefrancois (1996) notes that bonding in blended families may be more difficult for children whose fathers have custody as they may have spent more time with their natural mothers and may resent or reject a new mother figure. The new mother in the blended family can improve the children's sense of trust by spending special time with them alone, taking an active interest in their hobbies and school activities, and reaffirming that their relationship is different from that with their own mother, yet can be still rewarding and supportive.

Blended families that emerge due to the death of a spouse may be more difficult, especially at the outset, than families in which parents were divorced. Children may still be dealing with grief over losing their natural mother or father and may view their parent's remarriage as disrespectful to their deceased parent's memory. Children may, consequently, test the love of their new stepparent by acting out, confiding about their faults to their natural parent, or becoming isolated from family interaction. Moreover, others will take out their frustrations on their new stepsiblings as a way to get back at their stepparent, assuming the attitude of "no one in *your* family could possibly understand or appreciate what I have gone through." The adjustment period may be shorter in blended families where both parents have lost a spouse, as their children may feel that they have more in common with the new parent and stepsiblings. Parents can help greatly to assist with the process of cohesion by providing frequent family gatherings and activities and also by encouraging the children to form alliances for work and play. For example, stepsiblings may be asked to clean out the garage or mow the lawn together, rather than performing each family chore separately. In this way, the children have a chance to develop more respect for one another's differences and are more likely to perceive their parents as partners in parenting.

Children in blended families are likely to experience feelings of loss and alienation because they have lost or left behind not only a natural parent but also their grandparents, cousins, schoolmates, and other significant others. This is especially true for situations in which the creation of the blended family means moving to a new residence or even across the country. The children's sense of well-being and self-confidence may be enhanced by both parents' encouraging and ensuring them that these nurturing social networks will remain intact as much as possible. Children should not be made to feel that they are losing their old family but rather merging their previous family and social support system into an even larger network of relatives and friends. This may not be as likely to happen if the noncustodial parent is unwilling to work on keeping these relationships intact. The relatives, especially grandparents, can further these feelings of comfort and acceptance within the blended family by not taking sides, reaffirming their continued love and support, and encouraging new family rituals and experiences. In some extended family systems, this may involve including the stepsiblings in family gatherings and activities. In essence, children need not perceive their blended family as a totally new family but rather as one that is different yet accommodates their need to preserve and maintain previous family ties.

The APA Help Center (American Psychological Association, 1995) lists issues that stepfamilies should consider in planning for remarriage, parenting in stepfamilies, and stepparent-child relationships. They include completing "emotional divorce," the need for the couple to "build a strong marital bond," establishing a relationship with the children that is similar to a friend or "camp counselor," leaving discipline of the children to the custodial parent, and keeping some physical distance from stepchildren by providing "verbal affection rather than physical affection."

Moreover, Gestalt therapist Patricia Papernow (1993) presents four general issues that should be considered when working with new stepfamilies:

1. Competition for middle ground about ways to do everything in the newly formed family
2. Rigidly defined insiders and outsiders defined by two small units in the family (one parent and his or her children)
3. Differential attachment based on different experiences in previous family units
4. Differences in culture created by the insider-versus-outsider positions in the family

Papernow further proposes three normal stages of stepfamily development. In the early stages, each member of the family maps the territory. During middle stages, restructuring of the family occurs. Then, in the later stages, intimacy and redefined relationships develop. Despite many difficulties experienced in blended families, children will eventually thrive in stepfamilies if the parent and stepparent let the children know that they understand their feelings of grief regarding the unsuccessful marriage of their biological parents.

Carl Johnson, an African American, moved out of the house he shared with his ex-wife, Karen, and their five-year-old son, Kenny, when he and Karen divorced. They had purchased a newly built suburban homes near Atlanta, Georgia. He took an apartment in Atlanta, and Kenny stayed with him every weekend. Five months after Carl took a new position in a company as a customer relations supervisor, he was offered a promotion in New Jersey. Although Carl knew that he would miss having Kenny around, Carl agreed to take the position in New Jersey. He hoped to have a new life away from many bittersweet memories. Within two weeks after his move to New Jersey, Carl met Barbara, who was working at the same company. Carl found out that Barbara had pulled herself from a chaotic urban life after graduating from high school. She was a single mother of an eleven-year-old daughter, Kim.

Barbara invited Carl to live with them in a two-bedroom apartment instead of commuting back and forth from his tiny apartment. On the first vacation Carl and Barbara could arrange, they took Kim and Kenny to Disney World. They had a wonderful time. The most amazing thing was that Kim and Kenny hit it off so well that it was as if they were a real sister and brother. The following summer, Carl and Barbara married and Kim and Kenny were in the wedding party. Kenny participated in a day camp until the end of the summer. When Kenny had to leave for his mother in Georgia, Kim promised that she would call him every Sunday evening until he could return to New Jersey for the Christmas holiday. Carl accompanied Barbara to all the basketball games that Kim played, and Kim thought it was neat to have a father like Carl. When Kenny returned for Christmas, he told Kim he was not supposed to call Barbara "Mom," because his mother, Karen, was his mom. He also insisted that Kim not call his father "Dad" because he was not actually her dad. Carl took Kenny and Kim to McDonald's for lunch and explained that they could have two moms and two dads. They seemed to understand and had a great time.

## CHILDREN IN GAY AND LESBIAN FAMILIES

Children with gay or lesbian parents experience many stresses related to homophobia and rejection of their parents' lifestyle by other children and adults. Laird (1995) has estimated that the number of children living in such homes ranges between 8 and 10 million. Some parents hide their sexual identity and do not come out to their children; others discuss their sexual orientation with their children in an effort to enhance communication and family relationships. A study by Armesto (2002) found that the stresses of parenting are exacerbated for gay and lesbian parents because of their membership in a stigmatized group. He suggests that competent parenting by gay men seems to be affected by their ability to come to grips with their sexual identity and negotiate the stress of living in a homophobic and heterosexist society.

Those gay and lesbian parents choosing not to come out to their children may fear custody battles or may be concerned about the impact of this knowledge on their children (Zastrow and Kirst-Ashman, 2001). However, children who do not know their parents' sexual orientation may experience more harm if they discover this information from other sources, such as extended family members or family friends. Consequently, such children may become distrustful of their parents for not disclosing this personal and influential information to them. This can be especially difficult for teenagers who are in the midst of forming their own identities and may already be struggling to deal with their parents' separation or divorce. By not revealing his or her true identity, a parent may exacerbate the confusion that is inherent within this self-searching process.

When parents are open with their children about their own sexual orientation, the children not only feel better about themselves over time but are also able to come to grips with their own identity issues. Since many gay and lesbian parents have been in heterosexual marriages or relationships, the ex-spouses may have visiting privileges and therefore face questions about the lifestyle of the custodial parent. Openness about having a gay partner or significant other makes it easier for both the children and the parent to have a common point of reference for their life together. Children who feel that they have to keep secrets or give excuses may feel guilty and depressed because of their parent's perceived denial of sexual orientation or betrayal by not telling them the truth. The following case demonstrates a family system in which just the opposite chain of events occurred.

Betty, age thirty-seven, was married with three children, Lisa, age fifteen, Jack, age twelve, and Susan, age nine. Betty, a cosmetologist, and her husband, Tom, had decided to divorce after he started physically abusing her and having affairs with other women. Betty decided to begin attending a women's support group at a local community center. On her second visit she met Carol, a thirty-four-year-old lesbian who had been in several long-term relationships, the last one having just ended. Betty and Carol talked after group a few times and finally decided to go out for coffee one evening. Carol drove Betty home afterward. Before Betty got out of the car Carol gave her a kiss. That was the beginning of their relationship. They dated for a few months and Carol got to know the children well and became known as Aunt Carol. She was an avid sports fan, always checking the baseball box scores and watching televised games with the kids.

The children seemed to realize how much their mom liked Carol, and vice versa, and they were enjoying having another significant adult in their lives. They continued to visit their father on alternate weeks, but these visited dwindled after he met another woman with two children and moved in with them. Carol moved in with Betty and the children just before Christmas, and they had a wonderful holiday together. About a week after Carol moved in, Betty and Carol sat down and told the children about their relationship and their plans to live their lives as lesbian partners. The older daughter, Lisa, reacted by saying that she thought so and did not have a problem with it. The son, Jack, was quiet and only had a few questions. The youngest daughter was delighted because she missed her dad and kind of viewed Carol as a "daddy" figure. Betty and Carol planned regular family chats on Tuesday evenings to further address any questions the children had about their sexual orientation, relationship, or other family concerns.

After a short time, children at school realized that the Betty and Carol were a couple, as they would take turns taking the kids to school and also attended some school events together. Jack came home one day and told his mother that some boys called him a "big queer" because of her. He said, "I know it was hard with Dad, but I wish you guys were still together." Betty told Jack that she understood how painful name-calling could be and stated that those children were hurting themselves more than him with their bigotry and homophobia. This seemed to help him deal with his feelings of discomfort and rejection. In fact, when the children had their friends over for birthday parties and playing ball, they began to focus more on having fun rather than what their friends might think of their mother and her partner. Interestingly, many of these friends became so fond of Betty and Carol and their "cool ways" that they would make excuses to come over. Carol, who worked as a lawn and garden consultant, was able to get complimentary tickets to a Major League Baseball game, filling the van with kids from the neighborhood. The neighborhood, a fairly liberal middle-class community, seemed to accept the lesbian couple over time, and the whole family began to attend the local interdenominational church, with no repercussions. Betty commented to her friends, "We are just a normal family, and the children know we would do anything for them." Although at first the extended family had reservations about Betty and Carol's relationship, most family members were accepting of the couple within a year or so and even invited Betty and Carol to a cousin's wedding.

What is exemplary about this case is that Betty and Carol gradually came out to their children and did it in a way that was comfortable for all of them. The family meeting gave each child a chance to ask questions, reflect on his or her role in the family, and consider the challenges he or she would possibly face in society due to homophobia. Children, such as the ones in this family, are incredibly resilient and often will respond positively to problems of discrimination when the parents are candid and jointly supportive. Betty and Carol presented a unified front and consistency in discussing their sexual orientation with the children and that made the adaptation easier. This is not to imply that the coming-out process is smooth for all gay and lesbian parents, but the openness and honesty demonstrated in this family might help other parents in similar circumstances.

Some gay and lesbian parents do not have custody of their children but do have regular visitation rights and play an active role in the lives of the children. The parent's gay or lesbian partner also develops a role with the children and may be seen as an uncle or aunt, or just their parent's best friend. In the rural United States, gay and lesbian parents may decide not to disclose their sexual orientation for fear of being ostracized in the workplace and the community. The noncustodial parent often lives in fear of losing the opportunity to visit his or her children and thus may decide not to come out to avoid the possibility of this loss. In many regions and more rural areas, disclosing one's sexual identity may lead to a backlash of moralistic and legal indictments. This necessary secrecy may keep the children in the dark and bring on questions that will have to be addressed, especially as the children approach preadolescence and adolescence.

These parents may attend family reunions and church socials without their partners, or they may choose to associate with small groups of gay friends and go to the largest nearby city to interact with others in the gay community. This masking of their sexual orientation may make gay parents' lives easier, but it can confuse older children who are addressing identity issues in their own growth and development. Younger children tend to be accepting of their parents' friends and may not react negatively other than to resent the time the parent may spend with his or her partner during visits. However, this happens in heterosexual families as well, when the children come to visit the noncustodial parent. The following case example demonstrates how two gay male partners are dealing with their parenting role.

Ron, age thirty-four, and Peter, age thirty, live in a small southern town, about two hours from the closest city, which has 60,000 people. They both grew up in the same town and went to high school and college together. Ron is a psychologist at the local mental health center and Peter is an elementary school teacher. Ron was married for twelve years and has two children, Judy, age twelve, and Jimmy, age ten. Ron and his wife, Jillian, divorced two years ago, and she obtained custody. Ron admits that he had always been attracted to men, which in part led to the breakup. He and his wife stopped communicating, and she and the children moved in with her parents. Ron was granted visitation rights, and the children see him on alternating weekends. Meanwhile, Ron started seeing his friend, Peter, socially, going to movies, camping out, and visiting nearby cities. They were extremely close friends who eventually admitted their affection for each other. Within a month, Peter gave up his apartment and moved into Ron's house.

The children had known Peter all along as their father's best friend, so they readily accepted him. However, the children do not know that Peter is their father's life partner because Ron has decided not to come out to them. Ron fears that his position at the mental health center might be placed in jeopardy, and he also fears that his ex-wife might retaliate and accuse him of being unfit. Both men take responsibility in caring for the children during their visits, and they seem to view Peter as another father figure. Ron and Peter have a strong relationship, which they feel can only grow stronger. The children have become an important part of both their lives, and they believe that when the timing is right they will disclose their sexual orientation to the children. Until then, they feel comfortable relating to each other as roommates and withholding demonstrations of their affection for each other and intimacy when the children are around.

## CHILDREN IN MULTIGENERATIONAL FAMILIES

Children today are likely to live at some point in a trigenerational family due to a number of variables, including the high divorce rate, welfare reform, economic recession, and an ever-increasing ethic and cultural mix within U.S. society. With the high divorce rate, many mothers and some fathers will move back into their parents' homes for financial and emotional support, especially immediately after the separation or divorce. Data from the 2000 Census suggest that 5.8

million (42 percent) grandparents are responsible for the basic needs of their grandchildren ("Raising Children Again," 2002). These grandparents often provide coparenting for their children and become central figures in the lives of their grandchildren while the parents are working or preparing for a new career by going back to school. Welfare reform, which resulted in so many single-parent families losing benefits, has led to increases in trigenerational families. This arrangement may provide the family with an enhanced sense of security and well-being during this difficult transitional period. The grandparents can be instrumental in providing child care, transportation, and emotional support until the parent can get back on his or her feet financially and emotionally. In some trigenerational family units, both parents and the children may move into the grandparents' home because of unemployment or the need for both parents to retrain for new jobs.

Furthermore, with people living longer than ever before, it is now more likely that four generations of a family could be living together and interacting as one unit. The possibility of such family constellations is directly related to the growing continuum of care for persons in late life, many of whom remain with their children and grandchildren as opposed to entering a nursing home or community residence geared to the needs of senior citizens. Due to advancements in health care technology, older persons are not only living longer but also in better health. Many grandparents work part-time and are still involved in rearing their grandchildren and, in many cases, great-grandchildren on a daily basis.

Families from diverse cultures, who constitute a large portion of U.S. society, have long valued and even favored trigenerational living arrangements as a way of life. The trigenerational family allowed these families to adapt to economic conditions and, just as important, provide the children an opportunity to learn and celebrate their culture and national heritage through direct daily contact with the grandparents. African-American families have long been forced to live in joint households for economic and child-rearing purposes. These strong kinship bonds have helped families survive hardship from the era of slavery until today, with many African-American grandparents serving as surrogate parents when necessary, through the long-standing tradition of kinship care. Immigrant families frequently live in multigenerational households due to economic necessity or personal choice. Many ethnic families may prefer such living arrangements, especially immediately after the family's emigration from their home country, so that they will be able to pool resources and also help the children maintain their native language. Since the United States is becoming more and more multicultural, multigenerational living arrangements can be expected to increase in the future. The family scenario that follows is reflective of the advantages multigenerational families can provide to enrich the lives of all generations living under one roof.

Ordelia Corbett, age thirty-five, is a divorced, African-American mother of two children, Leonard, age eleven, and William, age nine, whose father left the family for another woman after a fifteen-year marriage. Ordelia could not seem to make it on her own after the divorce so she and her sons moved into the household of her mother, Mary Watson, age fifty-eight, a widow. Ordelia's father had died five years earlier from cancer. Mr. and Mrs. Watson had always been close to their grandsons and considered them to be special as Ordelia was their only child. Ordelia continued to work as an administrative secretary in an accounting firm, but she had difficulty paying for child care and maintaining the household on her own. Mr. Corbett had worked as a school bus driver, but they could never seem to save enough money for a down payment on a house. Ordelia's husband, unlike her, came from a large family of seven; he was the oldest child. Thus, he always helped his family out with money—not only his parents but also his younger siblings. This became a sore spot in the marriage, but Ordelia also believed in the power of extended-family support and was tolerant of her husband's aid to his family over the years.

She decided that moving in with her mother would be good for the boys and for her because they could spend more time with their grandmother, whom they call Nana, and she could save money for a down payment on a house. Mrs. Watson, a part-time beautician, still does hair in a small salon adjacent to the back of the house, so she is always at home. She watches the boys after school; they often hang out in the salon playing video games or watching television. And they enjoy hearing the many stories, funny and dramatic, told by Mrs. Watson who, like many of her beauty salon customers, grew up down South. Mrs. Watson also cooks the family meals, especially on the three days that the salon is not open. Ordelia, in turn, does the laundry for the whole family and cleans the house on weekends, while Mrs. Watson does the grocery shopping. Ordelia is especially grateful for her mother's overseeing the boys' homework during the school year, as well as her helping to fund a camp experience for them in the summer. The whole family attends the Baptist Church every Sunday and on Wednesday evenings without fail. And before church on Wednesday, Mrs. Watson, Ordelia, and the boys go out to eat at their favorite restaurant, Joe Louie's Hideway. The whole family enjoys this time together, and lately, when Ordelia has mentioned being almost ready financially to look for a house, the boys have said they would prefer to stay with Nana. Ordelia realizes that the boys have grown attached to living with their maternal grandmother, just as she has relished being able to be there for her mother to support her. Leonard and William visit their father and his live-in girlfriend and her three small children on alternating weekends and seem to look forward to these visits.

Multigenerational families assist on another financially and also emotionally. Parents may need to save money to be able to afford adequate housing or transportation in their efforts to adapt to a new way of life. Grandparents are often able to provide much-needed support during this process. In many families, the living arrangements become permanent. The children benefit greatly from having another parent figure in their lives and are enriched by the wisdom and experiences of their grandparents. In ethnic families and families of color, children become aware at an early age of the central role that older persons play within their lives and culture, and they begin to respect these traditions. The multigenerational household has helped countless families endure the trials of discrimination, racism, and disenfranchisement with society.

## CHILDREN IN FOSTER FAMILIES

In 2001, there were 542,000 children in foster care; that year 263,000 children also exited foster care. The average age of these children was 10.1 years and the mean length of stay in foster care after the termination of parental rights was thirty-three months. Approximately 126,030 of these children under the age of sixteen are waiting to be adopted. Of this total, 45 percent were African American and 12 percent were Hispanic (U.S. Department of Health and Human Services, 2003). Children in foster care are some of the most vulnerable, behaviorally and emotionally, as they have been displaced from their families of origin for any number of reasons. Some children, along with their siblings before them, have been beaten, sexually abused, or abandoned as babies by parents who were too emotionally or financially destitute to care for them. These children may learn early on that they have to fend for themselves and thus do not become too attached to one family or key individual in their lives. They may believe that, at any time, they could be moved to another home and neighborhood. Unfortunately, because of the volatility of the child welfare system and the shortage of qualified foster parents, many children may rotate through multiple short-term foster placements; others may even be maltreated within these settings. Care by a relative, in other words, kinship care, is now being considered for more and more children so that family ties and a sense of community and culture may be maintained. Still, foster care remains the most viable alternative to provide safety and security for the thousands of children who need out-of-home placement.

Despite the best efforts of child welfare officials, too many children remain in out-of-home placements, waiting for reunification with their families of origin or adoption into a stable home. National attention was brought to this ongoing crisis with the story of Rilya Wilson, a foster child from Florida who remains lost in the system. Eleven workers in Miami-Dade County, Florida, were fired during the investigation of how this tragedy could have occurred within the Department of Children & Families (see ongoing coverage in the *Miami Herald* at <www.miami.com>). Child protective agencies remain largely understaffed and worker turnover rate remains high throughout the system. Moreover, we know that children who live in multiple foster homes often experience attachment problems, which instills a lack of trust and the ability to cope with problems later in life. Delaney (1998) states very poignantly:

> Many foster parents find themselves trapped in déjà vu—unwitting prisoners of their foster child's past. They often become reluctant actors in a recurring drama. These foster parents undeservedly fall heir to their foster child's negative expectations—to his unresolved attachment issues. (p. 27)

Children who feel insecure upon being moved from one home to another may feel dejected, unloved, and mistrustful that any new home will work out for them. Hoarding of food and destructive behavior often occur for weeks as the child tests limits and also seeks attention from the foster parents. Many children go through a honeymoon period for a few days or weeks when everything seems to be going smoothly, but this pattern is soon disrupted with uncontrollable crying, nightmares, and lashing out at other foster children. In homes where there are natural children of the foster parents, extreme competition and rivalry may occur related to personal space and privileges, such as watching a favorite television show or demanding to use the computer all evening for games. Such children seem to cry out for recognition and inclusion within the new family unit.

Permanency planning and family preservation efforts have expanded and enriched the options available to children from the same family who are placed outside the home. Often, siblings bond more readily to foster parents when they are placed together in foster care and seem to receive strong emotional support from one another over time. Children who are placed together have joint experiences and memories of family stability that may encourage and sustain them. However, in some families children have experienced so many traumas that they reflect on these experiences with one another and continue the symbolic cycle of pain and fear.

Placement in kinship care may enable the relative serving as the parent figure to reframe these negative stories and help the children to adapt. For example, a grandmother might tell her grandchildren, "Your mother is a good person, but she is just not able to care for you kids right now. Once she gets some help, you may be able to go back home with her." This would be much more positive and empowering than her stating, "Your mom is a no-good junkie with no hope of ever getting off the streets or taking you kids back." The impact on the child's resilience and coping ability can be remarkable depending on how the natural parents' problems are described by significant adults in the child's life.

Ethical dilemmas often arise when sibling groups are placed together yet experience extreme conflicts in their relationship (Congress, 1999). Such problems may lead to the placement of one or more siblings in foster care settings or with another relative. When a child first comes into foster care, he or she may feel abandoned, confused, and uncertain about the future. These emotions should be recognized and anticipated by the foster family, which is why foster parent training is so significant within the field of child welfare. Children not only lose their families of origin but also often feel as if they are pawns, as foster family placements often fail and the social worker turnover rate is extremely high in the field of protective services and child welfare at large. A child may be separated from siblings, for the children in a family may be removed consecutively or all at once, depending on the nature of the family's and child's problems.

A child with extremely abusive and destructive behaviors may be placed in treatment foster care for specialized therapy and supervision, and the other siblings may be divided among several other foster homes. Child welfare officials do make an effort, whenever possible, to place children in homes thought to be best suited for their developmental and emotional needs. Children who are medically fragile, such as a child with juvenile diabetes, may be placed with a family who has specialized skills in caring for them and who can maintain close contact with medical and health care professionals to ensure optimum health and well-being.

Children sometimes react to foster placement by retreating into themselves almost as a tortoise would go into its shell. They may feel guilty about leaving their natural parents or, in the case of abuse, may believe that they brought on the abuse or neglect perpetuated by the parents. They may engage in any number of self-abusive behaviors, strike out at other foster or natural children in the home, and hoard food. Some children will even run away and attempt to find their natural parents regardless of the distance.

The little girl in the following case had serious problems adjusting to her new foster home, which led her parents to seek counseling. They felt desperate and were on the verge of taking the little girl back to child welfare officials and giving up on her forever.

Brandy Cooper, age five, was placed in foster care, along with her older sister, Patty, age seven, in the home of Gary and Louise Sanders, both age thirty-three. The Sanderses had not been able to have children of their own and had thought about adoption. However, they thought they would become foster parents first just to test the waters. They went through the necessary foster parent training and took Brandy and Patty into their home in the fall of the same year. They were so excited, and, at first, everything went well. They believed that they had made a wonderful decision that would change their lives. Then things changed. Brandy became totally disruptive to their household and the Sanderses began to regret their decision to become foster parents.

Patty seemed to blend in well with the family and made several new friends at school and in the neighborhood. However, Brandy cried at night and called out for her mother. She clung to a photo of her mother, which she put under her pillow each night. Brandy began taking food from the kitchen and hiding it under the bed. About a week after the placement, Brandy took a bag of cookies and stuffed them under her mattress, along with several bananas and a bunch of grapes. Mrs. Sanders smelled the rotting fruit while cleaning the girls' room and confronted Brandy when she got home from kindergarten. She starting crying and kicking the bed saying it was her food, and she deserved it. The foster mother tried to reason with her, but she just became angrier and more out of control. She ran downstairs and out into the front yard and would not come back into the house. Her sister, Patty, finally was able to get her to come back into the house for a before-dinner snack. Things went well for a few days, but then the parents discovered that Brandy had squirted ketchup, which she had in her book bag, all over the bedspread and wall in the girls' room. After the foster parents disciplined her and made her help clean up the mess, she said that they did not love her and loved Patty more because she was prettier and smarter.

The parents were very patient with Brandy but felt they were at their wit's end in knowing how to deal with her problems. They began family counseling at a mental health agency, which also offered a foster parents' group for parents of children with severe behavioral and adjustment problems. From counseling they learned that many of Brandy's problems were normal for a child who had experienced multiple traumas and foster home placements. Once the honeymoon period ended she had begun to measure her parents' commitment to her by testing their boundaries. She wanted to prove to herself that she truly had a place in this family along with her sister. The girls' mother did visit them a few times, but she was a long-term substance abuser and thief. She and her boyfriend robbed a bank for drug money and ended up in prison, at which time parental rights were terminated. The Sanderses did well in treatment and eventually adopted Brandy and Patty.

Some foster children do better in placement than others, even if they are from the same family. This difference in adjustment points to the individuality of children and their varied abilities to cope with change in their lives. Whether resilience is related to intelligence, temperament, age at the time of placement, or the degree of match with the selected foster parents is debatable. We do know that all children will go through an adjustment period, which may be manifested by manipulative and combative behaviors, often to get attention from the foster parents and win their love. As in the case of Brandy, she felt that the foster parents cared more for and favored Patty. Children will inevitably cling to ideal images of their natural parents over time, holding on to a letter or picture. They should not be discouraged from these attachments as they adjust to their new living environment.

## CHILDREN IN ADOPTIVE FAMILIES

Children who are adopted have an opportunity to grow up in a loving family environment and also enrich the lives of adults who might otherwise have remained childless throughout their lives. Children in adoptive families may not display remarkable differences from their adoptive parents and, in fact, may even look like them. In contrast, other adopted children may be quite dissimilar and may even be from a different ethnic or racial background than their new parents. However, it is essential that the parents tell the child that he or she is adopted at an appropriate time so that the child can incorporate this knowledge into his or her identity. Many families tell their children as soon as they are old enough to understand the concept of adoption, but others may wait until the child is in the third or fourth grade. Because children vary so much in their development, age becomes less important than the way the child learns about his or her adopted status. Children are likely to be hurt emotionally if they find out about their adoption from another relative, such as a grandparent, instead of from the adoptive parents themselves. Children will most likely begin to ask questions about why they were put up for adoption and will inquire about the whereabouts of the natural parents. Parents may help the child cope with this information by telling the child that they chose to adopt him or her and that the biological parent did what seemed the most logical plan of action at the time.

Parents who adopt a child should be clear about why they want to adopt and what type of child they want. Many childless parents are convinced that only a healthy infant will satisfy them and may also insist on adopting a Caucasian baby. However, many school-age and adolescent children need homes, and many belong to sibling groups in placement. An inordinate number of children waiting for foster care are children of color, with African-American children constituting a sizable portion of children needing permanent homes. The adoption social worker in charge of the home study and parental assessment should ensure that a good match occurs between the parents and adoptive child by considering such factors as personality, temperament, interests, and lifestyle.

Many adoption agencies are challenged by the large numbers of children of color who remain in foster and are likely to be there until they are twenty-one years of age. Interracial adoptions are still frowned upon by most child welfare professionals, with their rationale being that the child should be united with a family of similar racial, ethnic, or cultural background. Many private adoption agencies have facilitated successful adoptions of African-American children within Caucasian families, and the children have adapted well. However, when such children are not provided knowledge of and exposure to their birth culture, problems related to identity and sense of self may emerge as the child grows older. The popular film *Losing Isaiah* (1995) emphasized the importance of adopted children learning about their cultural heritage at an early age, as well as the adoptive parents' being open to interfacing with the adopted child's natural family regularly for multicultural support. Many child welfare professionals and U.S. citizens strongly believe that the quality of life the child experiences in the family is far more important than the color of the parents' skin. This debate is likely to become more intense as the country moves more toward a nonwhite majority in the latter part of the twenty-first century.

Foreign adoptions, though expensive and arduous to complete, serve as a viable option for families, especially for older childless couples who want to adopt a baby or toddler. Many children in Romania, Russia, Croatia, China, and other parts of the world remain in crowded orphanages hoping for adoption. In addition to applying with a local adoption agency in the United States, certified for international adoptions, the prospective parents must also apply to and be approved by the Bureau of Citizenship and Immigration Services. This process can take months and even years before the final stages of the adoption process can occur. In many cases, the parents are expected to go to the foreign country and bring their new baby home to the United States. In such adoptions, the child should be exposed to as little trauma as possible, with the transition to the new family involving those key persons, family, or residential staff who have been a part of the child's life. Older children should be prepared by counseling, which will help them to better understand the reason for the adoption and the opportunities that may await them in a family of their own. Moreover, just as important, the adoptive parents need to know as much as possible about the child's native culture, language, and placement history so as to better understand the child. Some adoptive families may also learn enough of the child's native language to communicate with him or her more efficiently as the child is learning English. Many families decide to maintain their adopted child's original language in an effort to instill bilingualism.

Many adopted children eventually choose to locate their natural parents and, even as adults, somehow try to put their lives in perspective in relation to their adopted status. Some will want only to know the identities of their natural parents, as well as limited demographics, but others will want to locate their birth parents in order to experience feelings of closure. Many adults believe that finding their birth parents will help them to achieve a sense of well-being about who they are. In many cases, there are practical reasons related to having children of their own and the desire to know as much as possible about their genetic heritage. Some adults who were adopted as children may have a child with a genetic or developmental disability, which might lead them to seek as much information as possible about their biological heritage in order to help their child. With more adoptions being performed with open records, more and more adopted adults are searching for and finding their birth parents and developing relationships with them over time. It is not uncommon for these unified adoptive families to interact frequently and get to know each other (Helton and Jackson, 1997). Still, as adults, other adopted children may have difficulty relating to the birth parent and may hold some resentment about their mother having given them up in the first place.

## CHILDREN IN RESIDENTIAL SETTINGS

Every year it is estimated that some 25,000 children will be emancipated or "age out" of the foster care system by turning eighteen or completing high school (Massinga, 1999). Most child care professionals today would perceive residential care to be an alternative to rather than an option for child placement. They contend that a variety of service options should be made available at all times and can point to the benefits of a range of child welfare programs. Curtis, Alexander, and Lunghofer (2001) state that in recent years residential group care and therapeutic foster care are more complementary than competitive with each other and exist on a continuum of services designed to meet the individual needs of children. Others would retort immediately that "orphanages" are outdated and have served their purpose in the history of child care in the United States. Orphanages may bring back historical images of the masses of children who were orphaned during the Civil War and the devastating cholera and smallpox epidemics that killed hundreds of thousands in this country. Others within and without the child care welfare field contend that residential or group home care is antithetical to normal child growth and development. Many parents, on the other hand, opt to send their children away to military or private boarding schools, where socialization for success and leadership serves as the key philosophy.

Although various residential or institutional facilities may have common characteristics, different types have been established to address the needs of diverse children with different problems. Group care facilities might be divided into six major categories:

1. Residential group facilities for dependent children
2. Correctional institutional for delinquent children
3. Treatment facilities for emotionally disturbed children
4. Residential drug and alcohol programs
5. Facilities for developmentally disabled children
6. Private boarding schools (Downs et al., 2000).

Fewer children are in these facilities today, largely due to the deinstitutionalization movement of the 1950s and child welfare amendments passed in the 1980s to preserve the family. Still, in 1996, out of the 530,000 children living in out-of-home care, 41,000 lived in residential care, 27,000 lived in community-based group homes, and 23,000 lived in therapeutic foster care (Petit et al., 1999). Children were placed in institutions because of neglect or abuse by their families, because they repeatedly ran away or refused to attend school, because they abused alcohol or engaged in sexual activities, or because they were born with developmental disabilities or developed severe mental illness at an early age.

Many troubled children seem to benefit from the structure and security of such a setting, especially when other options such as long-term foster care or adoption have proven inadequate. Based on research, it seems that children and youth living in residential group care are older, more likely to be male, more likely to have had contact with the criminal justice system, and are more likely to be minorities (Curtis, Alexander, and Lunghofer, 2001). The needs of these children are complex and perhaps can be best addressed in a twenty-four-hour care environment or milieu setting where interventions can be provided more often and more consistently. The group setting may offer more variation in relationships and structure than the home setting, and the impact of aggressive or acting-out behavior may be less because it is diffused among multiple individuals throughout the course of a day (Downs et al., 2000). Within this context, residential care might be offered within a continuum of care for those children who need long-term placement because other efforts for in-home care have fallen short. For instance, children with severe behavioral and emotional problems may pose unfathomable challenges at home, yet these same children tend to function better in a residential environment. Repeated attempts at placement with multiple foster families might, in fact, be more detrimental over time than caring for a child in a children's home or group setting.

Many children's homes today in the United States and around the world still espouse the philosophy that every child deserves to grow up in a nurturing and supportive family, yet homes are frequently not available. Tam and Ho (1996) found that children whose parents are also involved with them during the residential placement are more likely to be discharged to their families. A study of forty-eight children's homes examined children's responses to residential care and found that the influence of the child care staff was crucial to success or failure once the children returned home. Those children in homes in which the staff provided specific strategies for foster family ties were more likely to experience improvement in family relationships (Gibbs and Sinclair, 1999).

Despite family preservation, treatment foster care, and wraparound case management services, some children, especially sibling groups and those in the preteen and adolescent years, adapt better to residential care. Strong detachment from families of origin or the struggle for one's own identity may intensify feelings of connection within a residential setting. Some children become strongly attached to the staff in residential programs despite the high staff turnover rates. The case example below highlights a situation wherein residential care seemed preferable to foster care.

Rosa Fuentes, age eleven, and her eight-year-old brother, Eduardo, were placed in residential care three yeas ago, after their widowed mother was killed in an Amtrak train accident. They are originally from Mexico and have only one paternal uncle, a college student, living in the United States; the uncle, Jose, visits the children once a year but does not foresee being able to obtain custody of his niece and nephew. The maternal grandparents are deceased and the paternal grandparents do not want the children to return to

Mexico, believing that after coming of age they will have many more opportunities in the United States. The children were placed in four different foster homes, but each placement ended, largely due to Rosa's assumption of a surrogate parent role for her younger brother. This caused inevitable conflicts; once the children ran away for two days and were found hiding under a bridge. The children's services agency attempted placement of the children in a different foster home, but this placement failed as well, for each child demonstrated unmanageable behavioral problems. Nevertheless, these children have a strong bond with the cottage mother, Maria Trevino, age fifty-five; they often refer to her as Mama and respond to her as a mother figure. She speaks Spanish with them intermittently, something the other foster parents could not do as they were not bilingual. Mrs. Trevino and the other child care staff realize that the children might someday find a successful family placement; on the other hand, they may need residential care until they are old enough to care for themselves and each other.

## *CONCLUSION*

Some children seem to be able to adjust to certain family environments and others do better in other settings. In today's world there are many types of families in which children are able to thrive, grow, and develop into productive members of society. From gay and lesbian families to foster care and adoptive families, children are able to benefit from the nurturance, guidance, and support so important for social skills and relationship development. Some might conjecture that the many adjustments and coping challenges of children who grow up in blended families will make them stronger adults. Similar statements might be made about children who grow up in single-parent families, lose a parent to death at an early age, or join the ranks of children of divorce. The growing trend of kinship care, particularly grandparents raising grandchildren, points to the resilience of family life; older, often retired grandparents step in to care for their grandchildren when their own offspring are unwilling or unable. Children can grow and develop competencies in a large array of family settings; for those who cannot remain at home, residential settings may provide continued opportunities for enrichment and self-actualization.

## STRENGTHS STORY: JOANNA BROWN

Joanna was only five years old when her mother, Margaret Brown, ran away with another man whom she had met at her workplace. Margaret's husband, Eric Brown, was left with Joanna and her younger brother Andrew, three years old. Joanna was not too sad to see her mother leave them because she no longer had to bear her abusive parenting. She always tried to shield her brother from her mother's attacks. After kindergarten, Joanna's school bus dropped her off at the day care center where her brother spent the day. They waited there until their father could pick them up at six o'clock. Eric Brown was an accountant for a Midwest branch of a large manufacturing company. He struggled to raise two young children by himself, often leaving them alone while he shopped for food and ran errands. By the time Joanna reached the fifth grade, she was often sent to the principal's office by her teachers for disruptive behavior, and then had to wait for her father to pick her up. One Saturday, her father brought a young woman to the house and told his children that her name was Lily and that he planned to marry her the following month. Lily had just completed her master's degree in occupational therapy and planned to work at a nearby hospital. Lily and Eric married in a small ceremony at a friend's house.

Joanna's behavior at school got worse each year, and it was Lily who had to pick her up from the principal's office. In middle school, she was caught smoking a cigarette in the rest room with two other girls. When she was fifteen years old, she told Lily that her period had stopped. Lily took her to the doctor, suspecting that she was pregnant. The doctor confirmed that Joanna was indeed pregnant. As they drove home, Lily asked Joanna what she wanted to do. She just looked out the window and said, "I don't want to have a baby," and refused to disclose the identity of the baby's father. Lily was able to arrange a therapeutic abortion because of Joanna's young age. Joanna continued to be difficult with her stepmother, refusing to help her with household chores and playing her stereo extremely loud when her father was not there. She even told Lily that her father had a girlfriend and that Lily was stupid not to realize that. She waited for her father to come home to listen to her father tell Lily that Joanna was lying and trying to break them up. Joanna attended a state university located 150 miles away from home. She lived in a dorm on campus and came home for holidays. When she came home, she was out with her high school friends until late at night and then slept until noon. One day Eric phoned Lily at work and told her that Joanna had attempted suicide by taking a whole bottle of aspirin. Lily rushed to the psychiatric ward where Joanna had been admitted for observation. She sat on the bed and asked Joanna, "Did you really want to die?" Joanna replied, "No, I didn't want to die, but I was so lonely." Lily held Joanna tightly and said to her, "You are not alone, Joanna. I am here for you." Joanna clung to Lily and wept hard, mumbling that she was sorry for all the hurtful things she had done to Lily. Lily laughed and said, "I don't really remember those things." Joanna finally smiled and went to sleep in Lily's arms.

Joanna is now a teacher of students with behavioral problems. She is the mother of two young boys. Often she brings them to her parents' house to spend Sunday afternoon barbecuing in their backyard. She tells Lily that an older person should not be working so hard, taking over the cleanup. Eric claims that Lily is partial to Joanna as compared to Andrew, who is now a Navy officer.

## QUESTIONS FOR DISCUSSION

1. What are some of the problems faced by gay and lesbian families? Discuss whether a parent's coming out to his or her children is likely to help or hinder their psychological adjustment to the parent's sexual orientation and lifestyle.
2. What are some of the issues that blended families must face in order to help all family members come together as one family?
3. How can child welfare professionals help foster children prepare for independent living as they "age out" of the foster care system?
4. Discuss the emotional reactions that are likely to occur within the family when an adult adopted child decides to locate and develop a relationship with his or her natural parent.
5. Discuss how resilience may help single parents and their children to cope with the daily demands of maintaining the household.

# REFERENCES

American Psychological Association (1995). Families and relationships, get the facts: Interventions that work for stepfamilies. Available at <http://helping.apa.org/family/step.html>.

Armesto, J. C. (2002). Developmental and contextual factors that influence gay fathers'parental competence: A review of the literature. *Psychology of Men and Masculinity* 3(2): 67-78.

Beavers, W. R. and Hampson, R. B. (1990). *Successful families: Assessment and intervention.* New York: W. W. Norton and Company.

Congress, E. P. (1999). *Social work values and ethics: Identifying and resolving professional dilemmas.* Chicago: Nelson-Hall.

Curtis, P. A., Alexander, M. S., and Lunghofer, L. A. (2001). A literature review comparing the outcomes of residential group care and therapeutic foster care. *Child and Adolescent Social Work Journal* 18(2): 377-392.

Dacey, J. S. and Travers, J. F. (1999). *Human development: Across the lifespan,* Fourth edition. Boston: McGraw Hill.

Delaney, R. J. (1998). *Fostering changes: Treating attachment-disordered foster children.* Oklahoma City, OK: Wood and Barnes Publishing.

Downs, S. W., Moore, E. M., McFadden, E. J., and Costin, L. B. (2000). *Child welfare and family services: Policies and practice,* Sixth edition. Boston: Allyn and Bacon.

Erikson, E. (1963). *Childhood and society,* Second edition. New York: Norton.

Featherstone, D. R., Cundick, B. P., and Jensen, L. C. (1992). Differences in school behaviour and achievement between children from intact, reconstituted, and single-parent families. *Adolescence* 27: 1-12.

Gibbs, I. and Sinclair, I. (1999). Treatment and treatment outcomes in children's homes. *Child and Family Social Work* 4(1): 1-8.

Helton, L. R. and Jackson, M. (1997). *Social work practice with families: A diversity model.* Boston: Allyn and Bacon.

Laird, J. (1995). Lesbians: Parenting. In R. L. Edwards (Ed.), *Encyclopedia of social work,* Ninteenth edition, Volume 2 (pp. 1604-1615). Washington, DC: NASW Press.

Lefrancois, G. R. (1996). *The lifespan,* Fifth edition. Belmont, CA: Wadsworth.

Massinga, R. (1999). Aging out of foster care. Available at <http://search.csmonitor.com/durable/1999/04/22/P1151.htm>.

Palosaari, U. K. and Aro, H. M. (1995). Parental divorce, self-esteem, and depression: An intimate relationship as a protective factor in young adulthood. *Journal of Affective Disorder* 35: 91-96.

Papernow, P. L. (1993). *Becoming a stepfamily: Patterns of development in remarried families.* San Francisco: Jossey-Bass.

Perlmutter, B. and Miki, R. L. (2001). Stepfamilies: The new pioneers. Available at <http://stepfamilyseattle.com/constep.html>.

Petit, M. R., Curtis, P. A., Woodruff, K., Arnold, L., Feagans, L., and Ang, J. (1999). Child abuse and neglect: A look at the states. *The 1999 CWLA Stat Book*. Washington, DC: Child Welfare League of America.

Raising children again: More grandparents caring for families (2002). *The Post Standard,* Syracuse, NY, July 8, p. A-5.

Satir, V., Stachowiak, J., and Taschman, H. A. (1990). *Helping families to change.* Northvale, NJ: Jason Aronson.

Sims, S. (2002). Meet the parents. *Saratoga News*. Saratoga, CA, April 10. Available at <www.svcn.com/archives/saratoganews/04.10.02/cover-0215.html>.

Tam, T. S. and Ho, M. K. W. (1996). Factors influencing the prospect of children returning to their parents from out-of-home care. *Child Welfare* 75(3): 253-268.

U.S. Department of Health and Human Services (2003). The AFCARS reprot. Available at <www.ACF.DHHS.gov/Programs/Cb/publications/afcars/reports.htm>.

Zastrow, C. and Kirst-Ashman, K. (2001). *Understanding human behavior and the social environment,* Fifth edition. Belmont, CA: Wadsworth/Thomson Learning.

Chapter 4

# Child Socialization
# and Peer Relationships

The only way to have a friend is to be one.

Ralph Waldo Emerson

Peer influences on children have a great impact on how they learn the give and take of human relationships. Children are unique individuals, yet socialization adds a commonality to their experiences (Rose and Fatout, 2003). Children learn early on how they are perceived by others and how their emotions and behavior affect those around them. Many peer group relationships take on enduring and stable qualities, e.g., the characteristics of a group, wherein children find social acceptance as well as rejection. However, the sense of oneness that exists in the peer group allows children to experience the feeling of being included and knowing that their "inner experiences and emotional reactions" are shared by other members of the group (Pillari, 1998). Through peer relationships, children experience learning opportunities available nowhere else and play out their lives in a dynamic interaction with the social environment (Garbarino, 1992). They learn that the pendulum of social experience swings both ways, for they are constantly being molded by the social environment as they, in turn, impact all persons they encounter.

Children realize that in the peer group they can react to one another as equals and play a variety of roles not so readily available to them when they interact with adults (Kemple, 1991). At home, at school, on the playground, and at church or temple, children learn norms for behavior and look to other children as role models and even as heroes. Children rely on family members for early socialization in the home, but the school environment becomes a vital testing ground for learning how to communicate appropriately, provide social support for others, display competence, and engage in cooperation.

The ways in which children think about socialization help them to adapt to social and small group norms. Cognitive factors involve how children learn to think and act like others, act according to their expectations, and respond to socially relevant situational demands (Rose and Fatout, 2003). For instance, at a birthday party a child may join in to help break a piñata or to play Pin the Tail on the Donkey, when he or she would rather be playing computer games at home alone. Children learn that supporting others not only gains social acceptance but also helps them be successful in expressing their own wants and needs. Children learn to ponder the value of friendship and the pains of rejection at school and on the playground as they engage in praising one another, defending their rights, and resolving conflicts.

Shure (1994) states that cognitive factors involve the development of five interpersonal, cognitive, problem-solving skills within the social environment. First, a child learns to be sensitive to interpersonal problems and to pay closer attention to the new social rules that affect friendship. For example, children who talk only about themselves or constantly try to impress others may discover that their friends no longer invite them over to play on weekends. Second, means-end thinking helps a child to develop a social plan into action. If a child wants to make a new friend at school, he or she might ask the child to come over to play a video game. Third, alternative thinking helps children to succeed at socialization as they learn to develop different plans. An example might involve a girl who invites her friend for a sleepover. If the invited girl's parents will not let her sleep over, she might ask her friend to go to a movie the following week instead. Fourth, children learn to think about the consequences of their behavior within the social environment. A girl who wants to become a member of the cheerleading squad may not particularly like one of the girls on the team, but she knows that open criticism of this girl might hurt her chances of becoming a cheerleader. Last, children and adolescents learn the reciprocal nature of social relationships. A boy knows that if he is willing to let his friend borrow his baseball mitt then he can most likely depend on his friend for a similar favor (Shure, 1994).

Many children may be identified by several categories that have been ascribed to children in groups. Children who are athletic and play one or more sports may be referred to as jocks. These children tend to have high self-esteem, largely because of the ongoing accolades received from peers at school and in the community. A second group may be labeled popular because of club memberships, special talents, or just because so many other peers deem them to be "cool." The so-called tough kids constitute another group; peers may either gravitate toward these youths or avoid them because of drug and alcohol abuse or entanglements with the juvenile authorities. Children who have few friends and are loners may have poor interactional skills and survive on the margins of the peer circle. Santrock (2002) noted that jocks and popular adolescents have high self-esteem whereas children who do not fit into a peer group tend to have low self-esteem. However, most children fit into an average or middle group that is not popular, unpopular, or troubled; they are well liked, have a sense of well-being, and get along well with others.

Children seem to be accepted into peer groups based on their values, resources, and individual personality traits. Girls may be accepted by athletes or popular children because of their beauty, clothing, and material possessions (e.g., an expensive car or money for parties), and because their parents are permissive. Girls may find also that they are popular because they do well academically or are praised by their teachers for their success in the classroom. Boys, on the other hand, may not be rewarded for their intellectual abilities, but instead may be recognized for their athletic and physical prowess and even their defiance of authority. Most parents seem to prefer that their children fall into the more normal peer association of being well liked and content with an ample number of friends for support rather than engaging a highly competitive and power-oriented peer support group. Children who fall more along normative lines of peer interaction are perhaps more accustomed to the ups and downs of social interaction and would perhaps be more resilient.

Children may be harmed psychologically and emotionally by bullying or violence at school or on the playground. Bullying is a form of harassment that may include taunting, teasing, threatening, or hitting. Although boys generally engage in direct bullying, they may use more indirect or subtle tactics such as spreading rumors or forced isolation (Smith and Sharp, 1994). Fineran (2002) noted that since 1992 a number of lawsuits have been filed by students at all levels, including sexual harassment suits filed by males, as well as sexual harassment suits between peers of the same gender. This social problem has been gaining increased attention in the media since Erika Harold, Miss America 2003, made youth violence and bullying prevention her platform. A victim of racial and sexual bullying as a child, Harold championed this cause in personal interviews and talk shows across the country during her reign.

Bullying is a problem that can make children afraid to attend school, travel alone to and from school, or walk down the streets of their neighborhood. Both younger children and adolescents depend on peer relationships for validation and approval of their social skills and communication abilities. Children who become targets for bullying may feel inept and isolated. They are often afraid to confide in teachers, parents, or friends out of fear of teasing or being perceived as weak. Some children with low self-esteem related to obesity, physical size, or disabilities may blame themselves for the bullying; these children may ultimately withdraw. They may avoid association with others at school or in their communities out of embarrassment or fear, which impedes their capacity to develop and maintain friendships. Children who are unable to interact with peers may feel rejected and trapped in their own homes. Charach, Pepler, and Ziegler (1995) found that children perceived victims of bullying to be "weak," "nerds," and "afraid to fight back"; 43 percent said they would try to help the victim and 33 percent said they should help but do not do so. Some who confide in parents may be told to stand up for themselves or be encouraged to tell school officials. Children may feel that they are caught in a double bind: They do not want to fight back or report the bullies for fear of retribution. Neither do they want to disobey their parents nor lose their trust.

Prevention and intervention to address bullying takes a concerted effort by both parents and teachers. Smith and Sharp (1994) express the need for schoolwide policies as well as empowerment measures for students, such as conflict resolution, peer counseling, and assertiveness training. Olweus (1993) detailed several approaches to address the problem at individual, class, and school levels. Children and parents should be surveyed to obtain a benchmark level of occurrence and also to inform them of the seriousness of the problem and the need for systematic intervention. A parent awareness campaign may be implemented through parent newsletters, PTA (parent-teacher association) meetings, and parent-teacher conference days. These forums will also give schools an opportunity to ask for parental support in working toward a resolution of the problem. Teachers and school administrators can develop rules against bullying that are strictly enforced, and can disseminate materials against bullying at school. Teachers can incorporate role-plays in the classroom to address bullying and help the children affected use alternative methods of interaction. Teachers, coaches, and other school staff can attend workshops that involve role-playing and related assignments to help them understand and to intervene to stop bullying at school.

## FAMILY INFLUENCES ON SOCIALIZATION

Children are influenced daily by their parents, siblings, and extended family members. Children learn how to ask for help, share their ideas, and interact in prosocial ways that will assist them in meeting their needs. Family rituals, such as mealtimes and bedtime storytelling, give children an opportunity to interact with parents and siblings as they describe their ideas, ask for help with homework, or engage in dialogue about how they feel about themselves. Parents have a major obligation to ensure that children are not only seen but also heard. That is, children must be included in family discussions when their well-being is at issue, such as when the family is making a decision about moving to a new community or to another state. Children learn from family conflict resolution that issues affecting all family members should be discussed openly so that each family member will have input.

### Birth Order

Birth order in families inevitably affects how children resolve problems and make decisions. The oldest child, whether male or female, may be expected by parents to assist in child care and guidance of the younger children. Sulloway (1996) noted that the oldest child may have a difficult time forming friendships because of his or her emphasis on achievement and competitive role within the peer group. The younger children may go to sports events with the oldest child to learn firsthand about team sports and cooperation. Children may look up to an older brother or sister who is a star pitcher on the baseball team, which may inspire them to try out for a school sport. Also, younger children may be expected to stay close to home, ask permission of parents and older siblings before leaving the yard, or do their homework before going out to play. They may feel dependent on other family members, but this ascribed role serves as an effective way for them to maintain a sense of security. Toman (1993) noted that the youngest child may be spoiled or, conversely, feel deprived. The parents may dote on the youngest child and make him or her feel that he or she has more privileges than the other children, and this may be the case in many families. Or the youngest child may not feel special at all, sensing that belongings, such as bicycles or skates, or activities suggested by parents and siblings are "secondhand," or used by his or her predecessors.

Despite the stereotype of middle children feeling left out or not fitting in, middle children may be more resilient than older or younger siblings because they have to find a niche for themselves within the family. They may feel that more attention is being given by their parents to their older and younger siblings, so they may try their hardest to achieve recognition in academics or sports. Middle children may be more socially competent and form friendships at school and in the neighborhood at an earlier age than older siblings (Wilson and Edington, 1981). Forer (1976) stated that middle children learn negotiating and diplomacy skills at a young age in order to maintain positive relationships with both older and younger children, and they have a strong need for peer support.

One must also consider the unique socialization experiences of only children and twins. Only children may grow up to be adultlike in their thinking, emotions, and behavior, as they may be exposed more to adults-only relationships with parents and other relatives at home. They may feel more comfortable communicating with adults and at school may relate more effectively with teachers than peers; this may cause some competition with peers who may view their "in" with the teacher unfavorably (Wilson and Edington, 1981). In addition, the absence of competition while growing up seems to increase conscientiousness and self-esteem in task accomplishment at home and at school (Forer, 1976).

Twins seem to assume the overall social behavior and interaction preferences that correspond to their sibling position. That is, firstborn twins take on the behavior patterns of firstborn children, yet seek each other for friends, as well as other twins for life partners (Toman, 1993). Twins tend to develop close friendships with each other before reaching out to other siblings or peers. However, many twins believe that they must assert their individuality and a special identity for themselves, especially during adolescence. One twin girl, age thirteen, said that her mother had always forced her and her identical twin sister to dress alike and engage in the same social activities, such as tap dancing and ballet. She said she was tired of "getting up every single day and looking into the mirror," meaning spending time with her sister. Fraternal twins may find it less difficult to form peer relationships due to their differences, which may include gender, hair color, eye color, and stature, among other traits.

### *Children with Disabilities*

In families with a child with disabilities, there may be a role reversal where the child's socialization is concerned. The older child who has a disability may be socialized into a role of dependency and total immersion within the family. The younger child with no disability may be expected to look after his or her older disabled sibling at school, on the playground, or when the parents are at work. Moreover, this role of caregiver may lead to sadness and feelings of isolation as the sibling of the disabled child refrains from normal activities out of a sense of obligation to help the parents with child care. Self-esteem issues and resentment may occur in these situations if the child continues in such a role for a long time. In situations in which the youngest child has a disability or chronic illness, the oldest child may feel that an inordinate amount of the parents' time and energy is invested in the younger child in going to clinics, having psychological tests, searching for alternative treatments, or consulting specialists about resources. The older child begins to realize that his or her younger sibling will never grow up, so to speak, to do the things once expected by the other children and their parents. One ten-year-old boy whose brother was severely retarded said, "I know Mom and Dad love us both, but with [my brother], it's like having a baby brother every year of my life." Siblings of disabled children need time to adapt to a role within the family that allows the parents to give special attention to the sibling with special needs but also acknowledges the nondisabled siblings for their uniqueness and attributes as well.

## Foster and Blended Families

Children in foster or blended families are often socialized to a new role as well because their age may place them in a different position within the new family unit. Just as a child at a new school must live down the role of the "new kid," so must children in newly organized families find ways to relate with other family members that are both comfortable and rewarding. A foster child who was an only child in his or her family of origin may have to take on new responsibilities as the oldest child in his or her new family unit, for example. However, other emotional factors, such as parental attachment and acceptance as a "full" member of the family, may affect socialization.

In a blended family, children may have to negotiate new ways of communicating with siblings as they develop attachment to their new relatives while trying to maintain the closeness of previous family ties. Visitation with natural parents and grandparents may also be challenging, especially during the first few months of living with a new family. In stepfamilies, both parents must present a unified front to ensure that the children feel safe and trusting of these different but inclusive family relationships. All of these factors may affect social experiences of children in ways that lead the child to feel insecure and socially inept. Children whose roles are changed within the family often have to negotiate their wants and needs differently, which may invariably impact how they communicate and establish relationships within the social environment.

## Styles of Parenting

Gross (1989) identified four styles of parenting: overindulgent, permissive, authoritarian, and authoritative. These parenting styles inevitably affect adolescents' family and peer relationships in both positive and negative ways. Overindulgent parenting styles produce adolescents who are submissive to and/or dependent on others. Adolescents who receive permissive parenting may respond in any number of ways that affect their relationships with others. They may feel independent, confident, creative, or, on the contrary, they may be aggressive with peers or even their parents. Authoritarian parents set strict rules and compromise little, raising children who have low self-esteem and who may be aggressive with peers. Finally, authoritative parents are thought to provide the most effective model for peer relationships. They establish rules and routines and uphold them, yet they are willing to consider compromises with their adolescents. Consequently, these offspring generally have high self-esteem, a sense of self-control, a sense of their own limitations, and an ability to determine right from wrong. The last type of parenting fosters a sense of independence yet helps teenagers to realize the need for norms and boundaries, both at home and within peer relationships.

## SCHOOL AND PEER RELATIONSHIPS

Children today, as did their predecessors, broaden their social skills and abilities to get along with others when they enter school. Children have opportunities each day to make new friends, experiment with persuasion, learn cooperative strategies for problem solving, and try on new roles, be it president of the class or playground monitor. Children also are able to distinguish which rules they must obey faithfully from those that may be occasionally overlooked. Peers set examples with their clothing, styles of speech, or reading habits; children want to emulate one another's style of communication and interactional competencies. Many children will try to influence their parents to buy them clothes similar to those of their peers, or to take them on similar weekend outings or vacations. Children engage in daily "show and tell" in their free time, where they compare everything from their computer games to their bicycle tires.

Children often make their best friends through their experiences at school as they learn the importance of cooperation and teamwork. In the classroom, children may be expected to work on a group science or art project, which challenges them not only to be creative but also to learn to engage in mutual decision making and problem solving. Children generally begin to involve themselves in cooperative play around age five and refine these social skills as play and social relationships become more complex. Children may first learn what they do well on the playground, and peers are quick to tell them what they do poorly. Children learn from team play the importance of their role in a group and begin to learn that each person's contributions benefit the whole team.

Kerckhoff (1972) notes that up until around the third grade, children of both genders interact on the playground during recess and get along well. But then they begin to divide themselves into play groups along same-sex lines and continue to separate themselves from the other sex in play until around the fifth grade. This period is seen as an important developmental period in which children can "fashion a coherent gender identity" (Kerckhoff, 1972). This appraisal of the behavior of school-age children is consistent with Erik Erikson's developmental theory. Erikson (1968) emphasized that children between ages six and twelve must first develop a sense of mastery and success in their activities prior to forming their identity in adolescence. This same-sex affiliation evolves into an "us-against-them" mentality that may take the form of teasing, bantering, name-calling, and even open hostility, yet it seems to serve the purpose of emphasizing differences between the sexes (Kerckhoff, 1972).

An excellent portrayal of childhood socialization and the impact of peers on play is in the popular ABC cartoon show *Disney's Recess*. Breaking with the stereotype of boys playing only with boys and girls playing only with girls, *Disney's Recess* portrays four boys and two girls who constitute a close circle of friends. Although at times there may be some accentuation of gender differences and ascribed gender roles, the show highlights a strong friendship group consisting of six fourth-graders named Vince, TJ, Gretchen, Spinelli, Mikey, and Gus. They stick together through thick and thin, even if it means that all of them get in trouble for not telling on one another's misbehavior or infractions of the school's rules for playground behavior. During recess, the children learn about and reinforce one another's strengths while trying hard to ignore limitations. Vince makes the children realize their athletic abilities with his expertise in all sports offered at school, and TJ amazes the children with his clever ideas and maneuvers for helping the children to outwit Miss Finster, Principal Prickly, and other adults at the school. Gretchen is the brain who lends a scientific slant to commonsense solutions to problems, and Gus is the child who exhibits resilience because as a military brat he has lived in many places and knows the world. Spinelli proves that girls can be brave, beautiful, and equal to any boy on the playground, especially where arm wrestling is concerned. The obese but kind Mikey speaks in rhyme and constantly reminds his pals of their softer side and the importance of compromise and aesthetics.

The children abide by the motto, "All for one and one for all," on the playground and in the classroom. Like eight- and nine-year-olds in real life, they are embarrassed by their shortcomings but relish their accomplishments, especially when they are lauded by their peers and classmates. In one episode the children learn the significance of peer influence and pressure for conformity. Spinelli, the perennial tomboy, agrees to her mother's wish that she learn ballet, yet she does not want her pals to know, lest they make fun of her for breaking their image of her as a "tough kid." However, when she learns that her friend Mikey is secretly taking ballet lessons as well, she is willing to give the classes a chance and wants to help Mikey out because he does not have a suitable dance partner. When the kids at school are invited to the ballet performance, they are at first shocked but then gradually acknowledge that their two friends are talented and doing something they truly enjoy. Old images are broken and peer pressure yields to peer acceptance as they applaud their friends' success.

In today's world, families are mobile and ever-changing such that children have to change schools and make new friends several times during their childhood. Children may at first feel alone and different in the new environment, but most possess the resilience to adapt fairly quickly to new surroundings and social relationships. Making friends may happen immediately or may take some time, depending on the personality of the child and his or her level of comfort in the classroom and on the playground. Parents and teachers should carefully monitor how a child is adapting to the new setting and encourage efforts to bond with other children. A parent who attends a parent-teacher conference or volunteers to assist with a classroom party may help the child feel more settled, for he or she child realizes the parent's investment in the school and in his or her academic success. Children who move from another part of the country or who are immigrants may have a different accent or speak English as a second language. They may experience some teasing by other children, but this usually subsides as they share their interests and become members of groups. Children's acceptance of a new child into their friendship group is often contingent on only one other child's acceptance of the "new kid." Consider the following scenario of a boy who moved from the South to a large eastern U.S. city.

Danny Lee Whitehead, the youngest of three children, moved to Philadelphia from Castle, Tennessee, when he was eleven years old. His older brother and sister were both in college at the time, so he had to make the adjustment to big city life on his own. Danny Lee's father was transferred to

Philadelphia when his entire sales division was relocated in a company expansion. Danny Lee played on the softball team at Cooke Elementary where he was the star pitcher and also served as the goalie on his soccer team. He did not want to leave his best friend, Jay, although they promised to call and e-mail each other frequently.

The family rented a condominium while they looked for a house to purchase so Danny Lee did not have a place where he and his dad could throw a softball. He started school at a large central city school not far from the family's new home, but he immediately felt that he did not fit in. The children chided him about his accent and called him "cracker"; and he got a black eye the second day of school for fighting with a boy who kept pulling out his shirttail. No one saw the fight, so neither boy was sent to the principal's office. Danny Lee, however, had always been a good student and loved to discuss American Indian history and culture. His great-great-grandmother was part Chickasaw Indian, and he was quite proud of his heritage. Genealogy had become a hobby that he looked forward to working on each weekend when his parents allowed him to search for genealogy sites on the Internet.

He felt lonely, although he did talk regularly to a couple of boys in his classes. He felt that he did not belong and told his parents he wanted to return to Tennessee. His grandparents came to visit for a week at Easter, which made him feel a little better. Around the third week of school, a new boy from Virginia entered his social studies class and was also fascinated with American Indians and foreign culture. He told Danny Lee he wanted to be a photojournalist and study other cultures around the world.

Danny Lee got permission to have his new friend, Roger, over for dinner and the two boys spent hours looking at and discussing Danny Lee's genealogical records and collection of American Indian arrowheads. Danny Lee's grandfather used to take him on camping trips, and they loved to hunt for arrowheads. Roger told Danny Lee that he planned to join the baseball team and encouraged him to do the same. Danny Lee was uncertain but was encouraged by Roger's enthusiasm to engage in sports at their new school. Danny Lee said he would think about coming to the tryouts the following week. Encouraged by his parents, he tried out for baseball and made the team, as did Roger.

When the other children saw what a good player Danny Lee was, they dropped their teasing and were more accepting of him. He and Roger spent time together and also joined the social studies club, which planned a field trip to an American Indian reservation in New York State. The boys made several new friends through the baseball team and their school club and soon felt a part of their new school. Danny Lee said he still missed his old school and his home in Tennessee, but he also liked Philadelphia because of his new friends. In early summer, his parents bought an old house, which he enjoyed helping his parents renovate. He also became acquainted with two brothers, ages eleven and twelve, who lived two houses away. Danny Lee soon felt at home even in the big city, and he looked forward to visiting his friends back in Tennessee during his summer vacation.

As emphasized in the previous scenario, children who encounter new living arrangements and a new school may feel alone and even alienated from peers. If a child moves from another region, as was Danny Lee's situation, he or she may be teased and made to feel uneasy in the role of the new student. Children such as Danny Lee need time to feel comfortable with teachers and routines as well as the children in their classrooms. Children may need some time to adjust to the classroom dynamics before trying out for a sport or engaging in activities similar to those at their former school. Peer pressure can be painful as children attempt to find their way and prove themselves to be competent in a new environment. In Danny Lee's situation, meeting another boy who was new to the school and also had similar hobbies and interests made it easier for Danny Lee to adjust to a new circle of friends at school and in his new neighborhood. Children often realize that support by one other child in a peer group may help them to win acceptance and even admiration.

## CHILDREN IN THE COMMUNITY

Children learn early in life the importance of socialization in the community, whether on the playground in their neighborhood, at the local YMCA, or at the park. They learn to express their needs within a range of social contexts and better understand the concepts of diversity, friendship, loss, and change. Children learn how to play with and understand children from diverse social and cultural backgrounds and may first experience discrimination or the feeling of being different when interacting with others in their neighborhood. Children from a large family learn to accept and appreciate children who grew up as only children, as well as those who were adopted or spent time in foster care. They also have a broader opportunity to experience socialization with children of different ages and life experiences. For example, children who have lived in one house all their lives may be intrigued by their next-door neighbors who have lived in several states and foreign countries due to the military careers of their parents. Just as important, children learn to express their needs and concerns to other adults beyond their parents, be it the soccer coach, Sunday school teacher, or summer camp counselor.

In the community children learn to adjust to multiple changes, losses, and transitions. When a child's family moves for the first time to a new neighborhood, he or she may feel alone and that he or she will never be able to make friends as good as those left behind. However, children learn quickly that a new neighborhood may offer new and different ways of meeting people and making friends. Children whose parents divorce and remarry must often adapt to multiple neighborhoods and social situations. They may visit one parent during the week or on alternate weekends, where there are many children in the neighborhood, and yet have only a few friends in the neighborhood where they reside with their other parent. Also, remarriage brings about social situations involving new family members such as stepgrandparents, aunts, and cousins. Through their resilience, children are able to transition into new environments where they rely on their existing social skills to make friends and further test their communication and problem-solving skills. They learn to adapt to going to a different school, living in a different part of the country, having a new parent (e.g., a stepparent), or losing a friend who moves away.

Children learn the importance of community spirit and pride by interacting with others who live in their neighborhood or city. On the Fourth of July, a child may help build a float advocating safety or animal protection, or help prepare cookies for a big block party. A boy or girl who has a paper route not only learns to manage money more effectively but also has an opportunity to meet other adults and make decisions that will later be beneficial in the world of work. A child may work, along with other family members and neighbors, on a Habitat for Humanity project to rebuild a house that was lost in a natural disaster. Whether helping a parent to campaign for a seat on the school board or attending a community meeting with parents on recycling garbage, children learn that a community must work together as a system and that everyone has a role to play in maintaining the best quality of life possible.

## CONCLUSION

Children learn to interact with others within a range of social situations involving the home, school, and community. Children learn to make friends, give up friends, move from one city to another, or accept a new family configuration caused by divorce and remarriage. A significant factor in any child's socialization is his or her ability to learn to make decisions outside the family and to work with others to accomplish a joint effort, whether planning a block picnic or raising funds for the community swimming pool to stay open in the summer. Children are resilient in their capacity to comprehend and deal with all the changes that occur in their lives on a regular basis. They realize that their social situation will change, but that does not necessarily mean they will not be able to adjust to new friends, a new neighborhood, or a new school. They become increasingly more aware of their competencies and their self-concept improves as they learn to interact with peers and value the importance of negotiation and compromise on the playground. Children first develop a sense of community pride and belonging when they attend community events with their families and experience firsthand the importance of living with and getting along with a range of children and adults. Parents must include children in a variety of community activities at every stage of their development. Learning to be with others and around them, reach compromises when necessary, and achieve common goals are crucial elements for socialization and the establishment of strong peer relationships.

## STRENGTHS STORY: BILLY LAPAHIE

Billy Lapahie, a Navajo Indian, was born the youngest of four children to Martin and Sally Yellowhorse Lapahie on a reservation in Arizona. Billy's early years were difficult because his father was an alcoholic who beat Billy and his siblings. Once, when Billy was ten, his father beat him until he had to be hospitalized. He was placed with his aunt and uncle, whose children were grown and had left the reservation. Billy was a well-behaved child who enjoyed helping his uncle, who worked in forestry with the Bureau of Indian Affairs. Billy told his Uncle Raymond that he wanted to be a forest ranger and take care of the land. Billy felt close to nature and loved to help his uncle protect the forest and the animals that lived there. He also felt close to his culture and participated in native dances, especially at the beginning of each season. Billy was placed back with his parents after six months, and by that time his father had gone into a recovery program for alcoholics. Billy's older brother married a woman on the reservation, but his sisters left when they were still teenagers to look for work in the city. When they came back to the reservation, they seemed different somehow. Billy scolded them about giving up their true heritage and buying into popular American ways.

When Billy was sixteen, he began to drink alcohol and smoke marijuana. He started skipping school and fell behind on his assignments. He had been dating a girl from the Folded Arms People, his mother's clan. This caused a major rift within the family, as dating someone within one's own family clan is forbidden. Billy argued with his parents, and his mother felt especially betrayed by her son. Billy ran away to stay with his sisters in Phoenix, where they were working as housekeepers in a large hotel. The sisters did not want the family to be fractured further, so they advised him to go home. After four nights, they put him out, and he wandered the streets for three weeks alone, looking for food and shelter. Billy was given alcohol by men he met at a hobo camp down near the railroad tracks. He had no food other than what he could get from the garbage. He refused to go to a shelter at first, but eventually he encountered a counselor from Covenant House who convinced him he needed help.

With the help of a social worker in Phoenix, Billy agreed to go back home and finish high school. He had several more incidents with alcohol but finally was able to stop drinking after regularly attending Alcoholics Anonymous with his father. Moreover, Billy went to several sweat lodge ceremonies, conducted by a Navajo medicine man who also worked as a substance abuse counselor with the Bureau of Indian Affairs. Afterward, Billy was convinced that he could finally "face his demons" and conquer his cravings for alcohol. When his father would "fall off the wagon" and drink again, Billy would go stay with his aunt and uncle. Billy encouraged his father to attend a sweat lodge ceremony, and he did attend once.

Billy met Drucilla, a young woman from the Blue Bird People, at his high school, and they started dating. They became very close, and Drucilla helped Billy regularly with his homework, especially math. Billy and Drucilla graduated in the top 25 percent of their high school class and were able to receive scholarships to a four-year state university. Today both are seniors and doing well. Billy is majoring in fish and wild life management and Drucilla is majoring in nursing. They plan to get married on completion of their studies and will return to the Navajo reservation. Billy and his parents are closer now, but he gives his Uncle Raymond credit for all the encouragement and support in helping him meet his goals.

## *QUESTIONS FOR DISCUSSION*

1. Discuss the concept of birth order on the socialization of children.
2. Discuss the impact of the home, school, and community on child socialization.
3. Discuss the safety of children in the school environment and the impact of bullying.
4. What are some ways that parents can help children to develop positive relationships with other children?
5. How do successful peer group relationships serve children and adolescents in developing a positive self-image?

## REFERENCES

Charach, A., Pepler, D., and Ziegler, S. (1995). Bullying at school—A Canadian perspective: A survey of problems and suggestions for intervention. *Education Canada* 35(1): 12-18.

Erikson, E. (1968). *Identity, youth, and crisis.* New York: Norton.

Fineran, S. (2002). Sexual harassment between same-sex peers: Intersection of mental health, homophobia, and sexual violence in schools. *Social Work* 47(1): 65-74.

Forer, L. K. (1976). *The birth order factor: How your personality is influenced by your place in the family.* New York: D. McKay Co.

Garbarino, J. (1992). *Children and families in the social environment,* Second edition. Hawthorne, NY: Aldine de Gruyter.

Gross, J. (1989). *Psychology and parenthood.* Philadelphia: Open University Press.

Kemple, K. M. (1991). Preschool children's peer acceptance and social interaction. *Young Children* 46(5): 47-54.

Kerckhoff, A. C. (1972). *Socialization and social class.* Englewood Cliffs, NJ: Prentice-Hall.

Olweus, D. (1993). *Bullying at school: What we know and what we can do.* Cambridge, MA: Blackwell.

Pillari, V. (1998). *Human behavior in the social environment: The developing person in a holistic context,* Second edition. Pacific Grove, CA: Brooks/Cole Publishing Company.

Rose, S. R. and Fatout, M. F. (2003). *Social work practice with children and adolescents.* Boston: Allyn and Bacon.

Santrock, J. W. (2002). *Life span development,* Eighth edition. Boston: McGraw-Hill.

Shure, M. B. (1994). *Raising a thinking child: Helping your child to resolve everyday conflicts and get along with others.* New York: H. Holt.

Smith, P. K. and Sharp, S. (1994). *School bullying: Insights and perspectives.* London: Routledge.

Sulloway, F. J. (1996). *Born to rebel.* New York: Pantheon Books.

Toman, W. (1993). *Family constellation,* Fourth edition. New York: Springer Publishing Company.

Wilson, B. and Edington, G. (1981). *First born, second child.* New York: McGraw-Hill.

# Chapter 5

# Children and Learning

Education is not the filling of a pail, but the lighting of a fire.

William Butler Yeats

Children are so diverse that it should not be any wonder they display unique and creative approaches to learning. James and Jongeward (1971, p. 1) stated that each person is a new creation, "each has his own unique potentials . . . capabilities and limitations. Each can be a significant, thinking, aware, and creative person in his own right— a winner." Parents and teachers continue to be intrigued and even baffled by the depth and diversity of children's learning both inside and outside of school. Children have a natural curiosity for learning, which sometimes is hindered by the best intentions of parents and teachers. Each child has his or her own learning style that will enable him or her to learn new concepts and obtain valuable information about coping with any number of life's problems.

To be successful, children must be given ample opportunity to discover for themselves how to resolve various problems and dilemmas faced in everyday life. For example, a child who does poorly in math may need some regular assistance from parents with homework, but he or she should be given some additional time to figure out answers by himself or herself. Such learning can provide a sense of achievement and mastery and is as important as, if not more valuable than, being directed on how to solve a problem. Moreover, encouraging a child in another area of academic strength, such as reading, may provide motivation for enhancing overall academic skills and study habits.

## TEACHER EXPECTATIONS AND LEARNING

Teachers and educators have become increasingly aware that the teacher-student relationship is vital to the children's success and matriculation in the classroom. The classic study conducted by Rosenthal and Jacobsen (1968) gave new meaning to the term *self-fulfilling prophecy* and initiated a movement that has made teachers, school administrators, and parents more sensitive to teacher-child interaction. Robert Rosenthal, a Harvard professor, and Lenore Jacobsen, an elementary school principal in San Francisco, completed a study which suggested that teachers' expectations for student performance have a direct impact on learning outcomes. At the beginning of the school year, the researchers gave intelligence tests to all of the children at one school, which they referred to as Oak School, and then randomly selected 20 percent of the students, without any reference to their intelligence tests. They then informed the teachers that these children showed remarkable potential for growth and would manifest even more intellectual blossoming before the end of the academic year. Eight months later, the children were evaluated again, and the researchers found that the children who had been labeled by teachers as intelligent, and had been treated accordingly by their teachers, showed a significantly greater increase in test scores than those who were not singled out. Teachers were also requested to rate children on their intellectual curiosity, as well as on personal and social adjustment. Not surprisingly, the children who received higher teacher expectations, were rated to be more intellectually curious and happier, and had less need for social approval (Rosenthal and Jacobsen, 1968).

The way that children are treated in the classroom is largely contingent on how the teacher interacts with each child and sets expectations from the very first day of the school year. Children who are thought to be more intelligent may be placed at the front of the classroom and may be more likely to be called on to answer questions than other children. Children perceived to be less verbally adept may not be asked questions or expected to volunteer answers during a discussion of assigned readings. Moreover, children who are members of ethnic and cultural minorities may have different expectations for learning and social behavior that may conflict with the U.S. norm.

Teachers and school counselors must also be aware of how they compare students with previous students or siblings they have taught, and they should refrain from making gender-comparative statements. Some teachers may do children a disservice by stating, "Well, Sam, I had your older brother, Will, and your sister, Gwen, in my social studies class, and they were my best students." Sam may begin to worry that he will not be able to achieve a performance level equal to that of his older brother and sister. The anxiety over his teacher's expectations may affect his actual performance in a way that would cause him to do worse than his older siblings did in the class. On the first day of school, a teacher applying a strengths perspective might say something to Sam such as this, "Sam, I am so glad to have you in my class. Your older brother loved learning, and your sister was so motivated. She kept me on my toes. I believe that you will do your very best work in this class." Rather than creating specific expectations and causing unnecessary stress for the boy, the teacher has used statements that affirm her appreciation of children who enjoy learning and become excited about the learning process.

Furthermore, a teacher may unconsciously make references to boys doing better in some subjects than girls. For instance, some teachers believe that boys will do better in math and science and that girls will excel in reading, language arts, and spelling. Communicating these expectations to children in the classroom may lead them to have lower expectations for themselves throughout their educational experience. Teachers carry much influence in the lives of children and must not underestimate the powerful role they play on a daily basis. The same is true with parents who can easily communicate to a child that one subject is less important than another or that a child may not need to study as hard for a particular subject. The strengths and limitations of the child's abilities across the curriculum must be continually evaluated by teachers and parents in a collaborative effort.

## ELEMENTS OF LEARNING AND ACHIEVEMENT

Children's learning seems to occur in three major domains. First, children must acquire basic knowledge such as reading, science, and math skills. Second, children must learn prosocial skills, or ways of successfully interacting with both children and adults, as they unlearn less appropriate ways of socialization. Third, children must learn how to learn, that is, they must acquire tools for acquiring and maintaining information. These skills might range from learning to use computers effectively to gaining skills in making assertive requests about their learning needs (Rose and Fatout, 2003).

Children's learning styles vary. Teachers must be aware that children may need diverse teaching techniques in order to master classroom content. Some children are more visually oriented than others, meaning that they rely on having materials placed on the chalkboard or written down in a handout. These children do not do as well when the teacher lectures and expects them to acquire academic material after hearing them read out loud in class. By contrast, other children may acquire material more effectively by auditory means, which means that a written math problem placed on the board or handed out on paper may be difficult to grasp. Most teachers make an effort to understand each child's learning style, but in many schools the student-to-teacher ratio does not afford this type of individual attention. Still, achievement tests, the involvement of teacher's aides, and frequent parent-teacher conferences may assist teachers in better understanding how children learn best and how particular learning approaches can be accommodated in the classroom.

Stipek and Seal (2001) contend that for many years teachers and professionals have focused on improvement of self-esteem through reinforcement as the primary means of getting children to achieve in school. However, Stipek and Seal believe that the elements of success may be distilled into four areas: competency, autonomy, curiosity, and critical relationships. Every child must be given an opportunity to try things on his or her own, to figure out solutions to problems without constant involvement and supervision by adults. Through self-mastery children develop self-confidence and a sense of autonomy, an essential component for development of social and academic achievement. Moreover, children are inherently curious about what makes things work, whether it is a clock or a bicycle pump. This curiosity must be encouraged, too, in the learning of new skills such as decimals or multiplication tables. Finally, children need to know that there are adults in their lives whom they can depend on for guidance and direction when they reach an obstacle in learning and need clarification. Teachers and parents can work together to enrich a child's learning environment and to ensure that the child's success in school is predicated on these four critical dimensions of learning.

The ability of children to learn in school depends not only on their innate abilities but also on their level of motivation, attitudes, and emotional responses to school and other settings where achievement is expected. Psychologists have for some time referred to this aspect of achievement as achievement motivation. *Achievement motivation* is defined as an individual's tendency to evaluate his or her performance against standards of excellence, to strive for successful performance, and to experience contentment with a successful performance (Feld, Ruhland, and Gold, 1979). Still, children may show remarkable motivation to achieve in one subject, such as math, yet show little interest or effort in reading assignments, for example. Teachers, school counselors, and parents must recognize what motivates children to learn and how they go about learning. Understanding these processes will help teachers to encourage children to perform at a maximum level and enjoy their achievements.

Children spend a great deal of their time in educational settings and learn to move from the culture of home to the culture of school. Schooling fosters "cognitive, affective, and social development; and influences the development of a stable self-image, acquisition of interaction skills with classmates and peers, learning of social customs and mores, coming to like or dislike school and many other things" (Entwisle and Alexander, 1988, p. 450). The child's response to the school is largely contingent on the parental view of education. These parental views may range from perceiving the school as a necessary avenue for success in the United States to seeing the school as a major form of oppression (Schriver, 2001). Children themselves learn right away that the school environment is vastly different from the home environment and that there are distinctly different levels of power, rules, and codes of conduct.

## *ETHNIC AND CULTURALLY DIFFERENT CHILDREN*

Children of color may experience any number of cross-cultural conflicts as teachers begin to utilize relationship building and communication approaches that are unfamiliar with what the child experiences at home. Holliday (1985) noted that African-American children are socialized to be assertive and persistent in problem solving. However, teachers may view these approaches to learning as inappropriate, which may exacerbate a child's feeling of helplessness. Children's adjustment to learning and their feeling comfortable with themselves are vital elements to their future academic success in school. Ogbu (1987) observed cultural differences in the learning process and adjustment problems among African-American children. They may be discouraged by others in their community who have not been provided with an adequate education or who cannot find jobs.

In a study of fourth, fifth, and sixth graders of African-American, Mexican-American, Chinese-American, and Greek-American descent, significant differences were discovered in learning styles. These children were given the Learning Style Inventory to assess preferences among different ethnic groups in both rural and urban settings in New York and Texas. Chinese-American children responded to a variety of instructional approaches whereas African-American children felt more comfortable with patterns and routines. Mexican-American and Greek-American students had the least significant differences in learning styles. The researchers suggest that teachers use alternative classroom environments, methods, and resources to accommodate the learning needs of children from different cultures (Dunn and Gemake, 1990).

In a study of African-American and Mexican-American students in the third and sixth grades, Rotheram-Borus and Phinney (1990) found that Mexican-American children were more responsive to working together in groups under supervision than were African-American children. Second, African-American children were more likely to be more verbally and emotionally demonstrative as well as exhibit more active movement than Mexican-American children. Finally, both African-American and Mexican-American children were responsive to and relatively submissive to persons in authority. Mexican-American children tended to express bad feelings about scenarios involving authority figures, whereas African-American children were more apologetic. This study points to the importance of professionals understanding the differential reactions to communication and social situations among children from different ethnic and cultural backgrounds, especially where learning and achievement are concerned.

When considering American Indian children, school social workers, teachers, psychologists, and counselors must develop a strong cultural knowledge base for establishing strong working alliances and collaborations with their families. Six cultural characteristics have been identified as affecting the education of American Indian children: geographic isolation, cultural heterogeneity, extended family, role of children, group primacy, and traumatic educational history (Dykeman, Nelson, and Appleton, 1996).

Geographically, most American Indians live in rural areas where values are different from those in urban settings. Families on reservations may be reluctant to get involved with authority figures, may lack transportation, and may have difficulty paying for medical and baby-sitting services (Dykeman, Nelson, and Appleton, 1996). Moreover, American Indian culture is heterogeneous, involving 300 to 400 distinct ethnicities, with at least 250 languages. Cultural rituals in one tribe may not carry over into another tribe, and there are varying degrees of acculturation to the larger culture, based on tribal affiliation. Some American Indian children may feel bicultural whereas others may feel displaced in both their own and the dominant culture (Dykeman, Nelson, and Appleton, 1996).

Extended family members, such as aunts, uncles, and cousins, may be involved in rearing a child, and this arrangement may be approved by tribal council. This arrangement does not point to a family's inability to care for a child but rather an indication of family togetherness or close friendship ties. American Indian children are respected as much as adults are within the culture, and parents tend to use milder forms of discipline than their Caucasian counterparts do. Young children participate in powwows and are actively involved in learning storytelling and cultural legends. Group primacy as a value means that children are more accustomed to group activities and may not respond if the teacher addresses them individually across the classroom. Finally, many American Indians may be ambivalent about the school system based on historical events wherein children were removed from the reservations and placed in distant boarding schools. Still, by and large, education is viewed positively, as it offers a means of achieving success within the greater society (Dykeman, Nelson, and Appleton, 1996).

Children growing up in the Appalachian region are taught to value education as a means of making a better life for themselves. In a geographic area that includes all of West Virginia and parts of New York, Ohio, Pennsylvania, Maryland, Kentucky, Tennessee, Virginia, North and South Carolina, Alabama, Georgia, and Mississippi, many people still live in relative isolation and poverty. Many children live in remote areas where schools are some distance away and where parents and grandparents may have received less than a high school education. Children are accustomed to hearing stories of how their elders walked three miles to school and carried their lunches of crackers and eggs so that they could get an education. Still, children are taught the work ethic and the importance of practical learning that will be useful for making a living. Children are taught by the family that they must respect their teachers but must also be independent and always stand by their cultural values and beliefs. Children are expected to counter unfairness in the classroom and on the playground even if it means standing up to authority figures or children who are older.

Appalachian children learn early in life the cultural values of close family ties, strong religious beliefs, personalism, and the importance of place. Children feel obligated to look out for their younger siblings at school, which might be mistaken for overprotectiveness by outsiders. In some smaller communities, school officials are expected to understand that school comes second when there is a family obligation, be it helping the family to plant corn or attending the funeral of a distant cousin. Also, children are likely to discuss their religious and spiritual beliefs in reference to their learning and may verbally connect new ideas to their beliefs about fairness and the golden rule. In the Appalachian culture, children are taught that one person is not better than another, which may hinder them from running for class president or being captain of the baseball team. Similarly, Appalachian children may remain quiet during a classroom discussion even when they know the answer to a question. They learn at home that one must not be boastful or proud or "draw attention to oneself." Children are loyal to the family's sense of place and the strong ties to a particular area of the state or region. Schoolchildren whose families migrated to Midwestern cities often will recite stories about life in the mountains or coal mines even if they have never visited the Appalachian region.

Children whose parents or grandparents migrated to the Midwest for work after World War II and up until the 1970s may be misunderstood by urban school officials because of their unique cultural values. Children who are extremely quiet in class may be reluctant to speak up because of their southern dialect or because of past discrimination for being Appalachian. Children who are passive observers are generally not perceived to be successful in academic or career pursuits. Some Appalachian children may be misdiagnosed as having learning disabilities because of their nonverbal behavior in class, or, conversely, they may be more proficient in expressing their ideas verbally rather than on paper. This is perhaps related to the Appalachian expectation that children will describe what they see in nature, whether a bird's nest or an animal on the farm. Appalachian parents in urban settings value frequent contact with teachers and other school professionals, which allows them to voice their opinions and describe their children's interests and competencies, as well as learn about their strengths and limitations at school (Helton, Barnes, and Borman, 1994). Ongoing collaboration between Appalachian parents and teachers helps the child feel more confident about learning and helps the parents understand the value of education in their child's life.

Many cities such as Dayton, Columbus, and Cincinnati, Ohio, have tried to keep Appalachian culture alive, especially for the children and youth, with community projects such as a cultural wall, bluegrass concerts, and heritage festivals. In Cincinnati, Ohio, the Appalachian Identity Center was established decades ago by the Urban Appalachian Council to help children develop strong feelings about their cultural heritage and traditions such as storytelling, crafts, and genealogy. Appalachian professionals such as attorneys, college professors, teachers, and social workers go into the schools and discuss the importance of education and often tell stories of how they "made it." Also, the Urban Appalachian Council provides Appalachian storytellers who go into schools and preschools to tell stories of the mountains and colorful characters such as Jack and Mutsmag. The Urban Appalachian Council and the Appalachian Community Development Corporation have developed and maintain library resources on Appalachian literature, music, history, sociology, folklore, alternative medicine, the African-American Appalachian experience, and a range of other cultural topics. These agencies help children feel more positive about their cultural traditions by sponsoring street fairs and an annual Appalachian festival that brings entertainers, crafts demonstrators, and artists from all over the Appalachian region.

## CHILDREN AND SPECIAL EDUCATION

Until around three decades ago, children with disabilities were largely invisible within the context of the school setting. Children with disabilities were segregated in both learning and social activities. Rather than being viewed as whole people, students with disabilities were commonly labeled by their specific disabilities, such as, "a Down syndrome child" or "cerebral palsy child." The emphasis was on the child's problem rather than on his or her overall traits or potential as a human being who could grow and develop new skills, regardless of how long this process might take. The well-being of these children was at risk, and many dropped out of school or were taken out by their parents, who felt that they would never fit in or that they could do more to help children learn at home.

The well-being of children with disabilities in schools was addressed by the landmark legislation, Public Law 94-142, the Education for All Handicapped Children's Act in 1975. This law developed the concept of the "least-restrictive environment," which opened the way for children to be educated, to the maximum extent possible, along with children in regular classrooms. This law mandated that children suspected of having developmental disabilities have the right to a multidisciplinary evaluation of their cognitive, educational, language, motor, and social skills to facilitate appropriate classroom placement. Consequently, each child in special education was to have an Individual Educational Plan with specific and measurable goals, developed jointly by school staff and the parents. Also, via due process, parents were given the right to contest the school's lack of action in testing and placing children, as well as to go to court in order to obtain appropriate services for their children. Moreover, Public Law 105-17, the Individuals with Disabilities Education Act (IDEA) Amendments of 1997, reiterated the necessity for a least-restrictive classroom setting for children with disabilities and also advocated for access to such classes, as well as their progress in these environments (Cawley et al., 2002).

In between these important pieces of legislation came two amendments to Public Law 94-142; these were Public Laws 99-457 and 102-119, which instituted amendments to provide special education services for children in the birth-to-three-years age group. These significant laws mandated for the first time that children with disabilities under kindergarten age must receive special education services comparable to those of school-aged children, but they must also have a service coordinator and an individual family service plan. These laws gave special attention to the family's health and well-being as integral to a systems approach to assessment and practice in early intervention (Helton, 1994).

Many special education teachers have developed unique approaches for helping children get excited about learning and enhance their self-esteem. Animal-assisted therapy has proven to be effective with children with multiple disabilities (All and Loving, 1999), especially in improving their social and interactive skills (Edney, 1992). In Ohio, one special education teacher developed an activity program in which her twelve students, ranging in age from five to thirteen, are given the chance to go horseback riding to improve balance, self-esteem, communication skills, and motor coordination. A teacher's aide videotapes each riding session, and even those who are fearful of riding a horse benefit from the socialization and opportunities to use language. The horses and facilities are provided free by a retired police officer and several others volunteer their time, including a nurse who has said that the children's smiles are reward enough for her (Zeltner, 2002).

Children with learning disabilities are often misunderstood and, until special education legislation was passed in 1975 (Public Law 94-142), were frequently ignored, left in regular classrooms, or placed in classrooms with children who have mental retardation. Teachers and other school professionals tended to focus on their academic failure rather than attempting to unveil their strengths. Some children gave up trying to perform and dropped out when they became old enough. Others acted out behaviorally from the frustration and despair of being different. Although many children were placed in appropriate classroom settings, others, especially those with learning disabilities, were not always fully evaluated by the school system, due to a lack of understanding of learning disabilities or inadequate resources.

Miller (2002) found that college students with learning disabilities possessed resilient characteristics similar to others who have shown resilience in moving beyond various risks in their lives. Those with learning disabilities showed self-determination, acknowledged their strengths, relied on close friends who were supportive, had a dedicated teacher who always encouraged their efforts, and identified turning points when they beat the odds and achieved their goals. The turning points involved following their own instincts and believing in themselves rather than listening to the doubts of others regarding their school performance. Many students said that they would replay these turning points toward success over and over in their heads as a way to face new and even more challenging situations. These resilient students also thought it imperative to understand and acknowledge their learning disabilities so that they would be able to compensate for their limitations. Miller concludes that professionals can help to foster and maintain resilience in children with learning disabilities if they are willing to help them to identify, describe, and build on successful experiences.

By the late 1970s, however, increased federal funding was appropriated through the Department of Maternal and Child Health Services for interdisciplinary, university-affiliated diagnostic centers across the country. Children and families were thus given more options for obtaining a highly specialized, objective evaluation of their child outside the school system, which included referral for appropriate classroom placement and child and family counseling. These diagnostic centers were often established by faculty and practitioners within universities, where the latest advancements in research and practice were available for assessing and treating children with disabilities. These highly specialized centers advocated focusing on the whole child and family and incorporated key disciplines such as psychology, social work, special education, speech and audiology, developmental pediatrics, child psychiatry, occupational and physical therapy, nursing, and nutrition. Some programs were able to garner additional state and local resources for operating diagnostic preschools and specialized classrooms for children with autism and learning disabilities. A professional on the interdisciplinary team functions as case manager and coordinates a strengths-oriented assessment and intervention plan for each child and family.

Each team member addresses the unique needs of the individual child with a major concentration on what the child does well; the family can then be assisted in identifying and supporting the child's assets and strengths. The following case scenario demonstrates how such a team approach may help parents and family members empower a child to do his or her best and compensate for any weaknesses.

Ricky, age nine, was brought to the developmental center because he was not able to perform well in school, and his parents stated that he was slow. Ricky was making average grades in school but had more difficulty with math than other subjects. He had complained to his teachers and family that he was bored with school and was not motivated to complete in-class assignments. His parents noted in the social work assessment that they had gotten so frustrated with his inability to do his homework that they called him stupid a few times. The school system had done basic educational assessment, but the parents wanted a more comprehensive evaluation of Ricky. Ricky loved computers and amazed his parents with his computer knowledge. His parents had bought him a computer for Christmas but did not want it to interfere with his schoolwork. Ricky was limited to two hours a day on the computer and tried to get his parents to play video games with him. The father said that computers were all right, but he wished his son would play baseball with him. He indicated he gave up trying a long time ago as Ricky could not hit the ball. Both parents emphasized that they had only high school diplomas and worked at a local manufacturing company. They wanted Ricky and his four-year-old sister, Kelli, to someday go to college and have a better life.

Ricky underwent a complete assessment at the developmental center. The results indicated that he had an IQ in the gifted range, but he had rather serious visual, perceptual, and fine motor problems. He was placed in a gifted class part of the day and began to receive occupational therapy at school to improve his fine motor skills. His grades began to improve almost immediately, and he enjoyed the more challenging assignments in the classes for gifted learners. Ricky's parents had originally seen his fascination with the computer as maladaptive and isolationist, but when they showed interest, Ricky taught them to use spreadsheets, look up things on the Internet, and play video games. He even taught his sister to play video games, so the entire family started to spend more time together. The developmental center helped the parents help Ricky realize and celebrate his abilities rather than dwell on his limitations.

Teachers and parents must work closely together to ensure that the child's best interests are being addressed and that open communication is encouraged between the home and the school. The following scenario portrays a positive outcome of having open communication lines.

A school social worker met with a teacher who was frustrated that one of her nine-year-old special education students, Amy, had problems with basic reading. She stated that she was amazed, however, that the little girl had an incredible interest in animals and could name every animal in her reading book, as well as the ones in pictures in the classroom. The teacher and the school social worker went out for a joint home visit and talked to Amy's grandparents, who were raising her. She had been placed with them after being abandoned by her parents. Amy was found happily watching the Animal Planet channel with her grandfather, which he said was a daily ritual. The teacher was later able to use the knowledge of Amy's time with her grandfather to have her read books about animals, which improved her interest in and performance in reading.

Children in special education programs have a right to access all the educational resources available in their school and in their district. Until recent years most children with developmental disabilities were referred to as "slow learners" or even "retarded," with little attention being paid to how these children managed to barely survive from one school year to the next. Parents and teachers now work together much more closely to identify and reinforce a child's strengths and interests. Professionals and parents since the 1970s have begun to focus more holistically on the child's emotional, psychological, intellectual, and social well-being and use "people-first" language. In school, a child with an IQ of fifty is referred to as a child with mental retardation, with the emphasis being placed first on the child, not on his or her level of intelligence. Parents whose children once had little choice but eventual institutionalization are making arrangements for their children to remain at home as long as possible and then, as young adults, to transition into a community-based group home.

## *HOMESCHOOLING:*
## *AN EDUCATIONAL ALTERNATIVE*

Homeschooling has become increasingly popular in the United States, especially since the 1970s. In 2001, U.S. Census data indicated that as many as 2 million American children are homeschooled, with the number growing by as much as 15 to 20 percent per year (McDowell and Ray, 2000; Lines, 2000). The numbers reported by the Department of Education were around 15,000 in 1984 (Ray, 1989). Families today homeschool their children for a variety of reasons. Many families opt for homeschooling for religious reasons or because they believe they are capable of providing a more academically stimulating and creative learning environment at home (Rivero, 2002). Some simply believe that by educating their children at home they will be able to instill certain beliefs, values, and skills and, just as important, develop a stronger relationship with their children (Romanowski, 2001). Others may homeschool in response to the increasing incidence of violence and bullying in schools. Advocates of homeschooling contend that homeschooled children tend to have a better feeling about themselves. Taylor (1987) researched self-concept of children who were homeschooled using a random sample of 45,000 children and found that their self-concept scores on standardized tests were 47 percent higher for homeschooled children than for children who were educated in conventional schools. A smaller number choose homeschooling out of necessity because they live in remote, rural areas where commuting to school becomes a hardship.

Romanowski (2001) notes that homeschoolers are much more diverse today than in past years and seem to reflect a cross section of American society and culture. Once thought to be an educational approach reserved by families with fundamentalist religious beliefs, homeschooling is now embraced by various ethnic groups, social classes, and a rapidly increasing number of minority families (Wahisi, 1995; Ray, 1989; Long, 2001). However, homeschooling as a trend in U.S. society may lead to the development of new schools or school-like institutions built around the mutual needs of families choosing homeschooling (Hill, 2000).

Many arguments may be made for and against home schooling. In terms of the strengths of homeschooling, it has been noted that students are more likely to be more academically successful and maximize their potential when parents are highly involved in their learning (Simmons, 1994). Increased parental involvement in homeschooling may also enable them to develop stronger family relationships in an era wherein the family institution is falling apart. This is thought to be especially applicable to families where several siblings are being homeschooled together (Romanowski, 2001).

Homeschoolers argue that unlike their public school counterparts, children schooled at home are able to engage socially in multiage situations with a high level of confidence. These children are generally involved in numerous social activities, such as Scouts, dance classes, 4-H, and soccer, which provide them with important peer socialization skills. Homeschooling parents also contend that their children's individual needs are not being met in public schools, which are designed to meet the needs of many children and thus force adaptation

(Romanowski, 2001). Finally, families may feel that by not having the pressure of grades and competition, children schooled at home feel better about their learning accomplishments and learn for the sake of acquiring knowledge.

On the other hand, those who oppose homeschooling pose many questions about the benefits of this movement in education. First, many critics point out the vital socialization that a school setting provides and contend that children schooled at home are sheltered from the real world. Simmons (1994) points out that it is not only socially desirable but also essential that a child's education include interaction with other children of the same age group. By interacting with children from other cultures, social backgrounds, levels of ability, and worldviews, children are better able to understand others and develop socialization skills for problem solving in adulthood. These experiences ordinarily would not be available in a homeschool environment and would therefore restrict the child from important opportunities for understanding diversity. In addition, all children need to engage in discussions, share ideas, compete, and work with other students with a range of ideas and skills during their educational experience (Romanowski, 2001).

Another compelling argument is that families who homeschool their children may not have the necessary skills or adequate academic resources and facilities. This is especially challenging for parents of children with disabilities who attempt to arrange for special education services at home (Romanowski, 2001). Parents attempting to homeschool children with special needs repeatedly had their appeals for public-funded speech therapy to be delivered at home denied in the California Supreme Court (Walsh, 2001). Furthermore, it appears that we lack uniform standards throughout the states on the breadth and depth of knowledge and skills parents must possess in the core academic subjects for homeschooling their children. For example, California school systems have engaged in heated debates with parents who have tried to qualify their homeschooling as "private schools" under state law to avoid stringent requirements for teacher preparation (Zehr, 2002). Some emphasize the extreme difficulty of being able to simulate a classroom environment at home where everyday interruptions and routines of daily living may lead to fragmentation and gaps in a child's learning.

Homeschooling is expected to continue to polarize parents and teachers, who have divergent ideas and philosophies about how children should be schooled. Those whose ideologies are far from the madding crowd will advocate for expanded support of homeschooling, as those who are opponents will advocate for enriched and safer school settings which may better accommodate all children. Parents whose children have special needs, be they learning disabilities or gifted skills, may find homeschooling to be challenging; they may not be able to afford the necessary funds and resources for materials. Families who advocate for more control over their children's lives because of their fear of violence and negative influences in public schools may realize that a child's positive socialization begins at home yet is so dependent on the enriching interaction with other age mates.

## CONCLUSION

Children in the twenty-first century have so many more opportunities for learning and self-fulfillment than did children in previous decades. Children have diverse interests and competencies that may stem from any number of school and family activities. A child who is unable to achieve in math may excel in English and art classes, and should be encouraged for these successes. All children excel in some area, which is where they will shine and be able to feel good about their success. I think a third-grader's response to a science teacher's question begs us to ponder how children in their own words help us to understand their interests and strengths. When eight-year-old Ira was asked by the teacher to describe why rainbows occur, the boy looked at him quizzically and then retorted, "Sir, I thought rainbows were to be admired for their beauty, not explained." Parents, teachers, and school administrators must remain open to exploring what a child does best and then help him or her to find avenues for nourishing these competencies. Even the most intelligent child in the classroom may have a difficult time giving directions to his or her house or may not do well in sports.

In fact, special education strategies used in the classroom might serve as a model for educators and parents as the emphasis is on multisensory approaches to learning. Children who learn better by having materials on the chalkboard or on an overhead projector should be given copies of those materials, whenever possible, for review outside the classroom. Likewise, children who are better at learning by ear should have concepts repeated so that they can more easily encode and remember what has been said, along with receiving written materials. Both parents and teachers must encourage children to do their best, always praise their successes, and communicate expectations that are commensurate with the children's abilities and interests, without giving unrealistic hopes for achievement.

## *STRENGTHS STORY: HANNAH CARTER*

Hannah Renee Carter, age nine, is in the fourth grade at Eastern Elementary School and has an older sister, Cecily, age eleven, a sixth-grader. Hannah loves school, as does her sister, who usually makes the honor roll each grading period. Hannah finds learning a little more challenging and works hard to make average to above-average grades. She has had some tutoring by the teacher's aide in reading and spelling, but she still contends that these are her favorite subjects.

Her father is a butcher at the local grocery store and her mother is a real estate agent. Hannah's maternal and paternal grandparents have always lived in the same city, where they grew up, so Hannah is accustomed to a large, closely knit family with many reunions and celebrations. Hannah's mother and father have always read to her and her sister just before bedtime, and sometimes they ask the girls to make up stories about everyday events to be shared before bedtime.

Last year Hannah began to take an interest in the annual school spelling bee and spent hour after hour learning columns of words. Her parents and grandparents were proud of her when she entered the third grade spelling bee near the end of the school year. She worked hard and did her best but did not place among the top ten spellers. Sometimes her mother would sit down with Hannah after dinner and help her practice the harder words. Hannah was determined, however, and said, "Well, I will just enter again next year." Her sister, Cecily, had won the third grade spelling bee and encouraged her sister to continue learning words. In the fall of that school year, she was eager to begin classes and told her friends she was going to win the spelling bee. Her maternal grandfather,

Harry, encouraged her efforts and would call out words for her to spell when the family would travel in his camper for weekend outings.

One weekend in late October, Hannah set out with her maternal grandparents, Harry and Della, for a weekend at a state park about four hours from their home. Cecily stayed at home because she had a sleepover at a friend's house that Saturday night. There was a tragic accident in which Hannah's family's camper was swept off the highway by a tractor trailer and her grandfather was killed instantly. Hannah and her grandmother were trapped in the upside-down camper for two hours before they could be removed from the wreckage. Amazingly, Hannah and her grandmother had only minor bruises and scratches. Hannah would not talk much about the accident other than to say that she saw Papa (her name for Harry) die. All the family came together to support one another and Hannah was given many opportunities to express her grief with the love and support of her family.

Hannah went back to school after about a week and was able to catch up in her studies, as was Cecily. The two girls started studying words again and Hannah loved to talk about how Papa Harry had helped her to learn so many new words over the summer. Each week Hannah's spelling improved until the day of the annual spelling bee in mid-March. Hannah's whole family was there for the event, including her grandmother, aunts, and uncles. Hannah was so excited she could hardly wait to begin. She proudly spelled her way to being one of three semifinalists. When she was given the word *invisible,* she substituted the second "i" with an "a." She showed some sadness as she walked to where her parents and other family members were seated. Then, when her mother reached over and patted her on the shoulder, she began to sob, putting her face against her mother's side. Her mother said, "I know this is so hard for you. You have tried so hard and been through so much, honey, what with Papa passing and all." Hannah looked up to her mother and said, "No, Mom, I just wasn't ready to quit spelling."

Hannah was eager to do her best and in some small way wanted to honor her grandfather by doing better than she did the previous year in the spelling bee. She was given a ribbon for being second runner-up, which she proudly displayed on the door of her room. The family planned a dinner at her favorite restaurant with a big cake to celebrate her accomplishment. Hannah loved the spelling bee and its challenge and announced to the family, "Next year, I will be the winner." Hannah missed her grandfather and often talked about him, always adding that she wanted to win the spelling bee so that she could make her grandpa proud of her. Her mother and grandma told her that he was already proud of her and that she could win if she set her mind to it and practiced hard enough.

## *QUESTIONS FOR DISCUSSION*

1. Discuss how teacher expectations can influence how children learn and achieve in the classroom.
2. Discuss several cultures and how cultural values must be taken into consideration in educational and teaching methods.
3. Discuss the impact of the Education for All Handicapped Children Act of 1975 on education in the United States. How have various amendments to this act enhanced the educational experience for children with special needs?
4. Discuss some of the advantages and disadvantages of home-schooling.

## REFERENCES

All, A. C. and Loving, G. L. (1999). Animals, horseback riding, and implications for rehabilitative therapy. *The Journal of Rehabilitative Therapy* 65(3): 49-57.

Cawley, J., Hayden, S., Cade, E., and Baker-Kroczynski, S. (2002). Including students with disabilities into the general education science classroom. *Exceptional Children* 68(4): 423-435.

Dunn, R. and Gemake, J. (1990). Cross-cultural differences in learning styles of elementary-age students from four ethnic backgrounds. *Journal of Multicultural Counseling and Development* 18(2): 68-93.

Dykeman, C., Nelson, J. R., and Appleton, V. (1996). Building strong working alliances with American Indian families. In Ewalt, P. L., Freeman, E. M., Kirk, S. A., and Poole, D. L. (Eds.), *Multicultural issues in social work* (pp. 336-350). Washington, DC: NASW Press.

Edney, A. T. (1992). Companion animals and human health: An overview. *Journal of the Royal Society of Medicine* 88: 704-708.

Entwisle, D. R. and Alexander, K. L. (1988). Factors affecting achievement test scores and marks received by black and white first graders. *Elementary School Journal* 88(5): 449-471.

Feld, S., Ruhland, D., and Gold, M. (1979). Developmental changes in achievement motivation. *Merrill-Palmer Quarterly* 25: 43-60.

Helton, L. R. (1994). Strengthening efforts for a family systems approach in early intervention with disabled infants and toddlers. *Social Work in Education* 16(8): 241-250.

Helton, L. R., Barnes, E. C., and Borman, K. M. (1994). Urban Appalachians and professional intervention: A model for educators and social service providers. In Borman, K. M. and Obermiller, P. J. (Eds.), *From mountain to metropolis: Appalachian migrants in American cities* (pp. 105-120). Westport, CT: Bergin and Garvey.

Hill, P. T. (2000). Home schooling and the future of public education. *Peabody Journal of Education* 75(1/2): 20-31.

Holliday, B. (1985). Toward a model of teacher-child transactional process affecting black children's academic achievement. In Spencer, M., Brookins, G., and Allen, W. (Eds.), *Beginnings: The social and affective black children's academic achievement* (pp. 117-130). Hillsdale, NJ: Erlbaum.

James, M. and Jongeward, D. (1971). *Born to win: Transactional analysis with gestalt experiments.* Reading, MA: Addison-Wesley Publishing Company.

Lines, P. (2000). Home schooling comes of age. *The Public Interest* (Summer), pp. 74-85.

Long, J. F. (2001). Schooling at home. *Kappa Delta Pi Record* 37(2): 67-69.

McDowell, S. A. and Ray, B. D. (2000). The home education movement in context, practice, and theory: Editors introduction. *Peabody Journal of Education* 75 (1-2): 1-7.

Miller, M. (2002). Resilient elements in students with learning disabilities. *Journal of Clinical Psychology* 58(3): 291-298.

Ogbu, J. U. (1987). Variability in minority school performance: A problem in search of an explanation. *Anthropology and Education Quarterly* 18(4): 312-332.

Ray, B. (1989). Home schools: A synthesis of research on characteristics and learner outcomes. *Education and Urban Society* 21(1): 16-31.

Rivero, L. (2002). Progressive digressions: Home schooling for self-actualization. *Roeper Review* 24(4): 197-202.

Romanowski, M. H. (2001). Common arguments about the strengths and limitations of home schooling. *The Clearing House* 75(2): 79-83.

Rose, S. R. and Fatout, M. F. (2003). *Social work practice with children and adolescents.* Boston: Allyn and Bacon.

Rosenthal, R. and Jacobsen, L. (1968). *Pygmalion in the classroom: Teacher expectation and pupils' intellectual development.* New York: Rinehart and Winston.

Rotheram-Borus, M. J. and Phinney, J. S. (1990). Patterns of social expectations among black and Mexican-American children. *Child Development* 61: 542-556.

Schriver, J. M. (2001). *Human behavior and the social environment: Shifting paradigms in essential knowledge for social work practice,* Third edition. Boston: Allyn and Bacon.

Simmons, B. J. (1994). Classroom at home. *American School Board Journal* 181(2): 47-49.

Stipek, D. and Seal, K. (2001). *Motivated minds: Raising children to love learning.* New York: Henry Holt and Company Owl Books.

Taylor, J. W. (1987). Self-concept in home schooling children (doctoral dissertation, Andrews University, 1986). *Dissertation Abstracts International* 47: 2809A.

Wahisi, T. T. (1995). Making the grade: Black families see the benefits in home schooling. *Crisis* 102(7): 14-15.

Walsh, M. (2001). Court declines to hear case on home school special education. *Education Week* 20(32): 27.

Zehr, M. A. (2002). No end seen to flap over California home school policy. *Education Week* 22(9): 23, 26.

Zeltner, B. (2002). No horsing around in the saddle: Students riding high find self-esteem, self-control. *Plain Dealer,* October 16, p. B1-B5.

# Chapter 6

# Self-Concept and Self-Esteem

When children feel good about themselves, it's like a snowball rolling downhill. They are continually able to recognize and integrate new proof of their value as they grow and mature.

Stephanie Martson

Nothing is more important than a child's self-esteem. Children's self-esteem is first impacted by the way they are treated in the home by their parents and other family members. Children require ongoing demonstrations of affection and communication that they are worthwhile and vital to the family's functioning. At school, children should have a supportive environment where they gain self-confidence and approval for mastering academic tasks and improving social skills. Erikson (1968) states in his developmental theory that children must be able to prove their competence or industry during the school-age years in order to achieve a strong identity and sense of self in adolescence. Through engaging in team sports and community projects such as antilitter campaigns, children continue to recognize and appreciate their self-worth in reference to the images around them.

Although self-concept and self-esteem are often used interchangeably (Rosenberg, 1979; Garton and Pratt, 1995), self-concept should be distinguished. For example, Carl Rogers (1961) presents the concept of self that is "equivalent to self-concept that is a conceptual gestalt composed of perceptions of the characteristics of the self in relationship to others" (Zastrow and Kirst-Ashman, 2001, p. 105). As Zastrow and Kirst-Ashman suggest, self-concept is an individual's conception of who he or she is. The development of self-concept greatly depends on the individual's perceptions of his or her experiences. The same authors also state, "the person's perceptions of experiences are influenced by the 'need for positive regard' (to be valued by others)" (p. 105). Children are easily influenced to others because of their need for positive regard.

Cooley (1922) describes the process in which one comes to define the self:

> The social reference takes the form of a somewhat definite imagination of how one's self—that is, any idea he appropriates—appears in a particular mind, and the kind of self-feeling one has is determined by the attitude toward this attributed to that other mind. (p.183)

He further states, "Each to each a looking-glass reflects the other that doth pass." This self-idea has three principal elements: "the imagination of our appearance to the other person; the imagination of his judgments of that appearance, and some sort of self-feeling, such as pride or mortification" (p. 184).

According to Cooley, habit and familiarity are not sufficient to cause an idea to be appropriated into the self. Something novel and congenial in experience is appropriated and becomes the very heart of the self. Examples of such phenomena might include a child's new toy that other children admire, or a perfect score on a mathematics test a student has achieved. Such a newly acquired part of the self, Cooley claims, can thrive when the individual is surrounded by unconditional love. When one lacks the support of the other, with love closing, the self contracts and hardens. The self would continue to be closed until the rigidity is broken up by growth and renewal. In other words, the positive image of the self thrives when one is guided and nourished by sympathy.

Rogers (1961) applied Cooley's theory of the development of the self in his client-centered therapy. According to his theory, the self breaks off from the old definition of the self only in the absence of a threat to self, actual or implied, when one can examine various aspects of one's experiences without distorting them to fit the existing concept of self. Through this experience, one modifies his or her image of the self. Again, he or she must be in an environment in which such an exploration of the experience is fully supported in order for the client to appreciate it to the fullest extent. For example, a toddler attempting to gauge her own strength by splashing water while sitting in a wading pool on a hot summer day must feel that she is allowed to do so by observing her mother's smiling face, thus helping her to gain a new concept of her ability.

Markus and Nurius (1984) suggest that children must undertake four developmental tasks for adequate development of their self-concepts. Those include feeling obligated to meet others' expectations, understanding the complex nature of social interactions, developing expectations for oneself, and accepting responsibility for choosing certain behaviors. For example, a ten-year-old child comes to define himself as the oldest son born to a Jewish family who is expected to show positive examples for his younger siblings. He must perform well at school and should not miss piano lessons. He may define himself as "not very cool" because he is not athletic but rather an academic type. Nonetheless, he realizes that keeping up with his grades at school is very important because he wants to be, as is his dad, a dentist, in the distant future. He also knows that he is expected to carry on the Jewish traditions and attend Hebrew class one afternoon each week. His consciousness about these responsibilities and expectations from others mold his self-concept.

Fasig (2000) found that the concept of self extends beyond the physical self and emerges as early as eighteen months in development, much earlier than previously claimed. Based on her assumption that ownership understanding may provide evidence of the knowledge that an object belongs to that person or to another person, Fasig (2000) argues, the "recognition of the owned object and association of the object with the self requires knowledge of the self in conjunction with the object in the past" (p. 371). For example, a toddler who observes her mother letting another child climb into her baby carriage may protest the invasion of the object belonging to her by attempting to remove the invader from the carriage. In this case, the carriage is part of her concept of the self and she feels that her personal space has been invaded. Previous studies found that children showed knowledge of gender stereotypes for gender-based tasks, clothing, and other possessions as early as twenty-four to twenty-six months of age, becoming quite knowledgeable about these stereotypes by thirty to thirty-six months (Thompson, 1975; Weinraub et al., 1984). More recently, Johnston and colleagues (2001) found that a sharp increase in attention to gender occurs between eighteen and twenty-two months and infants can discriminate male and female faces as young as nine months of age. Johnston et al. (2001) conclude, once children actively attend to gender in the social environment, they are ready to use gender categories to derive association between gender categories and behaviors or objects, and to support inferences about behaviors and object preferences. In such a social environment, one learns to identify with one's gender category or another, and adopts behaviors and objects connecting with that particular gender. (p. 582)

Throughout the years of development, one's gender identity evolves through interactions with others in the immediate environment as well as secondary significant others. For example, a little boy sees his older brother playing with a toy truck, so he chooses to play with a truck instead of a doll or toy stove.

In addition, Egan and Perry (2001) produced empirical data to support the thesis that gender identity is multidimensional. Given that children develop fairly stable conceptions of self in terms of gender by their middle childhood, Egan and Perry (2001) conclude that the major dimensions of gender identity include the following:

(a) the degree to which they typify their gender category, (b) their contentedness with their gender assignment, (c) whether they are free to explore cross-sex options or are compelled to conform to gender stereotypes, and (d) whether their own sex is superior to the other. (p. 459)

The same authors further concluded that those dimensions are all related to children's psychosocial adjustment. In addition, Cramer (2000) supported Grotevant's (1987) hypothesis, based on her study of 200 male and female college students, that gender influences the identity development in ego resilience, openness to experience, self-esteem, and self-monitoring. Furthermore, gender itself makes a difference in the complexity of the development of identity. Josephs and Markus (1992) found that women's self-esteem can be linked to a process in which connections and attachments to important others are emphasized, whereas separation and independence increase men's sense of self-esteem. For example, through socialization and emulation of adult role models, adolescent males receive a strong message to be their "own man." Conversely, adolescent girls are socialized to bond with and spend time with one another.

Cramer (2000) also discusses the complex nature of identity development in females. The author theorizes that the beginnings of male sexual identity involve the boy separating from his mother to allow for identification with his father. For girls, however, the infantile emotional bond with their mother is not disrupted, leaving the adolescent girls faced with the task of loosening attachment ties to both their mother and father. For example, Silverman (1997) found that women with emotionally available fathers have more "androgynous," relatively neutral sex-role identities than do women with emotionally unavailable fathers, suggesting that the father influences the type of sex-role behavior his daughter attributes to herself.

In working with children, professionals should be cognizant of gender identity and the value attached to the particular gender in our society. Strong gender identity may help a child in navigating his or her development through childhood and adolescence, but if the child perceives that someone important to him or her values one gender more than the other, it would negatively affect the child's self-esteem. For example, Smith (1988) found that "teachers held differentiated expectations by the child's gender" according to the child's race; the "black male students received far lower expectations from their teachers, while the white male students received the highest expectations" (p. 114). Smith (1988) also found that the teachers in the predominantly black community held higher expectations only for the middle-class female students. These findings present an alarming prediction that teacher's expectations perceived by a child will significantly influence the child's self-esteem. A child with lower self-esteem tends to have less of the resilience that is necessary to buffer him or her from risk factors in the environment, which may lead the child into unfavorable peer groups—gangs, for example—to somehow improve the child's self-esteem.

Mary Ann was the youngest of three sisters born to Ian and Samantha Brenner. She was born when her older sisters were three and seven years old. Samantha was starting her career as a lawyer in a local law firm and Ian was completing his MBA while working at a bank when they first met. Samantha became the firm's partner by the time Mary Ann entered elementary school. Because she took frequent out-of-town business trips, Ian was the one who always read stories to Mary Ann at bedtime. He was a parent who regularly volunteered to drive Mary Ann's soccer team members to games, and he took his three daughters camping on weekends when they did not have games to play. When she was seven years old, Mary Ann's father opened a small consulting business. Immediately after that her parents divorced, agreeing to maintain joint custody of their children. Despite his busy business schedule, Ian managed to be home to cook dinner for the children on the days they stayed with him. Samantha was disturbed by the fact that May Ann preferred wearing jeans to dressing up in skirts or dresses. Mary Ann excelled in sports and competed well in math with the boys in her class. When she entered college, she thought that her roommates in a freshman dormitory were somewhat silly worrying about their makeup and hairstyles. They, in turn, teased her for her carefree attitude about her clothes and hairstyle. She reported their comments laughingly to her father during their weekly phone calls. Ian assured Mary Ann that she was beautiful without all that makeup and that many young men would be asking her for a date before she knew it. Mary Ann thought that her father was right as always. She was not surprised when a junior who was the president of the student government, with a blushing face, asked her to help him with his science project. They are now both working for their doctorates at another university, living in a married-student apartment near campus.

The concept of the self continues to develop throughout life. As a child grows older, he or she continues the task of defining the self in various dimensions through the interactions within the family, school, peers, and community at large. Into adolescence, the child learns that he or she will not be successful in every activity yet learns to recognize areas of competence and hold on to these strengths. This awareness of self in the context of life and its complexities prepares the child for the next challenge or crisis. This process continues during young adulthood, adulthood, middle age, and late life.

Robby, a fifth-grader, was obese and always a target of teasing among his classmates. He was never good at any sports, but he loved to listen to music. His teacher noticed that Robby was beating a table quietly to the music piped into the cafeteria. This teacher invited him to try out for the school band as a drummer. Immediately Robby excelled in the role of drummer and became a very important member of the band. His classmates saw him as a talented musician, rather than a fat boy. Robby felt good about himself now that he had a definite place in the class, and his schoolwork also began to improve.

## SELF-ESTEEM AND WELL-BEING

Many scholars have devoted time to studies of self-esteem because they believed that self-esteem is a critical variable for the healthy development of children. Although the term *self-concept* is used to mean self-esteem by some authors, including Rosenberg (1979), most scholars distinguish *self-esteem* from *self-concept.* Cast and Burke (2002) provide a compelling theoretical discussion on self-esteem. They present three conceptualizations of self-esteem: first, as an *outcome* as conceived by Coopersmith (1967) and Rosenberg (1979); second, as *self-motive,* a tendency for people to behave in ways to increase positive evaluation of the self (Kaplan, 1975; Tesser, 1988); and finally, as a *buffer* for the self, providing protection from harmful experience (Longmore and DeMaris, 1997; and Wells and Marwell, 1976).

Self-esteem plays vital roles in the process of self-verification within groups. In the context of structural symbolic interaction or identity theory (Stryker, 1980), self-verification occurs when an individual's conception of himself or herself matches meanings in an identity in the social structure. According to the theoretical framework of structural symbolic interaction, an individual understands the self in his or her perception of how others see him or her. For example, a child is able to verify his or her group-based identities as a good team member in a situation, such as playground activities. Upon conceiving others' appreciation, the child is likely to increase his or her self-esteem. Cast and Burke (2002) further claim that self-esteem works as a defense mechanism when one is unable to verify one's identities. In such a case, one uses a reservoir of self-esteem to protect oneself from distress caused by a lack of self-verification. For example, a child who could not contribute to a group game on the playground may use self-esteem that has been stored away in an attempt to convince himself or herself that this misfortune is a temporary condition. If such a misfortune occurs repeatedly, however, the child's self-esteem may diminish, exhausting the supply. This may also occur repeatedly with a child who is continuously exposed to family violence and abuse yet becomes a survivor. The child's self-esteem may increase again when he or she turns to a supportive teacher who consistently displays a great deal of belief in the child's ability in the classroom, providing verification of the child's perceptions of the self. Thus, self-esteem can be viewed as an outcome of successful self-verification.

Cast and Burke (2000) extensively discuss the second notion of self-esteem as a buffer. For example, they list studies claiming that individuals with higher self-esteem are more likely to perceive positive feedback consistent with their self-views and will work to discredit negative feedback (Blaine and Croker, 1993; Spencer, Josephs, and Steele, 1993). Other studies indicate that individuals with high self-esteem are more stable and resourceful in handling distressful circumstances (Baumgarder et al., 1989). Thus, Cast and Burke (2000) conclude that self-esteem protects the self from "stressors" (Longmore and DeMaris, 1997), distress (Rosenberg, 1979), and even depression (Mirowsky and Ross, 1989). For example, Palosaari and Aro (1995) found that although depression is most prevalent among persons from divorced families, youth with divorced parents who have an intimate relationship are protected from depression. They argue that adolescents' enhanced self-esteem through such a relationship reflects resilience against depression.

## A CASE SCENARIO OF RESILIENCE

Sarah's parents, Roy and Catalina, divorced when she was three years old. Her father, an African-American automobile factory worker, met her mother, a beautiful eighteen-year-old Puerto Rican woman, at a party. Catalina was very popular among the young men in the social scene. When Roy and Catalina found out that Catalina was pregnant, Roy's parents insisted that they should get married. After Sarah was born, Catalina continued her social outings. She often dropped Sarah off at Roy's parents before joining her friends for parties, taking advantage of the fact that Roy's mother could not get enough of her first grandchild. After her parents' divorce, Sarah spent more time at her grandparents' home because by then it became apparent that Catalina was an alcoholic. After Sarah's parents divorced, her grandmother continued to have Sarah over every weekend. When Sarah became a teenager, Catalina was working as a clerk at an office supply store. Her mother was often absent during the evening for socialization and came home late drunk. Sarah would put her mother to bed and then call her grandma to tell her that she was looking forward to spending the weekend at her house. Her grandmother always told her that she was an intelligent young girl and that she could be anything if she put her mind to it. Her grandmother spent her retirement money on her: she included Sarah in her trips to many distant locations in the world, including London and the Caribbean. Every fall, Sarah was frequently seen in her grandparents' yard on Sunday afternoon receiving instruction from her grandmother and planting bulbs to bloom next spring. Sarah maintained excellent grades at school. When boys in her class pursued her for her physical beauty, she just laughed and went back to the library to read more books by Charles Dickens. Sarah's grandfather died from cancer when she was in her first year of high school, and Sarah was at the grandmother's side all through his funeral. Watching her grandmother's grief, Sarah secretly promised herself that she would become a doctor and find a cure for cancer. Catalina told Sarah that she should come to work as a clerk at the store with her after her high school graduation because she was now old enough to contribute to the household expenses. A young man moved in with Catalina and she gave birth to a baby boy. By then, Sarah had been admitted to an Ivy League college with a full scholarship. When she was a junior in college, her grandmother died of a heart attack, leaving all her money for Sarah's academic pursuits. She is now completing her residency in oncology at a leading cancer treatment center.

## CONCLUSION

Children begin to acknowledge properties about themselves as early as two years old. They define who they are through a looking-glass self discussed by Cooley (1922). They imagine themselves as perceived by their significant others, including their immediate family members, and later at school and in the community. They learn about their own race, gender, and other characteristics as defined by people important to them. Self-esteem is the appraisal of the self as children perceive others' appraisal of themselves. Children's self-esteem is a reservoir of protective elements against adversities surrounding them. Self-esteem works as buffer when risk factors such as poverty, abuse and neglect, and domestic violence are present in the environment as children grow up. Self-esteem can be strengthened when children have one person in their lives who constantly reminds them to see themselves in a positive light, becoming a source of resilience for them. This resilience is a necessary property of children to accomplish all levels of adaptation.

### STRENGTHS STORY: MICHIKO TANAKA

Michiko was a miracle baby. Her mother, Yuriko, had a difficult birth with her. After ten hours of labor, the doctor informed Yuriko's husband, Genjiro, anxiously pacing in a small waiting room, that he had to choose either his wife or his first baby because Yuriko's vital signs were weakening. Genjiro told the doctor to save his wife's life if only one life could be saved. At the twelfth hour, the doctor pulled the baby's head out with forceps. The baby weakly cried and surprised the doctor and nurses. She was alive, but there was a large dent on each side of her head, which made her look like a space creature. Genjiro was afraid that the baby's life would be very difficult because of her deformed head. However, in a month, her head had returned to a normal shape. By the time Michiko was three years old, she became interested in the newspaper and asked her mother to tell her what those characters on the pages meant. Her sister and brother were born before Michiko turned five. Her parents had a modest income and rented a house in a rural community.

One day in early fall Michiko and her sister were playing under a persimmon tree in the yard, watching their baby brother while their mother sewed kimonos to sell to neighbors to supplement her husband's income. After dinner, all the children went to bed. In the middle of the night, Michiko was awakened by a loud noise from the shaking furniture and shelves. Her father screamed, "Michiko, this is an earthquake, and it's a big one. Get up and run to the persimmon tree!" Michiko saw her mother picking her baby brother up and her father carrying her crying sister. Michiko ran with all her might, following her parents toward the tree, realizing she had to fend for herself if she wanted to live. Michiko said to herself, "Okay, I can't depend on others. I am responsible for my own life."

When Michiko was in the second grade, her father opened a small shop in a city thirty miles away. He spent all his savings to buy a house on the same block as the shop. So Michiko and her sister were transferred to a new school. On the first day of school, the teacher introduced her to the boys and girls in the class. The girls exchanged chuckles about her country-style pants, and one boy whispered to another boy, "My older brother told me the kids from the countryside are all dumb." Michiko heard him and said to herself, "I will show them how smart some country girls are." The teacher continued her class, asking questions to review the previous day's lesson. Michiko was one of a few students to raise their hands. The teacher explained to Michiko that it was all right if she did not know the correct answers because she was not in class the previous day. Michiko stood up and gave the correct answer. The other children looked at one another with open mouths. When Michiko went home, she told her mother that she wanted to learn how to sew so she could alter her pants into city-style clothing.

Yuriko taught her how to use the sewing machine she had bought when she married Genjiro. The following week, Yuriko watched Michiko alter the bottoms of all her pants to make them look like the city-style ones.

When she was in the fourth grade, she asked her father to teach her to ride his bicycle. Genjiro told her that she was too small to ride an adult bicycle and that he did not have enough money to buy a child's bicycle. Michiko insisted that she could ride his bicycle the side way. Genjiro took her to a playground and let her learn how to ride his bicycle that way. Michiko looked very funny riding a man's bicycle that way, but she was grinning and shouting, "See, I told you I could." All through elementary, middle, and high school, she was always the highest achieving student in the class. Michiko had to miss her high school graduation, however, because she was being interviewed for admission to a prestigious women's college in Tokyo. Her father went with her. Michiko asked her mother to attend graduation to receive her academic achievement award during the ceremony. Yuriko was proud when she walked up to the stage to receive the award for her daughter, as Yuriko herself never graduated from high school. Yuriko had always told Michiko, "Get as much education as you can, and it will travel with you everywhere you go. You don't even have to pack it in your luggage." Michiko won a scholarship to college and hoped to continue her education through graduate school.

## QUESTIONS FOR DISCUSSION

1. Discuss the process of self-verification and peer group influence on a child's self-esteem.
2. Discuss how self-esteem can serve as a buffer against negative influences and risk factors in the life of a child.
3. How early in a child's life does self-esteem develop? Discuss the impact of the family environment on self-esteem.

## REFERENCES

Blaine, B. and Croker, J. (1993). Self-esteem and self-serving biases in reactions to positive and negative events: An integrative view. In Baumeister, R. F. (Ed.), *Self-esteem: The puzzle of low self-regard* (pp. 55-85). New York: Plenum Press.

Baumgardner, A. H. and Brownlee, E. A. (1987). Strategic failure in social interaction: Evidence for expectancy disconfirmation processes. *Journal of Personality and Social Psychology* 52: 525-535.

Cast, A. D. and Burke, P. J. (2002). A theory of self-esteem. *Social Forces* 80(3): 1041-1068.

Cooley, C. H. (1922). *Human nature and the social order.* New Brunswick: Transaction Books.

Coopersmith, S. (1967). *The antecedents of self-esteem.* San Francisco, CA: W. H. Freeman.

Cramer, P. (2000). Development of identity: Gender makes a difference. *Journal of Research in Personality* 34: 42-72.

Egan, S. K. and Perry, D. G. (2001). Gender identity: A multidimensional analysis with implications for psychosocial adjustment. *Developmental Psychology* 37: 451-463.

Erikson, E. (1968). *Identity, youth, and crisis.* New York: Norton.

Fasig, L. G. (2000). Toddlers' understanding of ownership: Implications for self-concept development. *Social Development* 9(3): 370-382.

Garton, A. F. and Pratt, C. (1995). Stress and self-concept in 10- to 15-year-old school students. *Journal of Adolescence* 18(6): 625-640.

Grotevant, H. D. (1987). Toward a process model of identity formation. *Journal of Adolescent Research* 2: 202-222.

Johnston, K. E., Bittinger, K., Smith, A., and Madole, K. L. (2001). Developmental changes in infants' and toddlers' attention to gender categories. *Merrill-Palmer Quarterly* 47(4): 563-584.

Josephs, R. A. and Markus, H. R. (1992). Gender and self-esteem. *Journal of Personality and Social Psychology* 63(3): 391-402.

Kaplan, H. (1975). The self-esteem motive. In Kaplan, H. B. (Ed.), *Self-attitudes and deviant behavior* (pp. 10-31). Pacific Palisades, CA: Goodyear Pub. Co.

Longmore, M. A. and DeMaris, A. (1997). Perceived inequity and depression in intimate relationships: The moderating effect of self-esteem. *Social Psychology Quarterly* 60: 172-184.

Markus, H. and Nurius, P. S. (1984). Self-understanding and self-regulation in middle childhood. In Collins, W. A. (Ed.), *Developing middle childhood: The years from six to twelve* (pp. 147-183). Washington, DC: National Academy.

Mirowsky, J. and Ross, C. E. (1989). *Social causes of psychological distress.* Hawthorn, NY: Aldyne de Gruyter.

Polasaari, U. K. and Aro, H. M. (1995). Parental divorce, self-esteem and depression: An intimate relationship as a protective factor in young adulthood. *Journal of Affective Disorders* 35: 91-96.

Rogers, C. (1961). *On becoming a person.* Boston, MA: Houghton Mifflin Co.

Rosenberg, M. (1979). *Conceiving the self.* New York: Basic Books.

Silverman, M. L. (1997). Fathers and daughters: Paternal presence and gender identity. *Dissertation Abstracts International*: Section B: The Science and Engineering, 58(1-B), July, 0428.

Smith, M. K. (1988). Effects of children's social class, race and gender on teacher expectations for children's academic performance: A study in urban setting. In Heid, C. A. (Ed.), *Multicultural education: Knowledge and perceptions* (pp. 101-117). Bloomington/Indianapolis, IN: Indiana University—Center for Urban and Multicultural Education.

Spencer, S. J., Josephs, R. A., and Steele, C. M. (1993). Low self-esteem: The uphill struggle for self-integrity of the self. In Baumeister, L. F. (Ed.), *Self-esteem: The puzzle of low self-regard* (pp. 21-36). New York: Plenum Press.

Stryker, S. (1980). *Symbolic interactionism: A social structural version.* Menlo Park, CA: Benjamin Cummings.

Tesser, A. (1988). Toward a self-evaluation maintenance model of social behavior. In Berkowitz, L. (Ed.), *Advances in experimental social psychology* (pp. 181-227). New York: Academic Press.

Thompson, S. K. (1975). Gender labels and early sex-role development. *Child Development* 46: 339-347.

Weinraub, M., Clemens, L. P., Sockloff, A., Ethridge, T., Gracely, E., and Myers, B. (1984). The development of sex-role stereotypes in the third year: Relationships to gender labeling, gender identity, sex-typed toy preference, and family characteristics. *Child Development* 55: 1493-1503.

Wells, L. E. and Marwell, G. (1976). *Self-esteem: Its conceptualization and measurement.* Beverly Hills, CA: Sage Publications.

Zastrow, C. and Kirst-Ashman, K. K. (2001). *Understanding human behavior and the social environment,* Second edition. Chicago, IL: Nelson-Hall.

# Chapter 7

# Adolescence

There are two lasting bequests we can give our children—one is roots, the other wings.

Anonymous

Adolescence is a period of life when one is neither a child nor an adult, neither totally dependent nor independent. It is a time of searching, a time for realizing that life is changing drastically and that one must adapt to these biological, psychological, and interpersonal transitions. Adolescents are beginning to sense that they do not fit into their peer groups and may feel compelled to bring about immediate changes in their lives in an effort to feel more comfortable with themselves and their new status as teenagers. Adolescence is a time when young people begin to sharpen the boundaries between the self and nonself, and to express autonomous decision making and self-determination (Garbarino, 1992). Often due to peer pressure, adolescents may attempt to shed the cloak of childhood by drinking excessively, using drugs, breaking curfew, running away, or changing their appearance in some drastic way. Teenagers with facial and body piercings, tattoos, and brightly dyed hair have become relatively common sights within U.S. culture.

Adolescents are also vulnerable to a range of risk factors because of the many changes they are going through. Adolescents and young adults are at high risk for contracting a number of sexually transmitted diseases (STDs) and have become a high risk group for contracting human immunodeficiency virus/acquired immune deficiency syndrome (HIV/AIDS). The Centers for Disease Control and Prevention (CDC) and the American College Health Association estimated that one of every 500 college students has contracted HIV (CDC, 1997). In December 2001 the CDC Surveillance Report indicated that of the

816,149 cases of AIDS reported to the CDC, adults and adolescents constituted 807,075, and children under thirteen constituted 9,074. When cumulative AIDS cases were broken down, persons between thirteen and nineteen comprised 4,428, and persons between twenty and twenty-four comprised 28,665. However, due to increased efforts to offer sex education in high schools and the dissemination of literature on HIV/AIDS, adolescents today seem to be more informed about the prevention and contraction of AIDS than in the past (Hyde and DeLamater, 2000).

Adolescents rank among the highest groups for attempting and committing suicide. Although suicide is linked with depression, not all depressed adolescents will attempt suicide. Suicide is the third leading cause of death for people age fifteen through twenty-four, outranked only by accidents and homicides (U.S. Bureau of Census, 1998). Moreover, some 9 to 13 percent of adolescents have attempted suicide, although few have received any mental health treatment (Newman and Newman, 1999). Stressors that might lead adolescents to suicide include unwanted pregnancy, family dysfunction and divorce, failing grades, loss of a friend, or a failed romantic relationship. Children who are overachievers are under an enormous amount of stress, which could lead to a suicide attempt (Santrock, 2002).

Adolescence is an awkward time for most in that body image and adaptation to peer group norms become paramount over maintaining a previous role within the family. Adolescents continually respond to peer pressure, and for many, body image becomes an obsession. They may gradually lose a large amount of weight and develop an obsession about being thin. This may lead to a condition called anorexia nervosa, which is characterized by a minimally normal body weight, defined in the *Diagnostic and Statistical Manual of Mental Disorders,* Fourth Edition-TR, as less than 85 percent of the expected body weight (APA, 2000, p. 583). Many of these adolescents, especially females, will also develop bulimia nervosa, which is characterized by repeated episodes of binge eating followed by inappropriate compensatory behaviors, such as vomiting; misuse of laxatives, diuretics, or other medications; or excessive exercise (APA, 2000, p. 585). In both conditions, the young people have a distorted body image and are bent on remaining as thin as possible at any cost. Both anorexics and bulimics seem to have some common characteristics. They generally come from middle-class families with overinvolved mothers and preoccupied fathers. They are dependent on their parents and are usually thought of as "good children." Bulimics, in particular, are over-achievers and tend to have high academic averages in college. Their vomiting after bingeing becomes a purification ritual to satisfy their self-loathing (Zastrow and Kirst-Ashman, 2001).

Adolescence might be described as a swinging footbridge because things seem to stay the same and yet are changing all at once. Similar to a swinging footbridge crossing a deep cavern, one must maneuver the path on his or her own, without using a vehicle or holding onto an adult for the trip. One must stand on his or her own two feet, despite the precarious motion that at times immobilizes the individual's progress across the abyss of change. When crossing a swinging bridge, moving ahead too fast, changing one's body position, or hanging on to the side rails of rope can cause a balance problem, impeding progress toward the other side. Also, anyone who has crossed a swinging bridge can attest to the impossibility of being able to turn around and go back to the beginning. The swinging bridge, unlike a stabilized bridge, may begin to sway and cause the person crossing to lose solid footing. Adolescence is a trying and uncertain time for most individuals, but crossing the chasm between childhood and adulthood becomes easier as the young person realizes his or her goal, which is to reach the other side with a sense of confidence and self-worth.

In his psychosocial stage theory of personality development, Erik Erikson (1963) perceived adolescents as experiencing complex identity issues that are largely centered on role assumption and adaptation. He referred to this fifth stage of his developmental model as "identity versus role confusion." As in the other seven stages of his theory, an individual may experience a crisis or multiple traumatic events at this stage of life and thus develop role confusion, which can negatively affect the subsequent stages. Erikson's concept of a moratorium during adolescence is described as a time when teenagers are given enough leeway by parents and other authority figures to explore their identities, personal interests, and ambitions. As such, they must in many respects be given enough room to test their boundaries and problem-solving skills in preparation for the adult world. During this time, adolescents typically experiment with membership in different peer groups, form cliques, build relationships with various mentors, and take different courses, all in an effort to find themselves (Hutchison, 1999). This period of self-discovery and exploration may be viewed as a testing ground for adolescents to examine both their strengths and limitations. This relaxing of the boundaries between parent and child can lead to resilience in considering life and career roles for the future.

Cross and Cross (1998) note that at first one may feel shaken and all alone in the universe as ties with parents are broken and individuality slowly emerges. The child often feels torn between two worlds as parents and other adults now have different expectations for their behavior. Some adolescents seem to acquire a strong sense of self relatively easily; others experience more difficulty in separating from their parents (Pillari, 1999). Children are expected to search for themselves on a path of self-discovery, yet they are still economically dependent upon their parents and are still expected to adhere to family norms and traditions. In general, children seem to move back and forth between the role of child and the role of adult, which is a normal expectation at this crucial stage of development. Still, adolescents must establish their own values and actions rather than adhere to societal expectations if they are to master the developmental tasks of adolescence (Goodridge and Capitman, 2000).

Many parents and professionals have come to view adolescence in a less-than-positive light because of problems that afflict some adolescents in their search for their true selves. Adolescents must be able to test their limits yet maintain a sense of balance as they try on various roles in an effort to prove they are worthy individuals who use good judgment and make credible decisions about their lives. White (1960) contends that the quest of competency lasts beyond puberty and becomes more intense in adolescence. He contends that many adolescents succeed in their sexual and social relations, and have for the most part not been overwhelmed by them. They develop plans for schooling, make career plans, develop a sense of their assets and limitations, and express concerns about modern society and the future. Adolescents begin to master multiple hobbies and interests, such as driving a car, engaging in sports, and expressing themselves creatively in writing, drama, and music.

## ADOLESCENT ETHNIC AND RACIAL IDENTITY

Identity formation in adolescence is an expected developmental hurdle, yet it can be more challenging for children who belong to a minority culture. Minority youth may assume a negative identity if they accept the stereotypes put upon them by members of dominant groups as well as their own ethnic group (Erikson, 1968). Marcia (1980) states that successful identity formation is achieved when one explores his or her ethnic identity and then commits to it. Minority adolescents need to feel a sense of self-satisfaction in order to feel good about themselves within the context of their ethnic group and society. Phinney and Alipura (1992) found that nonwhite children who have seriously examined their ethnic identity and its implications have a better self-image than do those who have not resolved these issues.

Adolescents who experience ongoing bicultural conflict may have difficulty managing dual skills and thus get "caught or stuck in a transitional state" (Robbins, Chatterjee, and Canda, 1998). This may lead to a state of transitional marginality, which Robbins, Chatterjee, and Canda (1998) describe as a state involving acculturation stress brought about by competing interests, values, and behavioral choices in the social situation, "accompanied by emotional discomfort and cognitive dissonance experienced by the individual" (p. 137). Ethnic minority children are much more affected by transitional states as they attempt to master the transition to adulthood, as well as forming their ethnic identity in the midst of the transition to a bicultural identity as an adolescent. However, adolescents generally resolve transitional marginality as they develop an ego-syntonic identity and behaviors that meet with social approval (Robbins, Chatterjee, and Canda, 1998).

Ethnic and racial group identity among adolescents is even more important at this time in history, as America's population is becoming increasingly multicultural, multiracial, and multilingual. Almost one-third of the adolescents in the United States belong to an ethnic group, such as African Americans, Asian Americans, Latinos, Jewish Americans and American Indians (Phinney, 1990). Ethnic identity formation has been divided into three phases, in which youngsters begin to identify with and appreciate their ethnic heritage. Phase one generally involves the belief that ethnic identity is not an important personal issue. In the second phase, young people begin to explore the personal impact of their ethnic heritage in an effort to learn more about themselves and their culture. In the final phase, these young people achieve a distinct self-concept, which combines that of their ethnic group and U.S. culture (Phinney, 1989).

A major component of self-concept comes from what other people tell us about ourselves (Uba and Huang, 1999). Minority adolescents seem to be more concerned with racial and ethnic identity than European-American adolescents are, largely due to racism, oppression, and social injustice in their everyday lives. Some ethnic and racial groups seem to be more at risk than others. For instance, Hispanic females are twice as likely as African-American and non-Hispanic white females to attempt suicide (CDC, 1996). This phenomenon is thought to be related to factors such as low self-image and family conflict, particularly when there are discrepancies in acculturation between daughters and their parents (Zayas et al., 2000).

Moreover, minorities are still underrepresented in the U.S. media and, when included, may be portrayed in subservient or marginal roles, such as servants or newly arrived immigrants with thick accents. Historically, minorities in films have been portrayed as secondary characters or villains or persons who always seem to be on the outside of the central action. Although media images are changing, African Americans, Latinos, and American Indians are often portrayed in roles that evoke humor or cultural stereotypes.

Atkinson, Moren, and Sue (1989) introduced a somewhat more comprehensive model of adolescent ethnic identity development that involves five stages. In stage one, minority group members look down on their own ethnicity and would prefer to be European Americans, and they adopt European-American values and behaviors. In stage two, these individuals have an experience that leads them to doubt their first-stage beliefs and values. They rethink their beliefs and feelings about both majority and minority persons and may identify with other oppressed groups. In stage three, these unstable feelings continue and lead the minority youth to reject completely the dominant group and unquestioningly accept their own ethnic culture. They explore in depth their ethnic group's culture and history and examine why they may have earlier been embarrassed by their minority group membership and identity. In stage four, these persons feel secure enough about their ethnic identity to identify, no longer reject the dominant group, and in fact recognize some positive elements of the dominant culture. In the stage five, ethnic individuals realize that they can accept and value their own minority group, and at the same time acknowledge that other groups have positive attributes.

The Anglo norm of individuality may actually conflict with the beliefs and values of other cultures which emphasize loyalty to the group and family (Lum, 1995). Mead (1928), in her landmark study on the Samoan culture, observed that an integrated set of activities characterized their way of being as opposed to the specialization, diversity, and fragmentation which are hallmarks of U.S. society. Robbins, Chatterjee, and Canda (1998) state that adolescents who experience ongoing bicultural conflict may be unable to handle dual skills and thus get caught in a transitional state. These authors define *transitional state* as "a temporary state of marginality that results from inconsistency in values and norms" (Robbins, Chatterjee, and Canda, 1998, p. 137). This marginal state is generally resolved when adolescents adopt adaptive behaviors and a firm identity that meets with social approval. Ethnic minority children have to forge an individual identity as they transition to adulthood, as well as form an ethnic identity within the context of a bicultural life experience. Those who are unable or unwilling to develop alternative coping devices may assume a permanently marginal adaptation (Robbins, Chatterjee, and Canda, 1998).

Alan Wizinski, age sixteen, is an example of a teenager who has successfully established a firm identity, in part due to his family's strong identity, peer acceptance, and individual fortitude. Alan is biracial, his father being Polish and Jewish and his mother being African American. Alan was always told by his parents that he was multicultural and that many strong intergenerational patterns of success were his legacy. Alan's father, like his father and grandfather, is a physician, and Mrs. Wizinski is a college professor of English, as were her mother and grandmother.

Last year, Alan traveled to Poland with his parents, and his father has made sure that he could both speak and read Polish. Alan is close to his mother's family, especially his grandparents, who live only three blocks away. He has visited many of his mother's relatives in Georgia and once spent part of the summer with his great-aunt, Virgie. Alan is a proficient in languages and has studied both French and Spanish in school. He next wants to learn Swahili and would like to spend his junior year in Africa. His career goal is to be an educational planner with the World Bank or to advocate for children by working for the United Nations. An excellent student, Alan aspires to obtain an advanced degree in international relations or international law. Alan is the head of the history and French clubs at school and is a star soccer player. He relates well to his peers who respect him and often go to him for help with their schoolwork. Alan has traced his genealogy on both sides of his family and is proud of his heritage.

## *GENDER ROLES*

Although adolescents have already been socialized to gender-oriented roles and expectations during childhood, they feel more pressure to conform to socially sanctioned gender roles and stereotypes during their teen years. During a developmental period wrought with change, including physical changes, sexual maturity, and increased peer pressure, adolescents begin to learn more about what is expected from them as males and females. Adolescents may have adapted to gender roles played out by their parents and other significant adults in their lives, such as teachers, community leaders, and persons in the media. They become confused in a society that is slowly beginning to relax its attitudes toward entrenched gender roles, behaviors, and communication styles. Parents may demonstrate one set of values regarding gender roles whereas movies and television may present other images. However, boys and girls are largely perceived as needing to carry out distinctly different roles in order to adapt to and cope with the challenges of daily living.

Girls are more resilient in the first decade of life than boys as they are more mature both physically and socially in the prekindergarten and grammar school years (Werner and Smith, 1982). However, they tend to be more vulnerable during the second decade of life when they are expected to be feminine and dependent. These expectations limit their sense of autonomy and accomplishment, which in turn may result in low self-esteem. On the contrary, boys are more vulnerable during the first decade of life and then become more resilient during the second decade due to cultural esteem and greater opportunities for independence and achievement (Turner, 2002). Self-direction, self-reliance, and individuation are highly valued behaviors for boys in the United States, but girls are more valued for their caretaking and relationship development abilities (Gilligan, 1982).

Masters, Johnson, and Kolodny (1995) have stated that adolescent males are expected to adhere to three basic norms. They are expected to be good at athletics, be interested in girls and sex, and avoid feminine behaviors and any interest in feminine things. To violate these rules often means that a young male will be socially ostracized and even mocked or derided. Many in our society still see male and female roles in terms of extremes; either one is exclusively male or does not fit this category. Thus, he may be placed in the feminine category and teased about his effeminate ways or being a homosexual (Zastrow and Kirst-Ashman, 2001).

Lott (1994) described three broad cultural expectations that affect how adolescent girls develop gender roles. Girls are expected to find the right male partner whom they can fall in love with and marry. Career goals and expectations must always be balanced with having a family, and some professionals will counsel girls to consider jobs as a nurse, teacher, or secretary, rather than focus on law or medicine. Adolescent girls may also receive the message that achievement in a career and caring for a family are incompatible roles (Zastrow and Kirst-Ashman, 2001). A second expectation is that a girl must be popular and feminine, that she must dress fashionably, smile, be friendly, and be available (Lott, 1994). These behaviors are connected with attracting men, presumably for marriage. Third, young women are socialized to be flexible and considerate, and to care for others. This expectation can leave adolescent girls feeling caught in between following their own interests and conforming to the needs of the family and society.

Today, we are beginning to see greater interest in promoting all of the talents and capabilities of adolescents, as opposed to determining how these traits may fit a particular facet of male or female behavior. Males are learning that it is acceptable to express their emotions and feelings openly and may choose nursing or elementary education as a career without having their masculinity placed on trial. Similarly, females are realizing that they can be construction workers, mail carriers, or physicians today and not turn many heads. Several years ago, a group advocating gender equality infiltrated a toy factory and changed the voices of Ken and Barbie to gain media attention in support of less gender stereotypic roles, even for dolls. At least for a day, Barbie talked about hanging out with the guys while Ken expressed his excitement about shopping. Adolescents respect and admire the world's top fashion and hair designers who happen to be male, and girls recognize that women excel in such traditionally male roles as dentistry and law. Most would agree that when it comes to adolescents' interest in music and pop culture, unisex styles and behavior are accepted and emulated.

Sports remain basically segregated for males and females, yet junior high and high school girls' sports teams may outrank their male counterparts in school tournaments. A few schools have even placed females on their football teams. But sports such as soccer and tennis, as well as karate and the martial arts, have become unisex sports in which effort and skills are weighted more heavily than one's gender. The Olympics have also influenced society's attitudes toward the stamina and adeptness needed by men and women to excel in sports. Both men and women are viewed as having the motivation, drive, skill, and dedication necessary to perfect their abilities in athletics.

## *ADOLESCENTS AND SEXUAL ORIENTATION*

Adolescents who realize that they are gay, lesbian, bisexual, or transgendered may feel alienated and alone. They may think they are the only ones who have these feelings or they may have a strong reaction to negative stereotypes of gays and lesbians in the media. Such youth may experience feelings of alienation when their straight peers engage in activities centered on dating, such as school dances and parties. Some young gay people, especially males, may engage in risky sexual behaviors with adults in public places in their effort to identify with and sense acceptance from others like them. In an era when more and more teenagers are becoming infected with HIV, this is a great concern. Professionals continue to be in dialogue about whether legislation should be more restrictive in allowing tests for HIV/AIDS and other sexually transmitted diseases (STDs) among children and adolescents. HIV/STD testing is available in all fifty states in the United States. However, many states do state that a youth must be twelve or fourteen to be tested, and some indicate that a physician may notify the parent. Others mandate parental notification if the test results are positive (Henry J. Kaiser Family Foundation, 2003). In some cases, youth have delayed much-needed testing for HIV/AIDS, fearing that their parents will be informed (Jackson and Hafemeister, 1999). Other gay and lesbian youth explore the Internet and are attracted to and use chat rooms that offer subjects related to being gay or lesbian where they may seek to explore their identity further or seek information about alternative ways to meet other gays. Such Internet encounters can put them at risk for abuse and exploitation.

Several stages have been identified in the coming-out process, which is defined as the development of gay, lesbian, or bisexual identity. Although highly significant during adolescence, the coming-out process can occur at any point in the life span (Mallon, 1998). These developmental phases have been referred to in the literature by several authors (Coleman, 1981; Moses and Hawkins, 1982; Cass, 1984; D'Augelli, 1994), but they generally outline similar processes. The coming-out process includes the following:

1. Exiting heterosexual identity
2. Developing a personal lesbian-gay-bisexual identity status
3. Developing a lesbian-gay-bisexual sexual identity
4. Becoming a lesbian-gay-bisexual offspring
5. Developing a lesbian-gay-bisexual identity status
6. Entering the lesbian-gay-bisexual community (D'Augelli, 1994)

Moses and Hawkins (1982) elaborate on the first stage as coming out to oneself, or signification, and state that this process can give lesbian, gay, and bisexual youth an opportunity to think and feel more honestly about themselves. Even though assuming a label with a negative societal indictment may cause anxiety and doubt, gay adolescents may begin to feel freer and experience a stronger sense of being honest with themselves. This is an important component of development for all adolescents, regardless of sexual orientation.

Cass (1984) developed a model based on the strengths perspective and focuses on the experiences and perceptions of gays, lesbians, and bisexuals. Cass's model differs from some others because she focuses on identity formation in both gay men and lesbians and does not assume that persons view homosexuality in a negative light. Her six-stage model includes cognitive, behavioral, and affective dimensions, and at any stage the decision not to develop a homosexual identity any further may occur (Schriver, 2001). Cass's six stages of homosexual identity formation are

1. identity confusion;
2. identity comparison;
3. identity tolerance;
4. identity acceptance;
5. identity pride; and
6. identity synthesis.

Substance abuse is known to be highly prevalent among adolescents today. Estimates indicate that as many as 50 percent report using illicit substances and 80 percent state they have used alcohol by their senior year of high school (Olson, 2000). Not surprisingly, gay and lesbian teens are even more at risk for substance abuse due to the added challenges of dealing with their sexual orientation. Stressors include their need to establish an integrated sense of self, although doing so puts them at further risk of peer and family rejection, increases their fear for their own personal safety, and subjects them to the ongoing experience of homophobia in today's high schools and communities (Olson, 2000). Gay and lesbian teens are also six times more likely to attempt suicide than their straight counterparts (Rotheram-Borus, Hunter, and Rosario, 1994). The Gay, Lesbian, and Straight Education Network (1997) reported that 19 percent of gay and lesbian students suffered physical assault associated with their sexual orientation, 13 percent skipped school at least once a month, and 26 percent dropped out all together. Many teens who feel they are adaptive or normal except for their attraction to same-sex peers may experience stress related to their strong need to fit in and just be "one of the guys." For example, a member of the track or soccer team may experience extreme success on the field and yet feel totally remiss in discussing dating or other peer activities with his or her team members. Still other youth who are bisexual may be even more confused about their attraction to both genders and may at times feel they are more alienated than even their gay peers because of this seeming double-bind condition.

Many adolescents who realize they are gay have great difficulty with the coming-out process. They may hide their attraction to and affection for members of their own sex for fear of being ostracized by peers and parents. Several research studies indicate that parents react to the coming-out process with disbelief, denial, negative comments, or hopes that it is just a "passing phase" (Savin-Williams, 1998; Ben-Ari, 1995; Robinson, Walters, and Skeen, 1989). Savin-Williams (1998) reports that almost half of the mothers of gay and lesbian college students reacted with denial and negative comments and half of the fathers reacted with silence or disbelief. However, 60 percent of siblings were supportive. Some 18 percent of parents in this study demonstrated intolerance, attempts at converting their children to heterosexuality, or threats to sever both financial and emotional support. In a study of gay and lesbian young adults and unrelated parents, Ben-Ari (1995) found that parents were less likely to reject their children but did react with shock, followed by feelings of shame, guilt, and finally acknowledgment. Mothers were more likely to react with guilt and anger whereas fathers were more likely to deny and reject their child's sexual orientation. In a cross-national study of more than 400 parents attending support groups for families of lesbians, gays, and bisexuals, Robinson, Walters, and Skeen (1989), discovered that almost two-thirds reported that their initial response to their child's coming out was negative, with grieflike qualities, and nearly half felt guilt. The parental support groups in Robinson, Walters, and Skeen's study were composed predominantly of mothers.

Gay and lesbian children's feelings must not be minimized, downplayed, or denied by professionals. To do so would cause even more confusion. Children need to understand that they can grow up to lead normal lives, even though they may be held in disregard by society and often by their own families (Baker, 2002). Such children need to be encouraged by their parents to communicate openly about their fears and concerns so that problems may be addressed before they produce inordinate stress within the family. Many children are reluctant to come out to their parents and are often more likely to disclose their sexual orientation to a trusted friend or sibling.

Transgendered youth often feel very disconnected from their adolescent peers and may find only limited support from a few close friends. They may be afraid to disclose their desire to live as a member of an opposite gender out of the fear of being socially banished or abused. Transgendered youth may suffer low self-esteem and depression because of misunderstandings and rejection by their families. Many gay, lesbian, bisexual, and transgendered youth refrain from disclosing their sexual orientation to parents during high school because they believe their parents would not provide adequate emotional support or information (Munoz-Plaza, Quinn, and Rounds, 2002).

Transgendered individuals are highly at risk for abuse, as pointed out by Lombardi et al. (2001), who found in a study of 402 transgendered persons that over half had experienced some form of harrassment or direct violence in their lifetimes. High-profile media cases, such as those of Brandon Teena and Gwen Araujo, have brought an increasing awareness to the dangers and lack of legal protection for transgendered youth at risk for bullying, violent attacks, rape, and murder (Gay and Lesbian Alliance Against Defamation, 2003). Brandon Teena, age twenty-one, a Nebraska native who was born female, was brutally raped and murdered when his male friends discovered his biological sex. Gwen Araujo, age seventeen, who was born male, was murdered at a party in California when an adolescent male became intimate with her and discovered Gwen's biological sex. These murders echo the bigotry and violent acts that led to the death of gay Wyoming teenager Matthew Shepard, who was brutally attacked, tortured, and left to die from exposure after two men he met in bar lured him to a remote location.

Some gay and lesbian youth seem to have more difficulty than others due to their birth order or status in the family. An oldest son may be reluctant to come out to his parents as he may feel an obligation to serve as a role model for his siblings. Moreover, if there is only one son, he may feel compelled to carry on his father's perceived masculine role in the family. Lesbians may experience similar feelings when they are the only female offspring and do not participate in similar socially sanctioned rituals, such as going to the prom or getting married. For both genders, the realization that they will not be getting married or producing grandchildren for their parents may bring about unnecessary chiding at family gatherings. They may also be pressured by family members to get married. Gay and lesbian youth who have another sibling who is gay may benefit from positive role modeling of the gay lifestyle, yet they may also experience guilt as they too may be seen as letting down their parents by also living an alternative lifestyle.

Two brothers only two years apart in age left home to get away from parental pressures. They attended the same college. Their parents had teased them both about not dating and had perhaps suspected their sexual identities, which made them feel increasingly uncomfortable during high school. They also occasionally experimented sexually with each other and were discovered by their mother and severely chastised due to her extreme fundamentalist religious beliefs. They had formed a pact always to be supportive of each other and to move away from their family so as to avoid further ostracism and embarrassment.

Another young man was the oldest of a Catholic family of seven children and left home to get away from the sibling abuse by his four younger brothers who constantly made fun of him, calling him sissy, queer, and pansy. He was a talented artist and loved sewing and design, talents of which he was most proud. During his preadolescence, he became an altar boy and also made and repaired kneeler cushions and church vestments. Unfortunately, he was sexually abused by the parish priest, which caused enhanced guilt feelings and a desire to flee his small town as soon as he could find a way. A college scholarship provided that opportunity, but he still went back regularly to visit his family on weekends and holidays.

More and more school systems, especially in larger cities, provide gay and lesbian youth with opportunities for getting together to share common experiences and mutual challenges in dealing with their sexual orientation. A two-year qualitative study of fifteen- to eighteen-year-old gay, lesbian, bisexual, and straight youth found that gay school alliances positively affect academic performance, school and personal relationships, and comfort level with sexual orientation. In addition, these students felt that they were more a part of the school environment (Lee, 2002). Moreover, many gay and lesbian adults provide avenues for adolescent self-discovery and coping with their gay and lesbian identity by conducting support groups in local gay community centers. Such involvement allows for ongoing support and role modeling by not only the group facilitators but also the group members themselves.

Despite the many newspaper headlines and talk show billings of gay teenagers in crisis, many gay teenagers have parents who understand their needs and try to seek help for their children and themselves. Robinson, Walters, and Skeen (1989) found that 97 percent of the parents came to accept their gay or lesbian children. Parents may become involved in organizations such as PFLAG, Parents, Families, and Friends of Lesbians and Gays, which impart and foster understanding of the gay experience by offering support groups and gatherings that accentuate the importance of assisting youth to develop a positive self-concept. Unfortunately, too many parents get involved too late, after a gay or lesbian child has threatened or actually committed suicide. A high school senior wrote an essay for his English teacher about his sexual orientation which led to his coming out to his parents, a collaborative school conference with the teacher, and the family's being referred to PFLAG. These kinds of role models outside the family unit often provide gay youth with an opportunity to express their true feelings and aspirations to have a normal life, despite the threats of homophobia and oppression as a minority group.

Gays and lesbians from divergent racial, cultural, and ethnic groups often experience discrimination from other gays and lesbians, and white gay organizations may not respond to their needs. This is true for African-American, Latino, Asian-American, and Native American men, who also may face discrimination and homophobia related to a range of cultural traditions (Shernoff, 1995; Berger and Kelly, 1995). In many ethnic cultures, being gay, lesbian, or bisexual leads adolescents to feel even more alienated due to their dual or even triple minority status when gender is also considered. In addition, they may feel that they are betraying their family's commitment to close kinship networks and strong religious affiliation by living an alternative lifestyle. By telling their parents about their sexual orientation, racial-ethnic minority youths may risk their association with, identification with, and support within their cultural communities; these extended support systems are likely to be more significant than for white youths (Savin-Williams and Esterberg (2000). Some racial-ethnic children are fearful of bringing shame or public humiliation to their families because of their sexual orientation. Chan (1989) notes that 80 percent of Chinese, Japanese, and Korean young adults in her study disclosed to a family member, usually a sister, and only one-quarter came out to their parents.

A nineteen-year-old Latino from a strict Catholic family in a large eastern city discovered his sexual orientation after a sexual encounter with another teenager at age seventeen. Afterward, he experienced guilt and remorse, thinking that he would be banished if his parents ever discovered his true sexual identity. Therefore, while he continued to date girls, play in a Latino community league, and put up other appearances of a heterosexual lifestyle, he began to meet men through clandestine liaisons formed on the Internet. In one instance, he traveled to a distant city to meet a middle-aged man so that his parents would not discover his sexual behaviors.

Such fear of ostracism may place many young ethnic gays and lesbians at risk for exploitation and further shame as they begin to seek alternatives to explore and live out their sexual orientation without their family's knowledge.

Guidelines for counseling gay, lesbian, and bisexual youth would be consistent with those set forth by the American Psychological Association for such populations in general (2000). These principles provide practitioners with (1) a frame of reference for the treatment of lesbian, gay, and bisexual clients and (2) basic information in assessment for intervention, identity, relationships, and the education and training of psychologists. The National Association of Social Workers and the Council on Social Work Education set forth standards for practice with gays, lesbians, and bisexuals, as well as policies for curriculum development.

## TRANSITIONS TO ADULTHOOD

In our society adolescents continue to strive for legal and social recognition as autonomous and independent individuals who can take care of themselves. In some sectors of society, adolescents may be viewed more as adults when given the same rights, privileges, and responsibilities as adults. In the United States, adolescents may vote at age eighteen, as well as purchase lottery tickets and cigarettes in some states. All adolescents may at age eighteen serve their country in the military. However, to drink and purchase alcohol, adolescents must be twenty-one years old. The age of responsibility has long raised dialogues in the fields of counseling, child welfare, and the law.

Across the United States, every state has laws that indicate when and under what circumstances a child may be emancipated or defined legally as an adult with all the rights and responsibilities the status brings. *Emancipation* is defined as a means by which a young person can be legally released from parental custody and thereafter be considered an adult. Some criteria used to determine when emancipation should occur include a young person who lives separately from parents, is able to self-support, has joined the military, or is married (Downs et al., 2000). Emancipation enables a minor to buy or sell property, sue or be sued, enlist in the military, and consent to medical, psychological, or social work services (Horowitz and Davidson, 1984). In some states children under age eighteen may petition the court to become emancipated, for example, California, where a law exists to empower a child to live separately from the parents, as long as the child is self-supporting and has the parents' approval, and as long as such a living arrangement would not be adverse to the best interests of the child (Davis and Schwartz, 1987).

In child welfare, children who happen to be living in foster care or residential care at the time of their emancipation may experience emotional and psychological problems related to going out into the world on their own. Every year some 20,000 youth age out of the foster care system and face the challenges of a new life (Child Welfare

League of America, 2003). Their adaptation to a world outside of a protective family or family-oriented environment may cause old attachment issues or feelings of insecurity to resurface. The child in placement may experience a dual loss: the loss of his or her "home" in the here and now, and saying good-bye to foster parents, school friends, or child care staff, as well as reexperiencing, perhaps even unconsciously, the original loss of the biological family (Downs et al., 2000). Many children will still face the harsh realities of perhaps never being able to work through or reconcile the reasons they were placed within supportive care. Social workers and counselors, as well as foster family members, must be sensitive about the reemergence of these adaptation issues and help the young person bolster his or her inner resources and strengths.

In 1999, the Foster Care Independence Act was passed to enhance the government's effort to help foster children prepare for independent living by ensuring that they get the tools they need to survive. Studies show that within two to four years of leaving foster care, only 50 percent of these youth have completed high school, fewer than 50 percent are employed, 25 percent have reported homelessness, 30 percent lack health care, 60 percent of the females have given birth, and less than 20 percent are completely self-supporting. The Foster Care Independence Act of 1999 authorized $700 million over five years to cover the following areas: earning a high school diploma or obtaining vocational education; requiring states to serve youth up to age twenty-one, which enables more youth to go to college; enabling states to provide financial assistance to these youth as they learn job skills for entering the workforce; and allowing states to extend health insurance coverage under Medicaid for foster care youth until age twenty-one (Child Welfare League of America, 2003).

Lyons and colleagues (2000) studied children and adolescents in residential settings in an effort to identify strengths and how these strengths might help these youth to prepare for independent living. These researchers developed a data-gathering instrument known as the Child and Adolescent Strengths Assessment (CASA) after an extensive review of the strengths-oriented literature and a series of focus groups with family members and service delivery professionals. The instrument contained thirty items and measured strengths in six different domains: family, school/vocational, peer, psychological, moral/spiritual, and extracurricular. The Childhood Severity of Psychiatric Illness (CSPI) was also used as a review measure. The sample consisted of 450 cases, 123 of which had already been discharged from residential care. The age range was four to nineteen years and was composed of 55 percent boys and 45 percent girls. All facilities were in the state of Florida. Thirty children were selected from each site, with the following ethnic backgrounds: white (49 percent), African American (35 percent), Hispanic (11 percent), and Native American and Asian/Pacific Islander (5 percent).

The results of this study demonstrated remarkable variation across individuals and types of strengths. The three most common strengths found were a sense of humor, the ability to enjoy positive life experiences, and having a strong relationship with a sibling. Conversely, the three least common strengths were involvement with a religious group, involvement in a community services group, and the identification of a career goal. Lyons et al. found that building strengths could enhance functioning independent of any success in alleviating psychiatric symptoms, which suggests the importance of addressing the strengths of children and adolescents in mental health service delivery. Implications point to the need for increased understanding of the strengths of children and adolescents in reference to their functioning and the likelihood of high-risk behaviors. Moreover, the authors suggested that mental health and residential care professionals need to provide tools, such as humor, coping skills, and social support, and emphasize the assessment of new strengths and strength development in the treatment process (Lyons et al., 2000). The case illustration that follows emphasizes the strengths and resilience of a young man who survived placement in multiple foster homes and was then placed in residential care.

James Eustice, age twenty, is now a sophomore in college, where he is studying computer science and making excellent grades. When James was three years old his father died and his mother remarried. James's new stepfather, a retired military man, had not wanted any children and always saw James as "a compromise." James remembers that his mother was afraid of Buford, his stepfather, and would always give in to his demands. James is now aware that his mother was also forced by Buford to have an abortion when she once became pregnant. When his mother left the house, Buford would tell James he was no good and that he had better not act up or he would "suffer the consequences," which meant he would be slapped across the face or made to put his head in the freezer until he could hardly breathe. Buford told his mother about his stepfather's abuse, but she denied that there was a problem, perhaps out of fear. Then, when James was five years old, Buford became furious when James broke an ashtray. Buford took a piece of the jagged glass and cut James across the forearm. The mother tried to chastise her husband, but he told her to shut up or get out. She chose compliance over action.

The next day, James went to kindergarten and his teacher noticed the deep cut, which had been treated with bandages and iodine. Upon additional questioning, the school social worker became involved and James admitted what had happened. Protective services became involved and, after an in-depth assessment, decided that James should be removed from his home. Since his natural father's parents were alcoholic and the widowed maternal grandmother was terminally ill, James was placed in foster care. He was never adopted, though parental rights had been terminated. He also lived off and on with his paternal grandparents, but they drank sporadically and never sought treatment. He missed his mother, but she had no additional contact with him and he heard that she and Buford had moved abroad.

James never felt that his foster parents really understood him and, in fact, they were often neglectful or abusive. Sometimes his caseworkers would listen; other times they would deny the complexity of the problems. James lived in one foster home where, at age eight, he was forced by an older foster brother to have sex many times. The older boy told James that if he told the foster parents he would see to it that James was thrown out and placed in an orphanage. This sexual abuse lasted for two years, until a new social worker on his case investigated and confirmed what had been going on. At age ten, James was placed in another foster home, which went well until the foster mother was killed in an accident. He subsequently was placed in another home at age twelve and adjusted fairly well. Nevertheless, the foster father was transferred to another state after a year, which meant another transition for James. At age thirteen, he was labeled "hard to place" by the child welfare system and placed in residential care.

In the residential program, James at first experienced many behavioral problems and at times felt rejected by the world. He got into fights on the grounds at the least provocation and was almost sent away to a home for extremely disturbed youth. He assumed a macho profile as a way to relate to other boys and girls in the facility, and many of the younger children looked up to him. He always dedicated himself to his studies, which he described once in counseling as his "escape." James was good at basketball and soccer. Within a couple of years he felt that he had finally found a home. Most of all, he developed a close and trusting relationship with Ryan Rose, age sixty, a counselor in his cottage. Mr. Rose was married, but he and his wife of forty years never had children. They had had several miscarriages and finally gave up and were resigned to view the children at the residential home as their children. Mrs. Rose, age fifty-nine, had retired from the local elementary school where she had been a cafeteria cook for thirty years. She also delighted in children and was open to taking James into their home for occasional weekends and holidays.

Some of the children at the home occasionally teased James about his "daddy," but he did not seem to mind. He felt that he could share anything with Mr. Rose: fears about the future, dating girls, and performing well in school. Sometimes Mr. Rose would help him with his homework and always praised him for his keen abilities with math. After James entered high school, Mr. Rose would sometimes allow James to stay up a little later and use the Internet to look up materials for school. He was always amazed at James's skills in accessing and processing information online.

James did so well in high school that he graduated in the top 10 percent of his class and won a tuition scholarship to a nearby university. Mr. and Mrs. Rose are supporting James's education by buying his books and giving him spending money. James has been able to get a part-time job as well in the campus computer technology center, where he delights in teaching students, faculty, and staff basic and advanced computer skills. He attributes his motivation to succeed to Mr. and Mrs. Rose, whom he refers to as Mom and Pop. He loves taking some of his buddies over from the dormitory as he knows Mrs. Rose will prepare a feast for them. The Roses feel that James is the son they never had, and they never fail to praise him. They attend all of his soccer games at the university and stay in touch with him regularly by phone and e-mail. James Eustice now has a strong positive self-concept and a strong sense of well-being because of the respect, love, and support he was given by one family who had much to give to a deserving child.


## CONCLUSION

Adolescence is one of the most trying stages in the life of a young person because so many changes are taking place as the individual attempts to form a firm identity. Children change physically and sexually, yet they find themselves leaning back toward parental values and injunctions and wondering what course to take in their lives. They question their worthiness and, at the same time, begin to realize and celebrate their uniqueness. Peer association and pressure help children to test their strengths and limitations through social interaction at school and in the community. Adolescence is a time when youth may worry about their weight, hairstyle, physical agility, or skills in sports in an effort to accommodate to the peer group and find social inclusion. Teenagers become more aware of gender roles and are sensitive to how gender factors into their identity as a male or female. Adolescents from racial and ethnic minority groups are doubly challenged to find a comfortable identity as they walk a bicultural road that is too often blocked by discrimination and social injustice. Gay, lesbian, bisexual, and transgendered youth may feel that they do not belong to any peer group, facing daily anxieties related to coming out to their parents or masking their true sexual orientation or identity until they can live independently of their families. Children in foster care who do not find a home may need a great deal of assistance in moving out of residential programs due to the feelings of uncertainty and exclusion for not having had a stable home environment.

Adolescents must be understood for their strengths and resilience at a time when their world may often seem turned upside down. Adolescents need a family environment that encourages individuality, creativity, and ambition—one in which parents and family members communicate openly about daily concerns. Teenagers have a responsibility to the family, yet they need the freedom to be a "child," to explore their interests, to engage in new experiences, and to identify their capabilities. Social workers, school counselors, and teachers must always encourage adolescents to maximize their potential and also advocate for policies that will provide support and opportunities for self-exploration and boundaries that are permeable enough to foster self-actualization. Adolescents are then more likely to develop strong self-esteem, which will help them to be more resilient in crossing the swaying footbridge from childhood to adulthood, with increased confidence, motivation, and self-respect.

## STRENGTHS STORY: ZOR HOLLIS

Born into an African-American family of six children living in a swampland of Florida during the tail end of the Great Depression, Zor Hollis did not know he was poor. His father, who had a third-grade education, drove a truck to haul fruits and vegetables, and his mother, who dropped out of high school when she became pregnant, stayed home. Her hands were always full, taking care of six children, each one year apart. They did not have running water or electricity in their home, and their tiny house shook violently when hurricanes hit the swampland. For a while, Zor had a pet alligator, which he found in the swamp. One Christmas, Zor went into the woods to cut a Christmas tree to set up in the house. His mother asked him, "Why are you doing that? You know that Santa will not stop at our house. It is useless." Zor replied, "He will when he sees this tree." That evening, Zor's father's first cousin stopped by and gave money to all the children. Zor knew that Santa had sent him to them because he himself was too busy to come this way.

His father woke all the boys up at five o'clock every morning to work in their vegetable garden and sell the harvest at a stand in front of the garden before heading for school. Zor and other children in the neighborhood rode a school bus that transported them to their school, which was located beyond the white schools. All the teachers at his school were African American and were respected in the black community. Zor always completed his homework because he liked it when his teachers told him that he would "make it," unlike other students in the class. When he was eleven years old, he began to make as much as thirty dollars a day shining shoes for white people. One of his favorite customers was a Klansman who tipped Zor generously, saying that Zor was a "good black boy." When he became hungry, he went into the woods to hunt for rabbits and opossums with his homemade weapons. He brought his game home to his mother so that she could cook them with rice. His regular clothing consisted of only a pair of overalls. When he went to a store for his mother, a patron asked him what he would wear for Halloween. Zor replied, "I don't know." This patron, laughing, said, "You should go just like that." Zor thought, "I should do something about this," and he spent the money he made to buy nice clothes. He became the best dresser in the class when he was in high school. Teachers voted him as most likely to succeed and students voted him best dressed.

Zor's aunt thought it was a shame for him not to go to college just because his parents did not have money, and she told Zor that she would pay for his college. The university he went to was segregated, and Zor did not think he was learning as much as his white counterparts in the other university. He did not feel right until he joined the Army when he was a senior. He knew there was a great wide world to be discovered where there would be no limit to his learning. When he left the Army, Zor went to Chicago with his Army friend, finished his college education, and later did graduate work through the GI Bill to become a principal of a public school system. When he returned to his hometown for his thirtieth high school reunion, the teachers who were still there remembered that they had voted him as the most likely to succeed.

## QUESTIONS FOR DISCUSSION

1. Discuss the metaphor of a swaying footbridge to explain the rapid changes and developmental crises involving adolescents.
2. Discuss some of the challenges faced by ethnically and culturally different adolescents.
3. Discuss the importance of the coming-out process for gay and lesbian adolescents.
4. Discuss the importance of gender roles during adolescence.

## REFERENCES

American Psychiatric Association (2000). *Diagnostic and statistical manual of mental disorders,* Fourth edition, Text revision. Washington, DC: American Psychiatric Association.

American Psychological Association, Div 44/Committee on Lesbian, Gay, and Bisexual Concerns Task Force (2000). *American Psychologist* 55(12): 1440-1451.

Atkinson, D., Morten, G., and Sue, D. W. (1989). A minority identity development model. In Atkinson, D., Morten, G., and Sue, D.W. (Eds.), *Counseling American minorities* (pp. 35-52). Dubuque, IA: William C. Brown.

Baker, J. (2002). *How homophobia hurts children: Nurturing diversity at home, at school, and in the community.* Binghamton, NY: The Haworth Press.

Ben-Ari, A. (1995). The discovery that an offspring is gay: Parents', gay men's, and lesbians' perspectives. *Journal of Homosexuality* 30: 89-112.

Berger, R. M. and Kelly, J. J. (1995). Gay men overview. In Edwards, R. L. (Ed.), *Encyclopedia of social work,* Nineteenth edition, Volume 2 (pp. 1064-1075). Washington, DC: NASW Press.

Cass, V. C. (1984). Homosexual identity formation: Testing a theoretical model. *Journal of Sex Research* 20: 143-167.

Centers for Disease Control (1996). Youth risk behavior surveillance—United States, 1995. *Morbidity and Mortality Weekly Report* 45: 41 (Table 10).

Centers for Disease Control (1997). *HIV/AIDS Surveillance Report* 9(2): 1-44.

Chan, C. S. (1989). Issues of identity development among Asian-American lesbians and gay men. *Journal of Counseling and Development* 68: 16-20.

Child Welfare League of America (2003). Legislative alert. Available at <www.cwla. org/advocacy/alrt030110.htm>.

Coleman, E. (1981). Developmental stages of the coming out process. *Journal of Homosexuality* 7(2/3): 31-43.

Cross, J. D. and Cross, P. D. (1998). *Knowing yourself inside out for self-direction.* Berkeley, CA: Crystal Publications.

D'Augelli, A. R. (1994). Identity development and sexual development and sexual orientation: Toward a model of lesbian, gay, and bisexual development. In

Trickett, E. J., Watts. R. J., and Birman, D. (Eds.), *Human diversity: Perspectives on people in context* (pp. 312-333). San Francisco: Jossey-Bass.

Davis, S. M. and Schwartz, M. D. (1987). *Children's rights and the law.* Lexington, MA: Lexington Books/D.C. Heath.

Downs, S. W., Moore, E. M., McFadden, E. J., and Costin, L. B. (2000). *Child welfare and family services: Policies and practice,* Sixth edition. Boston, MA: Allyn and Bacon.

Erikson, E. (1963). *Childhood and society.* New York: Norton.

Erikson, E. (1968). *Identity: Youth and crisis.* New York: Norton.

Garbarino, J. (1992). *Children and families in the social environment,* Second edition. Hawthorne, NY: Aldyne de Gruyter.

Gay and Lesbian Alliance Against Defamation (2003). Covering hate crimes. October. Available at <www.glaad.org/media/resource_kit_derail.php?id=3495>.

Gay, Lesbian, and Straight Education Network (1997). *Grading our schools: The national report evaluating our nation's schools and their progress on creating safe and affirming learning environments for gay and lesbian students and staff.* September. New York: Author.

Gilligan, C. (1982). *In a different voice: Psychological theory and women's development.* Cambridge, MA: Harvard University Press.

Goodridge, L. J. and Capitman, J. (2000). Adolescents at high risk for HIV infection: A growing concern. In Lynch, V. J. (Ed.), *HIV/AIDS 2000: A sourcebook for social workers* (pp. 123-137). Boston: Allyn and Bacon.

Henry J. Kaiser Family Foundation (2003). KFF state health facts online: 50 state comparisons: Minors' right to consent to HIV/STD services, as of August 2003. Available at <www.statehealthfacts.kff.org>.

Horowitz, R. M. and Davidson, H. A. (Eds.) (1984). *Legal rights of children.* Colorado Springs, CO: Shepard's/McGraw-Hill.

Hutchison, E. D. (1999). *Dimensions of human behavior: The changing life course.* Thousand Oaks, CA: Sage Publications.

Hyde, J. S. and DeLamater, J. D. (2000). *Understanding human sexuality,* Seventh edition. Boston: McGraw-Hill.

Jackson, S. and Hafemeister, T. L. (2001). Impact of parental consent and notification policies on the decisions of adolescents to be tested for HIV. *Journal of Adolescent Health* 29(2): 81-93.

Lee, C. (2002). The impact of belonging to a high school gay/straight alliance. *High School Journal* 85(3): 13-26.

Lombardi, E. L., Wilchins, R. A., Priesing, D., and Malouf, D. (2001). Gender violence: Transgender experiences with violence and discrimination. *Journal of Homosexuality* 42(1): 89-101.

Lott, B. (1994). *Women's lives: Themes and variations in gender learning,* Second edition. Pacific Grove, CA: Belmont.

Lum, D. (1995). Cultural values and minority people of color. *Journal of Sociology and Social Welfare* 22(1): 59-74.

Lyons, J. S., Uziel-Miller, N. D., Reyes, F., and Sokol, P. T. (2000). Strengths of children and adolescents in residential settings: Prevalence and associations with psychopathology and discharge placements. *Journal of the American Academy of Child and Adolescent Psychiatry* 39(2): 176-181.

Mallon, G. P. (1998). *Foundations of social work practice with gay and lesbian persons.* Binghamton, NY: The Haworth Press.

Marcia, J. (1980). Identity of Adolescence. In Adelson, J. (Ed.), *Handbook of adolescent psychology* (pp. 159-187). New York: John Wiley.

Masters, W. H., Johnson, V. E., and Kolodny, R. C. (1995). *Human sexuality,* Fifth edition. New York: Harper Collins.

Mead, M. (1928). *Coming of age in Samoa.* New York: Morrow.

Moses, A. E. and Hawkins, R. O. (1982). *Counseling lesbian women and gay men: A life-issues approach.* St. Louis, MO: Mosby.

Munoz-Plaza, C., Quinn, S. C., and Rounds, K. A. (2002). Lesbian, gay, bisexual and transgender students: Perceived social support in the high school environment. *High School Journal* 85(4): 52-63.

Newman, B. M. and Newman, P. R. (1999). *Development through life: A psychosocial approach,* Seventh edition. Belmont, CA: Brooks/Cole Wadsworth.

Olson, E. D. (2000). Gay teens and substance use disorders: Assessment and treatment. *Journal of Gay and Lesbian Psychotherapy* 3(3/4): 69-80.

Phinney, J. S. (1989). Stages of ethnic identity development in minority group adolescents. *Journal of Early Adolescence* 9: 34-49.

Phinney, J. S. (1990). Ethnic identity in adolescents and adults. *Psychological Bulletin* 108: 499-514.

Phinney, J. S. and Alipura, L. L. (1992). Ethnic identity in college students from four ethnic groups. *Journal of Adolescence* 13: 171-183.

Pillari, V. (1999). *Human behavior in the social environment: The developing person in a holistic context,* Second edition. Pacific Grove, CA: Brooks Cole.

Robbins, S. P., Chatterjee, P., and Canda, E. (1998). *Contemporary human behavior theory: A critical perspective for social work.* Boston: Allyn and Bacon.

Robinson, B. E., Walters, L. H., and Skeen, P. (1989). Response of parents to learning that their child is homosexual and concern over AIDS: A national study. *Journal of Homosexuality* 18: 59-80.

Rotheram, M. J., Hunter, J., and Rosario, M. (1994). Suicidal behavior and gay-related stress among gay and bisexual male adolescents. *Journal of Adolescent Research* 9: 498-508.

Santrock, J. W. (2002). *Life span development,* Eighth edition. Boston: McGraw-Hill.

Savin-Williams, R. C. (1998). *". . . And then I became gay": Young men's stories.* New York: Routledge.

Savin-Williams, R. C. and Esterberg, K. G. (2000). Lesbian, gay, and bisexual families. In Demo, D. H., Allen, K., and Fine, M. A. (Eds.), *Handbook of family diversity* (pp. 197-215). New York: Oxford University Press.

Schriver, J. M. (2001). *Human behavior and the social environment: Shifting paradigms in essential knowledge for social work practice,* Third edition. Boston: Allyn and Bacon.

Shernoff, M. (1995). Gay men: Direct practice. In Edwards, R. L. (Ed.), *Encyclopedia of social work,* Nineteenth edition, Volume 2 (pp. 1075-1085). Washington, DC: NASW Press.

Turner, S. (2002). Recognizing and enhancing natural resiliency in boys and girls. In Norman, E. (Ed.), *Resilience enhancement: Putting the strengths perspective into social work practice* (pp. 29-39). New York: Columbia University Press.

Uba, L. and Huang, K. (1999). *Psychology.* New York: Addison Welsey Longman.

U.S. Bureau of the Census (1998). *Statistical abstract of the United States,* 118th edition. Washington, DC: U.S. Government Printing Office.

Werner, E. and Smith, R. S. (1982). *Vulnerable but invincible.* New York: McGraw-Hill.

White, R. W. (1960). Competence and the psychosexual stages. In Marshall, R. (Ed.), *Nebraska Symposium on Motivation,* No. 8 (pp. 97-143). Lincoln: University of Nebraska Press.

Zastrow, C. and Kirst-Ashman, K. (2001). *Understanding human behavior and the social environment,* Fifth edition. Belmont, CA: Brooks/Cole.

Zayas, L. H., Kaplan, C., Turner, S., Romano, K., and Gonzalez-Ramos, G. (2000). Understanding suicide attempts by adolescent Hispanic females. *Social Work* 45(1): 53-63.

# Chapter 8

# Child-Centered Practice Approaches: Emphasis on Strength and Resilience

In youth, we clothe ourselves with rainbows, and go brave as the zodiac.

Ralph Waldo Emerson

Professionals working with children and adolescents must always carefully assess the youth's needs from a multidimensional approach, which takes into consideration biological, psychological, psychological, cultural, spiritual, social, and economic needs. Of paramount importance is that each child must be understood from a strengths perspective, in which his or her capabilities and competencies are readily identified and explored as a springboard for intervention. Children and adolescents have resilience, which enables them to cope with challenges and accomplish tasks, whether adjusting to a new foster placement or attempting to conquer a life-threatening illness such as anorexia or bulimia. Where resilience is concerned, helping professionals must ask which elements of a child's innate personality or makeup bring about resilience in problem solving, as well as consider the environmental factors that contribute to a child's coping capacity.

Child-centered approaches to counseling and human service intervention begin from the vantage point of the child and attempt to assess how the child will be affected by any plans of action executed on his or her behalf. In child welfare settings, social workers are constantly expected to look at what services might best serve the child's best interest in the long term, and they often must testify in court concerning these clinical assessments. Sometimes, however, what seems best for the child is pitted against what seems best for the family system, and the courts will ultimately render a decision affecting the child's future. However, social work assessment is a dynamic process that should not only result in a thorough understanding of the problem but also include the caseworker's best judgment about the strength of the client's capability in coping with a given situation (Jackson and Helton, 1997). In this case, the child welfare worker must decide and take a strong position in court regarding her belief about what is overall in the child and family's best interest. In school systems, school social workers and counselors attempt to understand why a child might be failing or not achieving his or her potential in the classroom. The child's poor performance is often related to a problem in the home environment, such as child abuse or a parent's substance abuse. In mental health agencies, counselors and therapists address serious emotional and psychological problems affecting children, such as hyperactivity, conduct disorder, and attachment disorder. In any of these settings, the counselor must consider the child's point of view in making assessments and intervention plans, which will affect the child's well being and quality of life, presently and in the future.

## GUIDELINES FOR INTERVIEWING AND ASSESSING CHILDREN

Before interviewing a child, the professional must consider the child's developmental level and ability to understand in language the situations being discussed. Spending some time observing the child helps the interviewer gain a better understanding of a specific child, as children vary in abilities. Play can help a child feel more at ease in talking about difficult topics. Before an interview, the room can be set up so that a child may access a variety of play materials, such as finger paints, clay, building blocks, puppets, dolls, dollhouses, and toy animals. Board games, cards, and electronic games may be considered for older children (Sheafor and Horejsi, 2003).

Engaging a child requires that the child knows who the interviewer is and how he or she wants to be addressed. A child may be reluctant to speak, so the professional may offer the child something to drink, comment on his or her clothing, or ask about his or her favorite television show. The professional must always attempt to accommodate or pace his or her voice tone to match that of the child. For example, if the child is smiling, the professional should begin the interview with a smile and an upbeat tone of voice. If the child seems sad and is soft-spoken, the interviewer should also speak with a soft voice while maintaining direct eye contact (Bourg et al., 1999). The interviewer may squat at the child's level to ensure face-to-face interaction. For children age six or seven, the interviewer may ask what he or she knows about the purpose of the interview. Once the child's expectations are assessed, the professional should then state why he or she wants to speak with the child. The professional cannot promise to keep the child's secrets, but he or she can ensure the child's safety by stating ways to protect him or her. The professional should acknowledge the child's anxiety and perhaps state that he or she, too, as a child had been fearful about talking to new people (Sheafor and Horejsi, 2003). Sheafor and Horejsi suggest that a game such as Hot and Cold may help a child be more open about sharing information. The interviewer may say he or she is going to make some guesses about what is bothering the child and then ask him or her to indicate when he or she is getting warm or cold in questions and statements. Humor may be used to get younger children to relax and begin talking.

In gathering and assessing information, the professional should communicate to children that they are the experts in relating what has happened in their lives. Children may view the adult interviewer as omniscient, or in other words, assume that he or she, as well as all adults, already knows what happened (Ceci and Bruck, 1993). A child-centered, strengths-focused approach views the child as an expert in telling his or her story. After the child talks about these events, the professional may want to emphasize that he or she does not know about other events in the life of the child (Bourg et al., 1999). Examples might be, "Gee, Kevin, I don't even know what your favorite sport is or what you enjoy most about school." The professional must always tell children to let him or her know when they do not understand a word that is being used or the way something is being asked.

Much of the information gathered on preschool-aged and younger children has to be based on observation, but this observation should occur across multiple settings to ensure that one's suppositions are valid. Since children under age six are impressionable and can be easily led to responding a particular way, the professional should avoid leading questions. Sheafor and Horejsi (2003) point out that young children are influenced more by the social context of messages (i.e., who said what and how, when, and where it was said) than by literal word meanings. Bibliotherapy or dolls may be used to help a child discuss feelings; it is much easier for children to project feelings onto an object.

The cognitive development of children must be understood in order to develop perspectives on how children respond the way they do when questioned by an adult. Children between the ages of three and six think in subjective, concrete, and egocentric ways and view others as experiencing life the same way they do. Preschoolers see life in absolute terms, good or bad, all or nothing (Sheafor and Horejsi, 2003). After age six children begin to see the world more objectively, yet they may still believe that they cause the hurts and problems of others. Piaget (1952) viewed children between ages seven and eleven as being able to understand the world more broadly, show empathy for others, and comprehend the multidimensional characteristics of objects. Consequently, such a child, who has been abused, should be able to integrate his or her knowledge and express valid information as to time, place, sequence of events, and persons involved. By age ten, a child understands that he or she may experience opposing emotions simultaneously and can also determine how another person might react to particular information. A child may be able to manipulate words to influence how others will behave. School-age children are generally eager to please adults and have good memories, which allows them to recall and describe events without continuous questioning (Sheafor and Horejsi, 2003).

## GUIDELINES FOR INTERVIEWING
## AND ASSESSING ADOLESCENTS

Interviewing adolescents can be challenging because adolescents are struggling with and attempting to develop an identity separate from the family. Adolescents are generally referred to social workers and other helping professionals for the following reasons: family conflict; alcohol and drug abuse; running away; behavior problems in school; violence; delinquency; pregnancy; and the need for out-of-home placement (Sheafor and Horejsi, 2003). The interviewer will make more progress with adolescents if he or she asks the youth to talk about life from their own perspectives and encourages them to examine current decisions and behavior in reference to hopes, dreams, opportunities, and goals (Sheafor and Horejsi, 2003).

Despite their challenges, adolescents can be interesting and fun to work with; they are persistently lively, inquisitive, and questioning (Sheafor and Horejsi, 2003). Some adolescents will test the authority of the professional by threatening to run away, commit suicide, or drop out of school. These behaviors often occur within the context of "doorknob conversations." That is, the adolescent may rise to leave the interview, yet hang onto to the doorknob with the door ajar in an attempt to determine whether the professional will set boundaries for counseling. Since most adolescents are involuntary clients, they will generally not terminate the session for fear of consequences from parents or juvenile authorities. But the professional may have to state firmly that leaving the interview is an individual choice that only the adolescent can make. Adolescents demand freedom and autonomy yet still expect rules and an environment that provides structure. In residential or group-home settings, professionals must establish rules that are reasonable and developmentally appropriate, and be consistent in enforcing all curfews and norms for in-house behavior.

Because of the strong peer group influence in adolescence, adolescent clients may respond more positively to group interventions as opposed to one-on-one approaches (Sheafor and Horejsi, 2003). Adolescence is a time of remarkable growth and change, which is characterized by resilience. Because of their energy and high activity levels, adolescents often are more relaxed about talking or sharing information if engaged in shooting baskets, walking, working out in a gym, or riding in the car (Sheafor and Horejsi, 2003). One young social worker has successfully engaged adolescents in her community center by demonstrating her bodybuilding and fitness expertise. Youth at this stage of life perceive the world as being full of opportunities and possibilities which means, if given the chance, they can be creative and open-minded in their approaches to addressing issues and challenges.

## *PRACTICE WITH CHILDREN IN CHILD WELFARE*

Children involved with the child welfare system are some of the most vulnerable children that social workers will encounter in their work. These children are moved from "pillar to post" as the professional social workers in the system evaluate their problems and consider how best to help the family. Ann Hartman (1990, p. 484) aptly described social work's role in child welfare as follows: "Social work has a very special role in the child welfare system. Our profession was born in that system. The social institution known as child welfare has been primarily a social work domain since the early 1900's." One hundred years later social workers continue to provide best-practice assessment and decision making to benefit all children and ensure their well-being. A secondary goal is to preserve the family unit whenever possible. Family preservation laws and child welfare statutes tend to be family focused in an effort to place the child back with his or her family in hopes of improving the quality of life for the entire family system. However, families are often given multiple opportunities to stabilize their home environments to no avail, and the child repeatedly ends up in foster care or residential placement. The mission of every social worker and child care professional must begin and end with the child's best interests, ensuring safety, well-being, and maximal chances for survival.

## *Physical Abuse, Sexual Abuse, and Neglect*

In child abuse and neglect situations, the child welfare professional must be aware of how the child feels and must also protect the child from emotionally harmful procedures, such as multiple interviews by police, medical professionals, and counselors. Children often shut down or refuse to talk about what has happened to them due to shock and feelings of loss. Children who are victims of sexual abuse are frequently misunderstood developmentally and psychologically by the plethora of professionals who are attempting to discover the truth about the traumas they have experienced. Sometimes children, especially adolescents, may become angry and lash out at those who are trying to assist them, or they may withdraw (Anderson et al., 2002). Social workers are recognized as sexual abuse experts in working with children; they work with this population more than any other human service professional does (Mason, 1992). In addressing sexual abuse, the traditional clinical role of the social worker might be expanded to integrate a number of roles to ensure the emotional and psychological well-being of the child. These might include interviewing the child, assessing his or her mental status, analyzing his or her developmental capacities for court testimony, evaluating the family's level of functioning in relation to the allegations, preparing the child for the court process, and recommending to the court ways to engage in testimony that might minimize retraumatization of the child (Strand, 1994).

Child-centered social workers may find themselves playing multiple roles in working with sexually abused children. Anderson and colleagues (2002) identify a process for working with sexually abused children that might also be applied to children who are victims of physical abuse and neglect. The roles assumed by the social worker include clinician, networker, broker, support person, educator, mediator, expert witness, and advocate (Anderson et al., 2002). The child-centered social worker will inevitably perform networker roles with a range of other professionals such as child protective workers, victim-witness social workers, schoolteachers, physicians, psychiatrists, and district attorneys. As a broker, such a social worker links the child and family with resources in the community, which might include day care, preschool, after-school programs, or family counseling. Moreover, the social worker may advocate with the court system to serve as a support person for the child in court. The worker, in such a role, attends all litigation and courtroom hearings and is there as a friendly presence during the child's testimony to help him or her cope with this challenging and often frightening situation. As an educator, the worker can help the child to prepare for court by teaching him or her relaxation and stress management exercises, as well as cognitive strategies for handling the courtroom process. The social worker can also educate others involved in the court proceedings about the child's developmental needs, cognitive abilities, and socioemotional state (Anderson et al., 2002).

The social worker as clinician or counselor involves an ongoing role as the worker attempts to help the family and other concerned professionals understand the impact of child abuse and neglect across developmental stages. Tomlinson (1997) noted that a child's recovery may be long and painful as some symptoms of abuse and neglect may show up later in life as the child grows, matures, and develops. As an expert witness, the social worker may use his or her knowledge of child development, psychological theory, and family processes to testify on the behalf of the child and what is considered his or her best interests. The expert-witness testimony of the social worker may actually prevent the child from having to take the witness stand (Anderson et al., 2002). Finally, a social worker may advocate for a child to protect him or her from current or future trauma that might be caused by the courtroom experience. Whenever possible, a social worker may advocate for adaptation of courtroom procedures that might include testifying behind a screen, using closed-circuit television, or hearing statements in chambers rather than in an open courtroom (Cashmore, 1992). The child-centered social worker may insist that a special attorney, known as a guardian *ad litem*, be appointed by the court to assess and protect the rights of the child at all stages of the court proceedings.

The social worker must be aware of the dynamics of sexual abuse: it is perhaps the most psychologically damaging form of child abuse. About 85 percent of child sexual abuse perpetrators are males (Petr, 1998), and they are often relatives or close acquaintances of the child and family. *Situational child molesters* are those who may not have a strong sexual preference for children but engage in sex with children because of low self-esteem, availability, feelings of power, experimentation, or insecurity. *Pedophiles,* on the other hand, have a strong preference for sex with children and are likely to be unsuccessful in their adult social and sexual relationships (Monteleone, Glaze, and Bly, 1994).

Errol Armstrong Jr. (a.k.a. Junior), age nine, and his sister, Julia, age eight, were placed in foster care after they were abandoned by their mother and father. Their mother was a cocaine addict and their father was an alcoholic. A neighbor had reported hearing children crying in their rental house next door. The children were found alone in a dirty house, with only a few pieces of moldy bread and a mattress on the floor to sleep on. The children were huddled together with a tattered quilt around them. Roaches and mice were scurrying all over the house. The children said that they had been alone for four days. They said their father had been arrested for drunk driving and was put in jail, and their mother had gone to get drugs and never returned. The phone had been disconnected so they could not call their maternal grandparents, who lived across town. The children were immediately placed in emergency custody within the foster care system. They were at first placed in a home with a foster family who had only one other child, a two-year-old boy. By the time the Children's Services Department decided to place the children with their maternal grandparents two weeks later, the foster parents were ready to give the children up. Junior and Julia fought constantly, called each other names, and stated they wanted to go live with their grandparents. Julia cried each night for her mother and said she feared her mother would never come back to get them.

The social worker assigned to the family was Lillian Vosdoganes, a thirty-one-year-old mother of two, who had worked for Children's Services for seven years since completing her master's degree. Ms. Vosdoganes met with the children separately and jointly to assess their strengths and competencies and was able to reassure the children that she would look out for them. Junior seemed aggressive and overly friendly with her and touched her often, which she overlooked at first but later suspected might be related to previous abuse. Ms. Vosdoganes noted that Julia was rather shy and reserved, looking at the floor when she answered questions. Julia seemed to be extremely concerned about her mother's whereabouts and needed much encouragement that she and her brother would be safe and able to live with their grandparents.

After a home assessment was completed, Junior and Julia went to live with their maternal grandparents, Les and Faye Elderidge, ages sixty-eight and sixty-seven, both retired schoolteachers in a suburban community. Besides the children's mother, Lee, the Elderidges had two older children who lived in another state. Mr. and Mrs. Elderidge were friendly and engaging, and they were affectionate with the children. They seemed bent on keeping Junior and Julia as long as necessary. The grandmother, who had diabetes and a disk problem in her back, was in relatively good health at the time of placement, but her condition declined after about three months. She was admitted to a nearby nursing home, but Mr. Elderidge was committed to keeping the children with him. He hired a part-time housekeeper to cook and manage the house, and the children adored her. Mr. Elderidge met the children at the bus stop each day after school and took them for ice cream. Once a week they went with him to the nursing home to see Mrs. Elderidge. The children seemed to have made an adequate adjustment to all the changes in their life.

Lillian Vosdoganes, the foster care worker, told the children in her weekly visit that their mother and father were both in jail and would be there for some time. Julia ran to the next room crying and had to be consoled. Junior was at first silent and appeared sad, but he then said, "Well, I can look after Julia, me and grandpa." Mr. Elderidge seemed worried about his daughter and son-in-law's incarceration, but he assured the social worker that the children were in good hands. He seemed knowledgeable of their homework assignments and had recently attended a parent-teacher meeting. Junior and Julia both became involved in soccer and went to games with the neighbor girls next door, whose father coached the team.

Everything seemed to be fine with the children until Junior was caught trying to kiss and fondle another boy in the rest room at school. When confronted by the principal, Junior began to cry and say he was sorry and did not mean to do it. The social worker was summoned to the school where she met with the school psychologist and principal. This was the first such incident noted at school. Junior's teacher was asked to join the discussion and reported that he seemed to be a "touchy-feely" child but that she had not suspected anything out of the ordinary. After the meeting, Ms. Vosdoganes took Junior to her office and talked to him about the incident. After a while he calmed down and was able to listen to her. She asked him about the incident with the other boy at school, but he would not talk about it. She told him that sometimes children have feelings that they need to share to help them feel better. Junior began to tell her how much he missed his parents and how he helped his grandpa take care of his sister, Julia. The social worker continued to ask Junior questions and he opened up a little more. He said that his parents had never touched him inappropriately and proclaimed his love for them. When the social worker asked about what he enjoyed doing for fun, he said he loved soccer and that he liked to hang out with his grandpa. He said they always had a lot of fun and liked to watch movies together when Julia went over to play with her girlfriends next door. When asked what type of movies they watched, he became quiet and started playing with a car. He appeared sad, discontinued eye contact, and seemed lost in his play activity. Ms. Vosdoganes moved to a chair right next to the table where he was rolling the car and asked him to look at her. She asked about the movies again, and he said, "I can't tell anybody. Grandpa made me promise not to." When the foster care worker asked if his grandpa had ever touched him in his private area, he said "No!" and started racing the car faster on the table. The social worker said, "It's okay, I am here to listen. Everything will be okay." Junior finally admitted that his grandfather had regularly shown him pornographic movies of men and women doing things. He admitted that while watching the movies his grandfather had kissed him on the lips, touched his penis, and made Junior touch his. At that point, Junior started to cry. Lillian Vosdoganes soothed Junior until he was feeling better and let him watch cartoons in the agency playroom.

The foster care worker acted immediately and was able to find a foster home for Junior and Julia that evening. The grandfather was arrested for child sexual molestation and was later convicted and incarcerated. Junior and Julia were placed in foster care with a young couple who had no children, and they adjusted well to the home. It seemed that Mr. Elderidge had not molested his granddaughter but had been accused of fondling a boy at a campground when the family had been on vacation almost a decade earlier. There had been no prosecution. Junior began counseling with a male psychologist who demonstrated a dynamic and engaging approach to working with children. Early in treatment there was another incident in which Junior touched a girl inappropriately on the bus, but this behavior ceased after a few months of weekly therapy. Ms. Vosdoganes met with the therapist regularly, as did the foster parents. Team meetings were held regularly as well to address the children's abilities to overcome their earlier trauma and adjust to a new living situation. The natural parents were released from prison and briefly exercised their visitation rights before being caught and resentenced for trafficking crack cocaine. Soon after, their parental rights were terminated, as neither had any other relatives who were willing to care for the children. Junior and Julia continued to visit their grandmother, who was a constant in their lives and provided some continuity of family contact. Within two years the young foster couple who had taken them in adopted the children, and the couple had a baby of their own shortly thereafter.

After the young couple, Greg and Tracy Tilly, adopted the children, Lillian Vosdoganes continued to see the children off and on and sometimes would take them out for ice cream on Sundays with her own children. She always praised the children's high energy and their agility in soccer and ice skating, a sport that was a family passion of the Tilly family. Mrs. Tilly had skated professionally before her marriage, so the family also attended most of the area and regional skating events. Julia was becoming quite a good skater, and Junior loved to boast about how she might one day join the Olympic team. Julia smiled coyly but knew that her brother really meant it.

Child abuse and neglect cases pose some of the most challenging dilemmas faced by social workers and other child care professions. As portrayed in the case of Junior and Julia Armstrong, social workers must take a multidimensional approach to assessment, always placing the immediate safety and security of the child at the forefront. Social workers may be influenced in their assessment and planning by past history, parent or family cooperation or defensiveness, child vulnerability, and other factors (Petr, 1998).

Foster care is generally advisable if a child is believed to be in harm's way, but often professionals may have differing opinions about whether the degree of abuse is moderate or severe, and they may consider related and ongoing risk factors. Likewise, social workers and other child care professionals involved may hold varying opinions about the amenability of the family to treatment and ameliorative services. Risk assessment has become a vital component of child welfare practice since 1980, and attempts to standardize data collection in an agency, help make decisions more consistent across different personnel, assist in prioritizing cases for investigation and services, and help determine the level and intensity of services needed (Petr, 1998).

Child welfare professionals must follow some important protocols and principles in conducting investigative interviews with children. Petr (1998) offers a set of principles that have been adapted from Garbarino, Stott, and Faculty of the Erickson Institute (1989):

- There are few fixed and specific formulas for communicating effectively with children; it is essential that the adult adapt to the characteristics of each child and each situation.

- In general, the more confident and mature the child, the more positively familiar the setting, and the more conversational the inquiry, the more effective the process of communication and the more valid the information will be.
- The more sources of information an adult has about a child, the more likely the adult is to receive the child's messages properly.
- Children rarely invent or fantasize allegations of sexual abuse on their initiative; adults are a more likely source of false allegations.
- In using play and storytelling, it is important to note the repetition of a theme, for it indicates that the theme has some special meaning for the child.
- Children are most likely to offer information that is reliable when talking about events that are part of or related to their own interests or part of their everyday experience.
- School-age children may feel that adult interviewers already know the answers to the questions that they are asking and thus may either severely curtail their responses or not respond at all.
- There may be powerful incentives for adults to suppress, ignore, or minimize information from children.
- Those who operate within the legal system must be—or at least must be advised by—informed and sensitive child development experts who can interpret the system for children and interpret children to the system. (Petr, 1998, p. 158)

Looking more comprehensively at how social workers and child care professionals can protect children, the NASW Policy Statement on Child Abuse and Neglect (Mayden and Nieves, 2002) highlights major approaches to safeguarding the lives and well-being of children who have been abused or neglected, or remain at risk. Social workers have as a profession always been at the forefront of developing and lobbying for legislation to ensure the rights and well-being of children. This statement, with some reordering, follows:

> Public agencies, such as child protective services, courts and law enforcement agencies, schools, medical and mental health providers, and national boards and commissions, must create an active collaborative network for treatment and prevention of child abuse and neglect. Prevention should be comprehensive and increase public awareness and family support services.

These programs might include parenting education and staff training for the identification of risk factors. Moreover, the child and family's quality of life will be enhanced by community-based programming, such as financial support, day care, recreation, counseling, case management, job training, and health and mental health services.

Furthermore, the NASW policy statement calls for a continuum of services for families ranging from prenatal care to parenting education. Public policy and resource allocations to protect children should support specialized law enforcement, child abuse investigative units, child advocacy services, early intervention, and mandatory reporting of abuse and neglect. Social work education and training must emphasize effective treatment for victims of abuse and neglect, an understanding of the psychological impact of trauma on a child's development, and family-focused intervention. Bachelor's and master's degrees in social work are specified as the most appropriate degrees for protective workers, with financial incentives being encouraged for child welfare workers to obtain these professional social work degrees. In addition, it is recommended that undergraduate and graduate students in such fields as nursing, education, psychology, law, medicine, and other disciplines be provided with curriculum on child maltreatment and prevention.

Moreover, the current NASW policy statement specifies that children are generally protected best by strengthening their family and kinship network. When the safety and well-being of children can be ensured, they should remain with their families with appropriate and adequate supports. Special services must be provided to recognize and address the special needs of populations, such as children with disabilities and very young children. Clear criteria and professional judgment should be used in making decisions regarding the maintenance, removal, and return of children to their biological or adoptive families. Social workers should be sensitive to the effect of spouse/partner abuse on the safety of children in the home and should not further victimize battered women by viewing them as passive abusers. In a broader sense, government, community and workplace policies should facilitate positive parent and child relationships that build on the strengths in each individual and family and kinship network.

Professionally trained social workers should take leadership roles in developing and strengthening policy, legislation, and child protection programs. School social workers especially should educate teachers, administrators, and support staff in identifying suspected child abuse and neglect. The NASW policy statement calls for implementation of the National Research Council's (1993) agenda on child abuse and neglect.

Sufficient public and private funding, staff, and resources should be provided to meet the needs of abused and neglected children and their families. Child protective services staff should be professionally educated, adequately trained, administratively supported, and legally protected. Management information systems that track the status of children and families should be developed and used in a way that protects children and supports families. A paramount issue is that standards for caseload and workload size need to be established to ensure the provision of effective case management services to each at-risk child. Finally, specialized treatment should be mandated for juvenile, Title I, and adult sex offenders (Mayden and Nieves, 2002).

The safety of children can never be guaranteed, whether they are placed back with the parents, in foster care, or in residential facilities. There continue to be ongoing and increasing reports of child abuse, neglect, and abandonment of children within the child welfare system. Social workers must address the policies and personnel procedures which will ensure that children have an opportunity to grow and develop in a safe and nurturing environment and that children be monitored closely in foster homes, residential care, and relative/family placements. Child-centered, strengths-focused child welfare practice mandates that children have basic, equal rights and should have a strong voice in determining their care and living arrangements. Child welfare professionals must never underestimate a child's thoughts, feelings, and responses to his or her living arrangements, and must always exercise sound clinical judgment in assessing, monitoring, and planning for the children in their care.

One effective tool for helping children in foster care or adoption placement to establish their identity is the life book. The life book serves as a kind of journal or record of a child's life, covering birth to present, and is written in the child's own words (Backhaus, 1984). The life book contains narratives about what has happened to the child, as well as the child's feelings about separation, change, and transitions in his or her life. A life book may contain such items as photographs, report cards, drawings, awards and certificates, a birth certificate, a genogram, and other personal items selected by the child. Sheafor and Horejsi (2003) note that a life book not only helps with continuity and identity but also allows the child to remember key people and events in his or her life. A life book can help a child deal with the harsh realities in his or her life, as well, and maintains in one place an important record of data. The life book generally becomes the focal point through which the social worker can discuss crucial events and the child's feelings about them.

## *SCHOOL SOCIAL WORK*
## *AND COUNSELING IN SCHOOL*

Professionals in the school environment have an opportunity to address a range of children's psychological, emotional, and social needs. School social work has proven to be an effective approach to help children adjust, utilize their strengths, and develop resilience in dealing with problems that place them at risk. The first school social work program was opened in 1913 in Rochester, New York, and involved visiting teachers. Although the visiting teachers were initially charged with educating and supporting parents to keep their children in attendance every day, they also worked to sensitize the school to the child's home environment and advocated for ways in which the school might meet the child's needs (Radin, 1989). For almost a century, school social workers have been addressing problems that hinder children in their academic learning and achievement as well as their development of social skills.

Torres (1996) reported that approximately 9,300 school social workers serve children in thirty-seven education jurisdictions across the United States. However, the distribution of school social workers is uneven, with many of them working in industrial states or in schools with greater resources. Early and Vonk (2001) evaluated twenty-one outcome studies of school social work practice and found that school social workers overall are effective in helping children and adolescents to develop skills for problem solving, improvement of peer relationships, and the enhancement of general functioning. In most studies examined, intervention by school social workers helped to reduce risk factors and increase resilience in those children and adolescents served. Still, the U.S. education system remains at risk as 30 percent of all first graders do not graduate from high school, and of many those who do graduate lack the required skills to enter the labor market (Mayden and Nieves, 2002).

Since social workers in schools are working as support personnel, they may not always be utilized to the fullest extent. Although many school districts have always hired school social workers as an integral part of the overall educational system, others have contracted full- or part-time school social workers through social agencies. Policymakers and other reformers have become increasingly aware that schools and human services agencies can serve their constituents better if they join forces in addressing the educational and social needs of children and families (Franklin and Allen-Meares, 1997). Consequently, when schools attend to the holistic needs of children by linking them with human service agencies, they do not have to decrease their focus on teaching and can be even more effective in their mission of educating students (Franklin and Streeter, 1998).

Since the passage of the Education for All Handicapped Children Act of 1975, school social workers have had increased involvement in interdisciplinary diagnostic teams, case management, and intervention with families. They often coordinate the diagnostic assessment of a child's developmental and educational needs, and play a major role in developing and updating the individual educational plan (IEP) for special educational placement. In preschool programs, social workers have become central players in implementing early childhood special education programs, which serve children from birth to five. Social workers in early intervention services have been instrumental in assisting families and sensitizing interdisciplinary teams to the complex needs of families. Social workers may serve as case managers or service coordinators in developing the individual family service plan in a range of early childhood special educational settings.

School social workers utilize a variety of prevention and treatment approaches that target the mental health needs of children. The interventions might range from counseling an adolescent with anorexia bulimia to facilitating the appropriate special education classroom placement of a child with conduct disorder or attention deficit-hyperactivity disorder (ADHD). Since the 1999 Columbine, Colorado, high school massacre, school social workers have been integrally involved in addressing issues of school violence, including bullying and intimidation of children who are different because of sexual orientation, race, disability, or any other reason (Indiana Education Policy Center, 2001). Although many lessons have been learned since the shootings at Columbine High School and other schools, many schoolchildren, faculty, and staff still feel at risk. Many schools are making a concerted effort to empower children with knowledge about threats of suspicious activities among peers and to encourage open communication among teachers, principals, counselors, coaches, and school social workers. Most schools now have a zero-tolerance policy for drugs, weapons, fighting, disruptive classroom behavior, and disrespect for authority. Some have also developed security measures, which include metal detectors, random searches, inspections by specially trained dogs, and the requirement of clear plastic book bags (Rose and Fatout, 2003). Under such unsettling circumstances, school social workers may serve as liaisons to the family, counsel children in the event of the sudden death of a classmate, or help mediate disputes and disagreements among students and school administrators.

Schools have recently been described as de facto mental health services systems (Burns et al., 1995), which implies that the extent and intensity of problems are ever increasing. The purpose of school social work has been described as follows by Allen-Meares (1991):

> The primary objective of social work services in schools is to maximize equal educational opportunity for all pupils: it is concerned not only with the cognitive aspect of learning, but also with the affective outcome in education. While promoting equity the worker is simultaneously attempting to strive for an educational environment that enhances social functioning and the mental health of all individuals within the school. The school social worker is the mental health professional in the school enterprise. (p. 15)

School social workers have an opportunity to work with children in one of the most important arenas for the development of communication skills, interpersonal skills, and self-esteem. School social workers should take a major role in identifying, assessing, and developing therapeutic interventions for children who are experiencing mental health problems. Unfortunately, the majority of children in special education programs are minorities, and African-American children are heavily overrepresented when compared to the general school population in all disability categories, including emotional and behavioral disorders. Although there may be a correlation with lower socioeconomic status, which in turn correlates with disability in many children, a strong likelihood exists that the large numbers of minority children in special education could be related to biased referral and inadequate assessment procedures (Artiles and Trent, 1994). School social workers can play a major role in determining how and when minority children are referred for special education services through classroom observation, regular teacher consultation, team collaboration, and ongoing support with the family to ensure their understanding and involvement. Smith (1991) calls for teachers to be interculturally sensitive, to avoid stereotypical thinking about other cultural groups, and to openly communicate with families in order to build each child's educational experience on his or her strengths.

Many children's mental health problems, such as attention deficit-hyperactivity disorder and conduct disorder, have long-term consequences. For children with ADHD, protective factors include the ability of the children to adapt to the environment through classroom management, behavior management, and social skills development (Early and Vonk, 2001). Between 30 and 50 percent of children with ADHD develop conduct disorder or oppositional defiant disorder between ages eight and twelve (Thomas and Corcoran, 2003). Sheridan and colleagues (1996) estimated that 60 percent of adults diagnosed with ADHD symptoms during childhood continued to have problems. School failure is thought to be a risk factor for alcohol and drug abuse, later affecting family and work roles, increasing mortality and suicide rates, and leading to more frequent admissions to state psychiatric facilities (Rumberger, 1987). Moreover, Hawkins, Catalano, and Miller (1992) found that peer rejection in the elementary grades is related to other school problems, delinquency, and additional risk factors for substance abuse.

Edgar (1996) studied the impact of a large-scale intervention aimed at creating "smaller communities" within a public high school to reduce risk factors among adolescents. Freshmen were divided into small groups of ten to sixteen and were then assigned to meet daily with a teacher, with the goal of increasing bonding and closer relationships. A total of 260 students were assigned to student homerooms or these small advisory groups, depending on their preference.

Evaluation involved three major areas of functioning: perception of relatedness to an adult in the school, ability to confront problems directly, and self-efficacy related to the school experience. Edgar believed that this intervention was effective in enhancing the students' general functioning and coping skills.

Hector de la Cruz, age ten, was referred to the school social worker for severe attention problems, hyperactivity, and aggressive behaviors, both in the classroom and on the playground. Hector, a fifth grader, is a third-generation Mexican American whose paternal grandparents came to the Midwest in the early 1960s to work in the vineyards and orchards. He is the oldest of three children and his parents are Don and Marta de la Cruz, ages thirty-three and thirty-one. Hector's brother, Joseph, is eight years old and his sister, Carmen, is five years old. Don de la Cruz is a computer analyst and Marta is a registered nurse. The paternal grandparents, Manuel and Lila, are both sixty-three years old and are retired. The paternal grandparents live only three houses away from the family, and provide child care on a regular basis.

Hector was tested for learning disabilities at another school in Michigan, where the family resided two years ago. However, no services were provided at that time as his scores were thought to be borderline. Hector has become increasingly more aggressive in the classroom and in the hallways. He picks on other children by knocking their book bags on the floor and is always touching other children even when they tell him to stop. This behavior has carried over into the home environment. Last week he got mad at his mother for telling him to come in and work on his homework, and he dumped a container of coffee grounds into the family's aquarium. Most of the fish died, for which he received a spanking with a belt from his father.

The social worker, Jackie Jarvis, age thirty-five, has been a social worker for twelve years and has worked at Brockton Elementary for five years as a school social worker. She has completed three observations of Hector in the classroom and has met with him once individually. She has scheduled a meeting with the school psychologist and counselor to review Hector's academic file, and she has also spoken with his parents. Mrs. de la Cruz cried on the phone, saying they did not know how to handle Hector's behavior any longer at home and were feeling desperate. Mrs. de la Cruz said that Hector had always been an active child but had never been this defiant and mouthy.

Ms. Jarvis met with the school psychologist, counselor, and classroom teacher to discuss Hector's learning and behavioral problems. This meeting served as a preliminary conference prior to their meeting with the parents. According to Hector's cumulative file, he had experienced erratic performance in most academic subjects in the past, generally receiving average grades. His records from the previous school had questioned his extreme activity levels and inability to get along with other children. Hector seemed to have above-average intelligence, which implied that his academic shortfalls could be attributed to a more serious problem. Ms. Jarvis also reviewed Hector's attendance record and discovered he had missed twelve days already this school year.

In the meeting with the parents, the school social worker served as spokesperson for the interdisciplinary team and welcomed Mr. and Mrs. de la Cruz's input regarding their son's difficulties. The mother, Marta, did most of the talking and her husband, Don, took a more reticent role. He did comment that he was also active as a child, but that his father had him "work off the steam" by picking and harvesting fruit. Still, Don had managed to complete high school with above-average to excellent grades and later earned a college degree. Marta became tearful and said she does not know any other parent in her neighborhood with a child like Hector. She said her sister had a son, Chester, age twelve, who was on Cylert, which seemed to help him concentrate more and improve his overall behavior. Mr. de la Cruz listened as Ms. Jarvis and the other team members described Hector's need for a multifaceted diagnostic evaluation, including a complete psychiatric evaluation. The parents agreed to the evaluation and were asked to accompany the school social worker to an observation room adjacent to Hector's class. The parents witnessed Hector's disobedience in the classroom, such as talking back to the teacher, pulling a girl's hair, and throwing chalk at another boy. Hector also got out of his seat more than a dozen times during the twenty-minute period they were observing.

The following week Hector underwent a battery of intelligence, psychological, speech and language, and educational tests to assess his emotional and behavioral problems, as well as his academic skills. The testing took two days to finish and proved to be challenging for Hector because of his extreme attention problems. The social worker and Mrs. de la Cruz were able to observe most of the testing procedures through a one-way mirror. Mrs. de la Cruz was deeply disturbed by her son's destructive and angry responses to the testing process, which convinced her even more of his need for special assistance. After all tests results were evaluated, the testing team and Ms. Jarvis met with the parents to discuss the findings and recommendations. The parents' anxiety was paralleled by their strong desire to know more about their son's problems and how to help him.

The test results were shared in great detail and the parents were given ample opportunities to ask questions about their son's needs. The battery of tests indicated that Hector had attention deficit-hyperactivity disorder, as well as conduct disorder. These two psychological conditions proved to be affecting his academic performance in all areas. In addition, the speech pathologist explained that Hector had an auditory processing problem that prevents him from integrating and understanding words even when he is paying attention. The parents at first thought this indicated a hearing problem, but the speech pathologist explained that this was a type of learning disability, not an actual physical problem with hearing. The parents asked a range of questions, but they seemed relieved to hear that their son's problems had been diagnosed and were eager to know what could be done to help him.

The school diagnostic team recommended that Hector be placed in a special education classroom for children with severe emotional and behavioral problems, receive speech and language therapy twice a week at school, and also be placed on the medication Ritalin to help control his disruptive behaviors. Furthermore, the team suggested that the family receive family counseling and attend a parenting support group for parents of children with similar problems. The parents agreed to all of these recommendations and met with Ms. Jarvis afterward to further discuss specific plans for counseling.

Jackie Jarvis provided additional clarification about Hector's problems and answered the parents' specific questions, especially about how the medication would work to help Hector focus his attention for longer periods and reduce his fidgety and aggressive behavior with other children. She explained to the parents that attention deficit-hyperactivity disorder can appear as early as age seven, and she said that Hector's symptoms had most likely emerged over the past several years. Moreover, she described the symptoms of conduct disorder and how Hector's aggression, destruction of property, and serious violation of rules and others' rights had led to this diagnosis. The parents admitted that perhaps they wanted to believe that Hector's problems would subside as he grew older, as they did not want him to end up like his cousin Chester who is on the brink of a juvenile detention admission due to having taken his parents' car and wrecked it. Mrs. de la Cruz said that maybe she is partly to blame as she has always worked as a nurse, opting not to stay at home with the children, as her husband might have wished. Mr. de la Cruz said that his wife's being at home most certainly would not have hurt the children. Ms. Jarvis intervened and advised the family that family counseling is often helpful for understanding and managing a child with ADHD and related behavior problems. Marta de la Cruz seemed interested in the counseling and shared that she is concerned about how Hector's behavior will affect her other children. She said that two evenings ago Hector and his younger brother climbed up on the kitchen island cabinet and mixed a box of salt into the sugar canister, spilling much of the containers' contents on the floor. Obviously, the children would have been punished immediately had the father been home, but he was away on a business trip. The mother said she tried grounding but Hector always finds a way to sabotage her discipline. Mr. de la Cruz seemed willing to go along with the counseling but was quiet, letting his wife do most of the talking.

When Ms. Jarvis questioned the father further about his concerns, he said that he would like to have his parents involved, in some way, in planning Hector's counseling since they provide regular child care for Hector and his siblings. Ms. Jarvis indicated that this was an excellent idea, as the grandparents need to understand why counseling seems to be indicated and also how they can provide a consistent environment for addressing and monitoring Hector's behavior while at their house. Mrs. de la Cruz expressed her obvious contentment with this plan. Then she told her husband she would arrange an evening off from work for the family meeting. After consulting with both parents about their work schedules, Ms. Jarvis scheduled a meeting with the family at Don and Marta's house for the following Wednesday night.

The social worker arrived at 7:00 p.m., as planned, and was greeted warmly by the family. Mrs. de la Cruz had prepared coffee and cake for the meeting, which took place at the dining-room table. Don de la Cruz's sister, Migdalia, had agreed to look after the children and her son in the recreation room downstairs. The grandparents were especially interested in hearing about their grandson's problems and how they could help him. They knew about the use of medication to treat ADHD because of their other grandson's problems, but they had concern about the prognosis for a child with conduct disorder, as did the parents. Ms. Jarvis listened carefully to each question and assured the family that Hector's special education placement, language therapy, and Ritalin would help to quell many of his disruptive behaviors. However, she emphasized that family counseling and a parent support group would greatly impact Hector's behaviors at school and at home, as well as their level of comfort in disciplining him and controlling his behaviors. She shared a story about a child named Scott who had similar problems and is now doing well in high school and is a star lacrosse player. She also rein-forced the parents' joining a local parent support group for children of par-ents with ADHD, which meets weekly. They agreed to attend regularly and also to share behavior management strategies with the grandparents. Ms. Jarvis also gave the family the number of the local mental health center for arranging the family therapy sessions, stating that she had made a referral and the family should be able to begin therapy within the next three weeks. The social worker concluded the family meeting by informing the family that they could call her at any time with questions. The meeting went well, and Ms. Jarvis left the family's home sensing that they were committed to doing whatever needed to be done to meet Hector's needs. She planned a meet-ing the following week with the interdisciplinary school team, including the new special education teacher, to review her meeting with the family and to ensure their compliance with the overall intervention plan.

## MENTAL HEALTH SERVICES
## FOR CHILDREN AND ADOLESCENTS

As mentioned, many children experiencing severe emotional and behavioral problems are referred by the school system and/or the family for treatment in community mental health centers or mental health counseling clinics. Some of these programs are affiliated with children's hospitals or diagnostic centers, whereas others are commu-nity based and perhaps located to serve specific geographic or "catch-ment" areas. Mental health services for children and adolescents carefully integrate individual counseling to youth with counseling for the family, and reflect an integrated approach to serving children within the context of family life, as did the child guidance movement. Mental health services might include individual and group counseling, case management, crisis residential care, intensive in-home services, family-based counseling, day treatment, psychiatric consultation, residential therapy, therapeutic foster care, tutoring, and child-focused treatment and advocacy services. Smith (1998) found a strong need for parents of adolescents with severe emotional and behavioral problems to become involved with mental health services in order to help their offspring develop and utilize a range of skills. These skills include but are not limited to learning how to listen to their children effectively, how to foster more independence by giving them increased responsibility, and how to expand their community networks.

According to the DSM-IV-TR (*Diagnostic and Statistical Manual of Mental Disorders,* Fourth Edition), published by the Americain Psychiatric Association (APA) (2000), a large number of disorders are diagnosed in infancy, childhood, and adolescence. These include mental retardation, learning disorders characterized by lower than expected academic functioning, motor skills disorders, speech and language communication disorders, pervasive developmental disorders which include schizophrenic-like and autistic behaviors, attention deficit and disruptive behavior disorders, persistent feeding and eating disorders, and other disorders such as separation and attachment disorders (APA, 2000).

Many children experience anxiety on a regular basis, and often this is manifested both at home and at school. About 10 percent of all children and adolescents have anxiety disorder; half of these youth have another mental disorder (Kashani and Orvaschel, 1990). Anxiety is potentially a serious problem that should be addressed when the young person feels that the anxiety is overwhelming or incapacitating. Family members and school personnel should be sensitive to levels of anxiety in children and adolescents that seem to interfere with daily functioning. This anxiety might be related to test anxiety, fear of failure, or a reaction to the threat of violence from a peer. Moreover, some children develop obsessive-compulsive disorders, in which they spend a great deal of time engaged in repetitive activities to the exclusion of normal peer relationships. Other children may manifest symptoms of panic disorder or post-traumatic stress disorder, which may involve flashbacks, intrusive memories, distressing thoughts, sleep disturbance, and the avoidance of places associated with the trauma (Rose and Fatout, 2003).

Children and adolescents may experience major depression, yet many adults are not aware of the potential dangers inherent in this condition. Estimates suggest that 3 to 6 percent of children and as many as 12 percent of adolescents experience depression (Rose and Fatout, 2003). The National Institute of Mental Health and the American Academy of Child and Adolescent Psychiatry estimate that 1.5 to 3 million children in the United States are seriously depressed (Brody, 1997). Such youth are likely to experience low self-esteem, have disturbances in eating and sleeping habits, withdraw from peer relationships, and avoid play activities they once enjoyed. Younger children may draw or paint sad pictures to express their depressed mood. Children with bipolar disorder experience exaggerated mood swings, experiencing excited or manic phases with more moderate moods interspersed. Many clinicians are challenged to diagnose bipolar disorder in children and adolescents because it often presents more like depression (Rose and Fatout, 2003).

Adolescent suicide is a major problem that has been on the rise in recent years. Suicide is perceived to be a form of violence against self, family, and community. It is important to realize that many depressed teenagers try to overcome their depression by using drugs and alcohol, which serve to intensify the depression and reduce their inhibitions (Fontes, 2003). Kirk (1993) estimated that between 1967 and 1987 the suicide rate among fifteen- to nineteen-year-olds increased from 3.6 to 10.3 per 100,000. It is estimated that 500,000 young people between ages fifteen and twenty-four attempt suicide each year, and nearly 5,000 children and youth between ages fifteen and twenty-four actually commit suicide (Peters, Kochaner, and Murphy, 1998). Consequently, suicide remains the third largest cause of death for those between the ages of fifteen and twenty-four (Peters and Murphy, 1998). Depression in adolescents may include depressed mood; significant weight loss or gain; insomnia; fatigue or loss of energy; psychomotor agitation or retardation; feelings of hopelessness, worthlessness, guilt, or self-reproach; indecisiveness; decreased concentration ability; suicide ideation, threats, and attempts; and recurring thoughts of death. These symptoms are generally considered to be very serious if they persist for ten days or more (Hepworth, Rooney, and Larsen, 2002).

Another serious problem for adolescents and young adults is eating disorders. Adolescence is the stage in which youth are more concerned than ever about how they look, how they dress, and how others perceive them. Adolescents continually respond to peer pressure, and for many, body image becomes an obsession, especially for females. This may lead to anorexia nervosa, which is characterized by a minimal body weight, defined as "less than 85 percent of the expected body weight" (APA, 2000, p. 583). Many of these adolescents will also develop bulimia nervosa, which is characterized by "repeated episodes of binge eating followed by inappropriate compensatory behaviors such as vomiting; misuse of laxatives, diuretics, or other medications; or excessive exercise" (APA, 2000, p. 585).

In both anorexia nervosa and bulimia nervosa, the adolescents have a distorted body image and both are bent on remaining as thin as possible at any cost. Both anorexics and bulimics seem to have a common psychological profile. They generally come from middle-class families with overinvolved mothers and preoccupied fathers. They are dependent on their parents and are usually thought of as "good children." Bulimics in particular are overachievers and tend to have high academic averages in college. Their vomiting after bingeing becomes a purification ritual to satisfy their self-loathing (Zastrow and Kirst-Ashman, 2001).

April Sands, age sixteen, lives with her divorced mother, Kay Sands, age forty-six, and her younger brother, Harold, age thirteen. Mrs. Sands is an accountant at a local bank and also runs a catering business with her married daughter, Jean, age twenty-three. Jean, a college graduate, is married to an engineer and has an infant son. Randy Sands, April's father, lives in California and is a marketing analyst. He sees the children only twice a year, at Thanksgiving and for a week in the summer. Mr. Sands has remarried but has no children by his current wife.

April has lately been spending more time by herself and seems depressed. She has always been close to her mother but has begun to resent the time that her mother spends with Jean at the catering business. She has told her mother this, but Mrs. Sands says that she wants to continue with the business until Jean can expand and hire some part-time staff. Mrs. Sands has been using the additional income to make extra mortgate payments. April used to talk to her mother about cheerleading when she was on the squad, as her mother was also once a cheerleader in high school. But at the end of last year, April dropped off the cheerleading squad and quit soccer, saying she needed to study more. Giving up her sports seemed to be precipitated by her having made only an above-average score on the PSAT exam. April has always had her hopes set on being the valedictorian of her school and obtaining a full scholarship to the college of her choice. She is determined to have the highest score in her school on the SAT test.

Also, April has over the past six months become obsessed with her weight. She has never been overweight but now skips breakfast, has fruit for lunch, and eats only a salad for dinner. She rarely does more than nibble at her mother's home-cooked dinners, and she has accused her mother of forcing her to eat. Mrs. Sands sometimes invites Jean and her family over for dinner, and everyone chides April about her being too thin and starving herself. April has lost about fifteen pounds within the past year, which on her thin frame makes her look emaciated. She recently yelled at her mother and Jean when they made a special birthday cake for Harold and catered his party. She called them "fatsos" and ran to her room when they teased her about picking at her cake and ice cream. Both Mrs. Sands and Jean are about twenty pounds overweight, but neither is obese.

April recently had the flu and missed two days of school although her mother sent for her homework assignments. Last week she had a midterm biology exam on which she received a B. This was the first B April has received in high school, so she took it pretty hard. She blames herself for being sick and now believes that her academic status in school is in jeopardy. In addition, she had another fight with her mother who said she had to go to Jean's house to prepare food for a major banquet. April's friend, Linda, had asked her to study at the library, but she declined. April stayed at home with her brother Harold, who remained in his room playing video games.

Around 10 p.m. Harold decided to get a snack in the kitchen and stopped by April's room to see if she wanted a soda. The music was blaring and she did not answer the door. He assumed she was still studying and he did not want to bother her. At 11:30 p.m., well beyond April's bedtime, the music was still going and keeping Harold awake. He yelled at his sister, but there was no response. He pushed open April's bedroom door and found her lying on the bed with a bottle of pills in her hand. She had passed out and could not be roused. Harold ran to the phone and called his mother, who called 911. Mrs. Sands and Jean arrived just before the emergency squad. They were hysterical and tried to revive April to no avail. April had taken more than twenty beta-blockers, which Mrs. Sands takes for hypertension. April had left a scribbled note, which had fallen to the floor. It read simply, "Nobody cares about me so now I won't bother you again." Mrs. Sands cried even harder and blamed herself as the emergency technicians arrived and began to work with April. They struggled but were able to revive her to the point where she opened her eyes a little.

At the emergency room, April was given immediate attention and within an hour or so was able to talk. She told her mother that she had not wanted to be in the way anymore, and that her grades had slipped at school. Mrs. Sands assured her that they would be spending more time together and would make that a priority. The psychiatric social worker, Lucy Hagen, was called in to meet with the family. She had already met with the doctors and had talked briefly with April, who was substantially underweight for her height and body structure. The social worker stated that she believed April was not only clinically depressed but also might have anorexia nervosa and perhaps bulimia. April had admitted that she did not eat much as she was afraid of getting fat and that she sometimes made herself vomit after eating at home. Also, she said that she was angry with her mother for spending too much time with her older sister and felt that her younger brother did not respect her privacy at home. April expressed her disappointment with herself because she did not feel that she was pushing herself enough to do her best in school. The social worker recommended admitting April to the psychiatric unit of the hospital to which her mother agreed. April began to cry and begged to go home, saying she was sorry and would not hurt herself again. She finally agreed to be admitted after the social worker assured her that she would be able to keep up with her schoolwork in the unit.

After admission, April was not allowed to see any family members for several days, although she could talk to them during brief phone calls. April was among eight teenagers on the children's psychiatric unit, most of whom had attempted suicide. Another girl on the unit had been diagnosed with bulimia nervosa but was not as thin as April. In group sessions April discussed her displeasure with her family for not giving her the attention to which she felt she was entitled. Moreover, April complained of her looks, expressed anxiety about school, and shared her desire to be more popular among her peers. At age fifteen, she had dated a boy for six months, but that relationship ended when he moved out of state.

She developed a strong relationship with Dr. Alvin Clifford, the team psychologist, who had done a series of psychometric tests and provided individual counseling, in addition to cofacilitating the adolescent group with Ms. Hagen, the social worker. April began to feel better after the first week and had gradually begun to eat more each day. She met three times a week with the teacher on the unit and was able to keep up with homework assignments. At first there was much tension between her mother and her during visits, but this improved during the second week.

At the end of the second week of psychiatric hospitalization, April was ready for discharge and agreed to continue counseling on an outpatient basis at the hospital clinic. She was enrolled in a treatment group for girls with anorexia and bulimia that would meet once a week. The nutritionist had also met with Mrs. Sands to discuss ways that she could prepare foods in small amounts that might be more appealing to April. Moreover, the family, i.e., April, Mrs. Sands, and Harold, agreed to attend family therapy sessions at a group practice, where Dr. Clifford and Ms. Hagen worked part-time.

After April arrived home and was getting settled into her room, Mrs. Sands began to prepare dinner, and had invited Jean and her family over to welcome April back home. Harold came home from school that Friday and started shooting baskets in the backyard. April called her friend Bonnie and talked about school and some new rap CDs that Bonnie had just bought. After a while, April came down to the kitchen table where her mother was preparing a dinner salad. Everything seemed to be back on an even course until Mrs. Sands opened the refrigerator and showed April that she had stocked up for her return home. She had bought eight two-liter bottles of diet soda for April, and that infuriated her. April started screaming at her mother and called her a "food pusher" and "a hopeless mess." She ran to her room and started crying, but did come back out for dinner that night. She was rather quiet but managed to eat a small amount of salad, baked chicken, and a morsel of chocolate cake, her favorite dessert.

The next family therapy session, Dr. Clifford and Ms. Hagen addressed the incident and talk about the communication problems that persisted between April and Mrs. Sands. The mother agreed to spend more time with April and informed Jean that she needed to be relieved more from the catering service to spend more quality time with April. She also informed April that she would respect her eating habits as long as she would agree to eat nutritiously and try to eat more over time in order to gain back some weight. Harold agreed that he would not take April's CDs without asking and would not invade her privacy when her friend Bonnie comes over for sleepovers. The family seemed to realize how their problems had largely stemmed from a breakdown in communication and their tendency to be focused on their own priorities, neglecting to work together as a single-parent household.

After eight weeks of family counseling, the family seemed to be doing well and April had gained back nine of the fifteen pounds she had lost. April continued to attend the weekly treatment group for teens with eating disorders at the outpatient clinic and once again excelled in all her subjects at school. Mrs. Sands also started taking April shopping every other Saturday and afterward they would attend a movie or matinee play. Mrs. Sands made an effort to compliment April's looks as she began to gain weight and look better in her clothing. Mrs. Sands was pleased with April when she returned the compliment, acknowledging her mother's having lost enough weight to fit into a smaller dress size. April's self-image improved and she and her friend Bonnie joined the soccer team at school. April expressed an interest in trying out for cheerleading again in her senior year.

## CONCLUSION

Counseling children and adolescents from a strengths perspective enables them to realize their assets and build on them. For too many years the helping professions of social work, psychology, child psychiatry, and counseling approached the difficulties experienced by children from a problem-oriented, medically focused framework. Beginning with the strengths of children and emphasizing their right to express their preferences has made a major difference in the way children and adolescents are served in the human services. A guardian *ad litem* may be appointed by the court system to highlight the needs of children, even the potential needs of infants who are facing placement in foster care. Moreover, therapeutic foster care and wraparound child welfare services attempt to address the individual needs of each child and family served and to offer culturally competent programs to encourage children to be proud of family traditions and rituals. Teamwork in child welfare has introduced innovative measures for assessing risk factors that contribute to child abuse and neglect and the perpetuation of violence against children. Likewise, the strengths perspective has been infused into many agency interviewing and assessment tools, which encourages professionals to acknowledge the child and family's resilience and determine ways to enhance their ways of coping. Community-based programs for children who witness violence also provide treatment and recreation programs to help children feel better about themselves and their families.

During the past three decades the family has become the central focus for the empowerment of children through child guidance clinics, early intervention, and home-based family preservation programs. School social workers have been instrumental in developing school-based programs that address diverse social problems, including learning disabilities, teen suicide, violence, eating disorders, conduct disorders, behavior disorders, and other problems faced by children and teens. Mental health agencies have become much more specialized and offer an interdisciplinary approach to evaluating and treating the psychological, emotional, and social problems of children and adolescents. Many more schools have contracted social workers from mental health centers to assess and treat the increasingly complex problems of youth today. Professionals serving children and adolescents must have a solid grasp of child development and be willing to give children some flexibility in addressing their own problems. Children and adolescents have a remarkable ability to express what they do best and how they can enhance their feelings of well-being if only families and professionals are willing to take the time to hear them and to offer them help.

### STRENGTHS STORY: INA ABRAMS

Ina Abrams, a young adult, is a journalist in Chicago, where she coanchors the evening news. Ina believes her current job has fulfilled all of her dreams. She sometimes thought she would never make it this far, but she always says, "Mom never gave up on me." It is that spirit, along with the help of key others, that has gotten Ina through many difficult times.

Ina, an only child, was born to a single Jewish mother, Liz. Ina never knew her father, but when she was a teenager she tried unsuccessfully to locate him. Liz Abrams was never married to Ina's father, and he abandoned Liz when she became pregnant. Liz Abrams always worked as a secretary and struggled to make ends meet for herself and her daughter. They sometimes went to temple on the Sabbath but were not a religious family. When Ina was two and half years old, her mother learned that Ina had a speech disorder. Ina's speech was delayed and she also had a problem with stuttering. Ina was immediately enrolled in speech therapy at her preschool and made remarkable progress.

Until second grade, Ina had a difficult time in school as the other children teased her about her stuttering. The teasing was so embarrassing for her that during the second grade she only occasionally volunteered to answer the teacher's questions. Liz Abrams, however, was unfailing in her support of her daughter. She went to every teacher conference and worked with Ina at home on her articulation to boost her self-esteem. By the beginning of third grade her speech and language scores were within the average range, and she no longer stuttered.

Ina and her mother grew closer as Ina grew and developed into an attractive young woman. The mother and daughter especially loved to go to matinee movies on Saturday, which was their major form of recreation. Liz Abrams dated occasionally but was never serious about any man in particular. She had several male and female friends from work who would come over for dinner and holiday celebrations. They always brought their children along, and Ina laughingly called them her "borrowed" brothers and sisters.

When Ina was fifteen, she met Adam, sixteen, and they began to date. They would go to the roller-skating arena on weeknights and occasionally to a ballgame. They were intimate but had not had sex because Ina said she was waiting for marriage first. Adam liked to bring beer on their dates, but Ina drank only a little. One night, when Liz Abrams had to work late, Adam picked Ina up and took her over to his house for pizza and a pay-per-view rock concert. His parents were at a banquet that evening and would not be home until late. Adam's paternal uncle, Rick, age thirty-one, was attending a conference in Chicago and was staying with the family that week. The three of them were having a great time when Rick went to his room and came back with marijuana. After some coaxing, Ina joined Adam and Rick in smoking and began to get dizzy. Adam fell asleep on the couch, and Ina had to go to the bathroom. She went upstairs and felt sicker as she climbed the steps. She did not realize that Rick was following her. When she came out of the bathroom, he grabbed her. Ina pulled away but could not resist his strength. He pulled her into his room and brutally raped her. She ran downstairs crying, telling Adam that she did not feel well and had to go home. She felt humiliated and did not want him to know what had happened to her. She said the marijuana had made her very ill. Adam's uncle was still upstairs, and Adam informed him that he was taking Ina home.

Ina was at first determined not to tell anyone, even her mother, but she became terrified and knew she must confide in someone. When Liz Abrams entered the apartment, Ina was in her room, pretending to read. However, her mother knew something was wrong and kept questioning her daughter. Ina confessed that she had been raped and gave all the details. Her mother then called the police and rushed Ina to the emergency room to be evaluated. A social worker, Brenda Johns, came to speak with the family before the physical evaluation and was there afterward to console Ina and Liz, assuring Ina that she did the right thing to report the rape. Ina was gasping for breath as she described the incident and started to stutter. Even after returning home, the stuttering continued.

Through several follow-up counseling sessions with Brenda Johns, the stuttering persisted and Ina was devastated. She was out of school for a couple of weeks but upon returning rarely was her talkative self in the classroom. She was referred to a psychologist who specialized in working with persons who have experienced post-traumatic stress disorder. After about ten months of counseling, the stuttering stopped, and Ina regained confidence in herself. She and her mother were closer than ever. Ina graduated cum laude in journalism, and her mother has continued to be her shining star. Ina is engaged to a fellow journalist, and her mother is also dating an accountant from work. Ina and her mother still go to the movies every other Saturday which they laughingly refer to as "our time."

## QUESTIONS FOR DISCUSSION

1. Discuss several techniques that have proven to be effective in interviewing children and adolescents.
2. How may a social work advocate ensure that a child's rights are considered and protected in the courtroom?
3. Discuss some signs that are at-risk indicators for suicide in children and adolescents.
4. How may a school social worker work with other professionals to address the problems of a child and family?
5. Discuss the role of the school social worker or counselor in assessing and developing an intervention plan for a child with conduct disorder or attention deficit-hyperactivity disorder.
6. How may a social worker use a strengths approach in assessing a child with learning disabilities? How may the family be helped to understand the child's special needs?

## REFERENCES

Allen-Meares, P. (1991). The contribution of social workers to schooling. In Constable, R., Flynn, J. P. and McDonald, S. (Eds.), *School social work: Practice and research perspectives,* Second edition (pp. 5-16). Chicago: Lyceum Books.

American Psychiatric Association (1994). *Diagnostic and statistical manual of mental disorders,* Fourth edition. Washington, DC: American Psychiatric Association.

American Psychiatric Association (2000). *Diagnostic and statistical manual of mental disorders,* Fourth edition, Text revision. Washington, DC: American Psychiatric Association.

Anderson, L. E., Weston, E. A., Doueck, H. J., and Krause, D. J. (2002). The child-centered social worker and the sexually abused child: A pathway to healing. *Social Work* 47(4): 368-378.

Artiles, A. J. and Trent, S. C. (1994). Overrepresentation of minority students in special education: A continuing debate. *Journal of Special Education* 27: 410-437.

Backhaus, K. (1984). Life books: Tool for working with children in placement. *Social Work* 29(6): 551-554.

Bourg, W., Broderick, R., Flagor, R., Kelly, D. M., Erwin, L. E., and Butler, J. (1999). *A child interviewer's handbook.* Thousand Oaks, CA: Sage Publications.

Brody, J. E. (1997). Invisible world of the seriously depressed child. *The New York Times,* December 2, p. B15.

Burns, B. J., Costello, E. J., Angold, A., Tweed, D., Stangl, D., Farmer, E. M. Z., and Erkanli, A. (1995). Children's mental health service use across service sectors. *Health Affairs* 14: 147-159.

Cashmore, J. (1992). The use of closed-circuit television for child witnesses in the act. In Briere, J., Berliner, L., Bulkley, J. A., Jenny, C., and Reid, T. (Eds.), *The APSAC handbook on child maltreatment* (p. 310). Thousand Oaks, CA: Sage Publications.

Ceci, S. J. and Bruck, M. (1993). Suggestibility of the child witness: A historical review and synthesis. *Psychological Bulletin* 113(3): 403-439.

Early, T. and Vonk, M. E. (2001). Effectiveness of school social work from a risk and resilience perspective. *Children and Schools* 23(1): 9-32.

Edgar, S. (1996). Advocacy: The evaluation of a high school advisory program. *School Social Work Journal* 20: 28-41.

Fontes, L. A. (2003). Reducing violence in multicultural schools. In Pedersen, P. B. and Carey, J. (Eds.), *Multicultural counseling in schools,* Second edition (pp. 211-233). Boston: Allyn and Bacon.

Franklin, C. and Allen-Meares, P. (1997). School social workers are a critical part of the link. *Social Work in Education* 19: 131-135.

Franklin, C. and Streeter, C. L. (1998). School-linked services as interprofessional collaboration in student education. *Social Work* 43(1): 67-69.

Garbarino, J., Stott, F. M., and Faculty of the Erickson Institute (1989). *What children can tell us: Eliciting, interpreting, and evaluating information from children.* San Francisco: Jossey-Bass.

Hartman, A. (1990). Children in a careless society. *Social Work* 35: 483-484.

Hawkins, J. D., Catalano, R. F., and Miller, J. Y. (1992). Risk and protective factors for alcohol and other drug problems in adolescence and early adulthood: Implication for substance abuse prevention. *Psychological Bulletin* 112: 64-105.

Hepworth, D. H., Rooney, R. H., and Larsen, J. A. (2002). *Direct social work practice: Theory and skills,* Sixth edition. Pacific Grove, CA: Brooks/Cole.

Indiana Education Policy Center (2002). *Preventing school violence: A practical guide to comprehensive planning.* Safe and Responsive Schools Project. Bloomington: IEPC. Available at <www.indiana.edu/~safesch1/psv.pdf>.

Jackson, M. and Helton, L. R. (1997). A new look at traditional social work methods. In DiNitto, D. M. and McNeece, C. A. (Eds.), *Social work: Issues and opportunities in a challenging profession,* Second edition (pp. 68-84). Boston: Allyn and Bacon.

Kashani, J. H. and Orvaschel, H. (1990). A community-based study of anxiety in children and adolescents. *American Journal of Psychiatry* 147: 313-318.

Kirk, W. G. (1993). *Adolescent suicide: A school-based approach to assessment and intervention.* Champaign, IL: Research Press.

Mason, M. A. (1992). Social workers as expert witnesses in child sexual abuse cases. *Social Work* 37: 30-44.

Mayden, R. W. and Nieves, J. (2002). *Social work speaks: National Association of Social Worker policy statements 2000-2003*, Fifth edition. Washington, DC: NASW Press.

Monteleone, J. A., Glaze, S., and Bly, K. M. (1994). Sexual abuse: An overview. In J. A. Monteleone and Brodeur, A. E. (Eds.), *Child maltreatment: A clinical guide and reference* (pp. 113-131). St. Louis: G. W. Medical Publishing.

National Research Council (1993). *Understanding child abuse and neglect.* Washington, DC: National Academy Press.

Peters, K. D., Kochaner, K.D., and Murphy, S. L. (1998). Deaths: Final data for 1996. *National Vital Statistics Report*, 47(9): 1-100.

Petr, C. G. (1998). *Social work practice with children and their families: Pragmatic foundations.* New York: Oxford University Press.

Piaget, J. (1952). *The origins of intelligence in children.* New York: International Universities Press.

Radin, N. (1989). School social work practice: Past, present, and future trends. *Social work in education* 11(2): 213-225.

Rose, S. R. and Fatout, M. F. (2003). *Social work practice with children and adolescents.* Boston: Allyn and Bacon.

Rumberger, R. (1987). High school dropouts: A review of issues and evidence. *Review of Educational Research* 57: 101-121.

Sheafor, B. W. and Horejsi, C. R. (2003). *Techniques and guidelines for social work practice*, Sixth edition. Boston: Allyn and Bacon.

Sheridan, S., Dee, C., Morgan, J., McCormick, M., and Walker, D. (1996). A multimethod intervention for social skills deficits in children with ADHD and their parents. *School Psychology Review* 25(1): 57-76.

Smith, M. K. (1991). Cross-cultural perspectives in education: Valuing differences. In Harris, J. J., Heid, C. A., Carter, D. G. Sr., and Brown, F. (Eds.), *Readings on the state of education in urban America* (pp. 123-132). Bloomington/Indianapolis, IN: Indiana University–Center for Urban and Multicultural Education.

Smith, M. K. (1998). *Adolescents with emotional and behavioral problems.* Lewiston, NY: The Edwin Mellen Press.

Strand, V. C. (1994). Clinical social work and the family court: A new role in child sexual abuse cases. *Child and Adolescent Social Work Journal* 11: 107-122.

Thomas, C. and Corcoran, J. (2003). Family approaches to attention deficit-hyperactivity disorder: A review to guide school social work. *Children and Schools* 25(1): 19-34.

Tomlinson, B. (1997). Risk and protective factors in child maltreatment. In Fraser, M. (Ed.), *Risk and resilience in childhood: An ecological approach* (pp. 50-72). Washington, DC: NASW Press.

Torres, S. Jr. (1996). The status of school social workers in America. *Social Work in Education* 18: 8-18.

Zastrow, C. and Kirst-Ashman, K. (2001). *Understanding human behavior and the social environment*, Fifth edition. Belmont, CA: Brooks/Cole.

# Chapter 9

# Media-Directed, Creative Child Therapies

> It should be noted that children at play are not playing about;
> their games should be seen as their most serious-minded activi-
> ties.
>
> Montaigne

Children may respond to a range of media-directed and creative
child therapies that basically put them in charge of expressing their
feelings and ideas in both verbal and nonverbal ways. These therapies
may be referred to in the professional literature as play therapy, but
each has a distinct purpose and philosophy for helping children use
their strengths and coping abilities to overcome problems. In addition
to traditional play therapy, which may involve single or mixed media,
media-directed, creative child therapies may involve puppet therapy,
bibliotherapy, art therapy, and music therapy. Some therapists use the
overall term *play therapy* to describe various kinds of play that are
used to bring about therapeutic change in children. In a children's services setting, each child may have a preferred medium of play, which
means that a variety of techniques should be offered to accommodate
their needs. Whereas one child may respond to finger painting and
watercolor drawings, another may prefer listening to music or dancing to the rhythms presented in different songs. Board games can even
be used to help children develop social skills, self-discipline, cooperation,
frustration tolerance, and a sense of mastery (Petr, 1998).

## *PLAY THERAPY*

Children are often able to project their feelings onto or through objects of play, whereas talking directly to an adult about traumatic
events or problems could be too emotionally painful (Tyndall-Lind,

Landreth, and Giordano, 2001; Irwin, 2000). Through play, children discover ways to enjoy their interests and talents, express their feelings, and practice growing up (Timberlake and Cutler, 2001). Hutchison (1999) notes that play is an element of development that is universal regardless of culture. Play is what children are all about; one might say it is their "work." Play helps children develop motor skills, learn problem solving and communication skills for cognitive development, and express feelings and acquire the self-confidence essential for emotional growth (Hutchison, 1999). Sometimes even the most unresponsive children will open up to play therapy, as Virginia Axline (1967) reported in her seminal work with a little boy with autism. Media-directed or media-centered approaches to counseling, which have long been popular in hospital wards and child life programs, are now becoming more common in mainstream mental health and child protective agencies.

Children often respond in play therapy because play is such a familiar and comfortable activity for them. Prior to an interview with a child, the counselor should consider the child's developmental age and select play materials that will help the child feel at ease and facilitate communication. Kaduson and Schaefer (2001) note that play therapy not only helps children relax and feel more comfortable with the therapist but also allows them to link their play therapy sessions to their everyday lives, with the shift of focus moving from the therapy room to the children's home and school environments. Before the interview begins, the interviewing area should include art materials, e.g., finger paints, modeling clay, building blocks, as well as objects that can be used to bring up family issues, e.g., dolls, puppets, dollhouses, and stuffed or model animals (Sheafor and Horejsi, 2003). Introducing dolls, paint and paper, puppets, and storybooks allows children to relax and open up and to discuss themes that will lead to sharing of true feelings. Because children are masters at play, they feel at ease in taking charge of play situations and talking about these experiences. Whether a therapist is using anatomically correct dolls to persuade a sexually abused child to talk or asking for a family drawing, he or she can use media-directed therapy to help a child express deep-seated fears and frustrations. Older children may have a keen interest in card or electronic games, which may facilitate their relaxation and opening up to the counselor.

Selecting the appropriate media for play therapy is important to successful outcomes in therapy, and the children's interests, feelings, and viewpoints should always be explored. Carroll (2002) completed a research study involving fourteen children, ages nine through fourteen, to analyze their feelings about their experiences with play therapy. All of the children saw their therapists as engaging and kind, yet some said that the endings of sessions were difficult for them. More than half of the children enjoyed their relationship with the therapist, which they considered an important part of the play therapy process. However, some children did not like to be prompted to express their feelings throughout the process of therapy and felt more comfortable with open-ended questions and dialogue. Many saw the play activities as "just fun" (Carroll, 2002). Most children believed that their problems had been alleviated substantially by the end of therapy.

Children in hospital settings use various forms of play in individualized ways that seem to meet their needs. Whereas some children may respond to puppets or art tools, others will select toys brought from home with which they feel more comfortable or skilled in using. A social worker in a pediatric ward found that children with critical and life-threatening diseases were able to face one hospitalization after another with a strength and resilience not found in many adults. These children seem to make the best of multiple hospitalizations, surgeries, and grueling treatment regimens, even as their medical conditions seemed to worsen. They often resorted to play as a way to cope with the uncertainties of their day-to-day lives.

Sigee Dunlap, age five, was admitted to the hospital often for treatment of cystic fibrosis, yet she almost always had a smile. She lived on a small farm with her father, Mark, and her mother, June, in eastern Kentucky. Her grandparents lived on an adjacent farm. Her older sister, Dorothy, had died of cystic fibrosis one year earlier. Sigee loved to play with her baby doll and take care of her. She would tell her doll that "Mommy will be back soon and everything will be okay." She sometimes would talk about Dorothy and say that she was "living in heaven now."

Sigee loved to come to the social worker's office with her mother and would invariably bring her Velcro dartboard and darts, so she could play a game of darts while her mother talked. She was ecstatic when she would hit the bull's-eye and always looked to her mother for approval. The doctors would often come to get Sigee themselves if there was a procedure to be done, and she would go willingly. One of the interns always carried her on his shoulders, and the whole ward could hear her laughter as she played cowgirl. Then, one day the laughter ended when the disease took Sigee's life.

Children today are so in touch with telecommunications through telephones, televisions, and computers that they may be willing to tell a doll or role-play talking into a cell phone about their problems, or act as if Barney (the purple dinosaur) were telling them how to solve their problem. The approaches that can be used are as diverse as the children who require therapeutic services. Children with ADHD, for example, have responded to puppet therapy and have been able to identify perceptions and feelings they could not bring out in traditional counseling. A therapist may facilitate discussions by asking the child how the puppet feels or how he or she might keep or make friends (Timberlake and Cutler, 2001). Gilliland and James (1997) suggested that play therapy has been found to be helpful in assisting children because it allows the therapist to enter the counseling process at the child's cognitive level and determine the child's coping abilities. Such engagement and development of trust can be much more challenging in a traditional therapy session with a child diagnosed with post-traumatic stress disorder.

## *DRAWING AND ART THERAPY*

Art therapy has been proven effective in working with children having a range of emotional and psychological problems, including grief, adjustment to a parent's remarriage, and trauma brought about by natural disasters (Sontag and Graham, 2001; Cobla and Brazelton, 1994; McDougall Herl, 1992). Children are amazingly gifted at expressing their emotions through pencil or crayon drawings or painting. Putting their feelings on paper seems to enable them more freedom to express themselves in an individualistic way. Counselors and social workers may give a child general instructions to draw a picture of his or her family or may ask the child to paint a picture that tells something special about him or her. Some children will ask specific questions about what the counselor wants in an attempt for further clarification. The counselor or art therapist must choose his or her words carefully so as not to lead the child into producing a particular kind of drawing or painting. The following example highlights the importance of letting a child choose what he or she wants to draw, without any coaching by the counselor, and is derived from play therapy with siblings of children with developmental disabilities.

Tristan, age seven, was experiencing some difficulty with his mother's authority and blamed her for paying too much attention to her older child with profound disabilities, per the mother's report. After some free interaction with the child, wherein he allowed the child to play with various toys in the office and explore the room, the social worker asked Tristan to draw a picture of his family. The boy immediately asked, "Which family do you want me to draw?" The worker responded by saying, "Draw me a picture of your family, any way you would like." The boy continued, "You mean both of them?" The worker answered, "Yes, if you want to draw both families, that would be great."

Tristan sat down and painstakingly drew a picture of two houses with a big figure in one, presumably his father, and a small figure in another house at the opposite corner of the page. Each figure was holding a phone and the phones were connected with large, dark spirals that Tristan had drawn. The boy figure had words in a bubble that said, "But Dad, I cannot help it." When the social worker asked Tristan to discuss the drawing, he said, "That is me there. My dad hates me. He has a new family now and does not want me to call him anymore."

In a follow-up family meeting, the social worker learned that Tristan's father had remarried and had an infant son. He had moved to another city and had become distant from Tristan and his brother. The mother said that Tristan's dad did say that he could not take the children for visitation for a while and was not paying child support, an added complication for the family's communication. This explained Tristan's wanting more attention as he had been rejected by his father and was trying to make up this loss by clinging more to his mother. The drawing exercise revealed information that may not have been revealed totally in family counseling, or it might have taken longer to discover the troubling family dynamics between Tristan and his father.

Not all children like to draw or color with crayons. Some are much more creative in using paints and collage. The counselor may have a box of photographs, representing multiple life situations and images, that may be glued on paper or cardboard by the child. This is another way for a child to express feelings in a less threatening way as he or she will be using images that are already there, without having to produce his or her own. Moreover, some children may feel more comfortable with art therapy if the therapist states that they may explore all the toys and materials and then draw a picture during the next visit. Children love to play games as well and may be more encouraged to draw or paint a picture if the therapist draws a picture as well. This technique may be expanded to family meetings wherein everyone draws a picture, perhaps of an emotion or experience each had during the week.

## *PUPPET THERAPY*

Puppets may be used to help children express their feelings without guilt or anxiety because the puppets do the talking (Timberlake and Cutler, 2001). Puppets may be used by an individual child and counselor to explore emotional reactions, or by a group of children with the counselor as a facilitator. By using puppets, children are able to act out specific scenarios they have experienced or reenact a chain of events that has caused intense pain. Likewise, children may use puppets to anticipate what might happen to them in the future, thereby dealing with future safety and security issues. Children in foster care or children living in a domestic violence shelter with their mother may be able to play with a family of puppets to create a play about what they want to happen when the family is reunited. Puppets can provide an opportunity for children to test reality, express their needs symbolically, and relieve anxiety (Carter, 1987; Machler, 1965).

One of this book's authors, who worked in medical social work, helped establish a play therapy program for children on the general pediatrics hospital ward, as well as for children admitted to the neurosurgery service. Several media were used to engage the children including finger painting, role-plays, and puppets. Puppets became one of the children's favorite methods of play, as they were able to use them to better understand their illnesses and hospital procedures. Puppets representing doctors, nurses, and children were used, with children also being provided with stethoscopes, tongue depressors, and IV lines without needles. The children would often choose to have the doctor puppet explain the type of surgical procedure that was being scheduled or would reassure the child puppet that the surgery would go well and make him or her feel much better. Often, the children would put the puppets aside and take the stethoscope to examine the social worker, social work intern, or recreation therapist involved in the play episode. Children responded to puppet therapy in both a group play setting and on a one-on-one basis. Similar to Doherty and Phillips (2001), the author of this book who worked in hospital settings realized the importance of taking time after the play activity ended to help each child discuss any additional feelings or ask questions related to the play therapy.

## CLOWN THERAPY

A social worker in a mental health center had long been in charge of children's therapy services and had tried many successful ways to reach the children, including field trips, talk groups, story hour, drawing, and music therapy. However, he felt that he needed to introduce something innovative and creative, a type of counseling that would be fun and perhaps benefit a larger range of children. He was a great collector of clown paraphernalia and had been fascinated with clowns and the circus since childhood. So, he created a group work program which he called clown therapy, perhaps somewhat similar to the hospital antics and play techniques of Dr. Patch Adams (1998). He was already providing group sessions for children with attention deficit-hyperactivity disorder, conduct disorder, and learning problems in school. The children who came to his talk group were surprised one Friday when he walked in wearing a clown costume, with full painted face and a bag of tricks. He entertained the children and was able to engage some of the most depressed and hyperactive children to laugh and express themselves openly. He played circus music, provided clown puppets for the children, and invited them to release the "clown within."

In clown therapy, the children used the clown puppets to talk about things they would not have normally shared with an individual or group worker in a traditional counseling program. Even the most emotionally distraught children responded at some level to this play therapy medium, and the therapist gave them small plastic clowns to take home with them. The addition of humor seemed to help them find the words to discuss troubling thoughts and experiences. Unfortunately, when this master's-level social worker retired, this innovative clown therapy program was not continued as the agency thought that a major component of its success lay in the personality and informal style of the therapist who developed it.

Clown therapy has been used in a variety of other hospital and therapeutic settings and has been especially successful in reaching children with life-threatening illnesses such as cancer and heart disease. Carp (1998) notes that the trickster, fool, and clown are archetypal images and states that the clown is "a connection between the conscious and the unconscious," and that clown therapy allows the clown to emerge from the unconscious. She also notes that clown therapy provides the capacity for individuals to internally experience the qualities embodied by the clown and to express in play the spontaneity, lightheartedness, humor, and creativity necessary for healing (Carp, 1998). As a form of play therapy, clown therapy may facilitate children's abilities to open up and express their feelings, even their deepest secrets and most dreaded fears. Child life programs in hospitals across the United States have implemented play therapy programs involving the clown image. Some utilize professional clowns from the circus who are adept at aerobics, juggling, tumbling, balancing, and face painting; others incorporate amateur "clown" nurses, medical students, and recreation specialists to perform the antics that will bring laughter to the faces of seriously ill children and their families. At the Big Apple Clown Care Unit at Babies & Children's Hospital of New York, grants were given out in the pediatric surgery unit to ensure that professional clowns, also known as "doctors of delight," could continue to amuse hard-to-reach children. This program was so successful that it spread to hospitals within the New York metropolitan area and around the world (Big Apple Clown Care Unit, 1996; Dayton, 1997; Sabo and Platzer, 2000). These clown therapy programs are carried out with the true spirit of humor and laughter, perhaps the most potent of all forms of natural medicine.

## *BIBLIOTHERAPY*

Another effective media-directed therapy is bibliotherapy, which simply means therapy with books. As with various forms of play therapy, bibliotherapy uses books to explain some of life's major challenges, as well as common everyday events, in words that children can understand. Petr (1998) states that bibliotherapy is a nonadultcentric way to help children cope with life's problems by communicating with them in their own language. Bibliotherapy books may deal with such traumatic and life-changing events as surgery, disability, adoption, foster care, sexual abuse, or the death of a parent. Based on the child's age, reading level, and particular needs, a social worker or counselor may choose books for a child to read and discuss with an adult. It is a known fact that children have a natural ability to identify with and express themselves through children's books.

In most cases, it is important for the child to make direct, overt connections between the events in the bibliotherapy story and his or her own life. A social worker may encourage a child to discuss "events, themes, and feelings of the characters in the book" (Petr, 1998, p. 159). This indirect approach used in bibiliotherapy allows children to be able to emotionally distance themselves from the actual story being read. Yet in doing so, they gain valuable insight into their own feelings and emotional challenges. Adolescents whose parents have mental illness have benefited from reading and discussing young adult fiction books about children whose parents suffer from mental illness (Tussing and Valentine, 2001).

Bibliotherapy was first used in hospital settings as a way to help hospitalized children prepare for procedures as simple as a tonsillectomy or as serious as neurosurgery. Children in hospitals are already experiencing remarkable stress related to separation from parents and siblings, peers, familiar toys, and activities. Reading about other children who are undergoing similar circumstances helps them be able to allay some of their fears and anticipate a positive outcome from their hospital stay. Some classic bibliotherapy books, such as *Johnny Goes to the Hospital* (Sever, 1961), have been printed as coloring books so that a child can individualize his or her experience with the reading materials. Many hospitals have a teacher assigned by the school district who helps children keep up with their studies and also integrates bibliotherapy materials into the lesson plans. In addition, most large public libraries have bibliotherapy sections and lists of problems and life issues for which these materials are suggested. More and more bookstores also have bibliotherapy sections located within the children's literature area.

Children with severe behavior problems may respond well to bibliotherapy paired with traditional cognitive-behavioral approaches, such as in the treatment of obsessive-compulsive disorders (Tolin, 2001). Still, books may engage children in understanding themselves within the context of peer relationships and help them deal with such issues as low self-esteem, competition on the playground, or how to make and be a good friend. Through bibliotherapy, real-life issues are woven into children's stories, along with powerful emotions and pictures that help the child to become engaged in the problems and solutions to someone else's life challenges. Through allowing the child to discuss the events of the story, either individually or in a group setting, the therapist enables the child to indirectly experience, even in a small way, the reactions and emotions of the characters in the book.

Bibliotherapy has been used effectively to help children cope with a range of psychological, social, and developmental problems (Pardeck 1998; Pardeck and Pardeck, 1998a). Not surprisingly, many children's book authors are utilizing themes such as family togetherness, helping an unfortunate neighbor, or finding an abandoned pet in an effort to help children express their emotions about everyday problems in life. Through these books these children can forget about their own problems and for a short time become totally engrossed in the lives of fictional characters whose lives may be close to their own in many ways. Children's books have for centuries been using similar bibliotherapy themes of helping those in need and proving that good prevails over evil. Take for example the moral that is communicated through *Jack and the Beanstalk* (Opie and Opie, 1974) or *The Three Little Pigs* (Weisner, 2002). Leo Buscaglia (1982) in his classic story *The Fall of Freddie the Leaf: A Story for All Ages* helps children understand that death is natural and an essential component in the cycle of life. In *Aunt Flossie's Hats (and Crab Cakes Later),* Howard (1991) addresses the power of family history and rituals in the African-American family and how two little girls learn to appreciate the joy that their elderly relative brings into their lives.

Pardeck and Pardeck (1998b) have written extensively about how to reach children using bibliotherapy and have many suggestions for helping children understand persons with disabilities. They emphasize helping able-bodied children better understand and appreciate children with a range of special needs. They also provide annotations of books that teachers and other professionals may use to present the concept of disability as a type of cultural diversity. These books are excellent resources for school systems that have implemented programs similar to the southwest Ohio program, Everybody Counts. This program engages children with disabilities, their parents, and their siblings to discuss the problems, as well as the normalcy in their lives. Bibliotherapy books on disability often emphasize the humanity and equal rights of all children, which may help children to cope with and accept diversity in their own lives.


## MUSIC THERAPY


Music therapy can be an effective way of helping children express themselves in nonverbal ways and can also stimulate motor involvement as children begin to identify with and respond to various rhythms. Music therapy has been used effectively with children having autism and other psychological problems that can affect their abilities to communicate and develop interpersonal skills. Barrera, Rykov, and Doyle (2002) found interactive music therapy to be effective in increasing comfort level and overall sense of well-being of children hospitalized with cancer. Whether country-western or rap, many children respond to music, which, just as the medium of play, is a constant presence in their lives. Children are exposed to music on television, in movies, on the radio, and even through computer games and programs. A five-year-old autistic youngster who would not communicate with anyone except his parents, and even then on a small scale, opened up to music.

Mikey was enrolled in a specialized classroom for autistic children located within a diagnostic center for children with developmental disabilities. Both his classroom teachers and parents had been attempting to get Mikey to respond to any stimuli within the school and home setting. He responded only occasionally to his father's attempts to engage him in a video game with bright colors and loud sirens. The teachers routinely tried sand paintings, drawing, modeling clay, and other methods to get Mikey's attention, yet he spent much of his day rocking and banging his head. Then one day a Christmas concert was announced and the children were invited to participate. The concert was being offered by two parents whose children had been clients at the diagnostic center. One mother played the guitar and sang, while the other one played a flute. The children present had various types of developmental disabilities and most were accompanied by their parents, including Mikey. As the festive sounds began to fill the room, the children started to sing along and clap their hands. After a while, Mikey stood up and smiled faintly. Then he started jumping up and down and clapping his hands. He began to hum one of the carols and also rang a small bell that each child had been given. His parents were amazed, as were all present. They realized the power of music to reach this little boy and discovered it was the guitar that actually stimulated his response. The father began to take guitar lessons and played for Mikey regularly at home while his mother sang nursery rhymes. Thus, music continued to be used as a medium for reaching Mikey at home and in the classroom.

## COLLABORATION WITH PARENTS

Collaboration with parents or involved professionals is important so that they may better understand some of the emotions the child has expressed in counseling and also encourage the child to use this media again for self-expression. Parents face the multiple challenges of understanding the impact of problems on their child, learning to address their child's needs more effectively, and renewing their sense of self-fulfillment in parenting and daily life (Timberlake and Cutler, 2001). Parents often do not understand that various forms of media may be used to help their children cope with problems. In cases of post-traumatic stress disorder, children react differently than do adults by expressing their fears through nightmares with themes of monsters, disasters, and helplessness, and they may have intrusive recollections and dissociative flashbacks (APA, 1994). Children may draw or paint pictures of what happened to them, which can be discussed in therapy. Collaboration with the parents becomes crucial; they need to be able to observe and monitor the child's expression of these fears at home.

Media-directed, creative child therapy allows an opportunity for working with parents throughout all stages of therapy. Many settings, such as hospitals and classrooms, have facilities in which the parents may observe their children in play therapy sessions, or the parent and therapist may jointly observe the child in individual play scenarios. A hospital social worker may collaborate with child life personnel or recreation therapy staff to offer concurrent parent groups while their children are involved in play therapy sessions. It is extremely important for the counselor to able to explain to the parent or involved family members the themes that the child is bringing out in the play therapy sessions, whether these are anger, sadness, extreme anxiety, fear, or remorse. Timberlake and Cutler (2001) consider parenthood a reciprocal parent-child relationship and describe this bond as follows:

> [W]hen parents feed, guide, or play with their child, they integrate their mental representations of this actual child with their mental representations of their inner child of the past, the wished for ideal child, and the child of their future hopes and dreams. (p. 111)

Dealing with these issues in counseling may help the parent to better understand the depth and breadth of the child's painful experiences in light of their own problems and challenges as a parent. Many parents who seek help for their children may be overwhelmed with their own problems and may have difficulty differentiating their own problems from those of their child (Timberlake and Cutler, 2001). By working with the parents concurrently, the counselor is able to obtain and assess the parents perceptions and concerns as well as receive valuable feedback about how the child is responding at home or in their presence or when with other family members or peers.

## CONCLUSION

Children have active imaginations that are unrivaled during any other stage of life. This innate ability enables them to be creative and to address problems from a natural perspective that can be successful in allowing them to share thoughts and emotions. Children have a natural resilience for being able to cope with problems that some adults would not even attempt to resolve. The use of media-directed therapies and counseling approaches give children fuller opportunities for utilizing the skills that come naturally to them. They are much more likely to respond to play materials such as toys, dolls, and paints than to a more sterile, adult-centered approach of questions and answers in counseling. Whether a child is talking through the mouth of a puppet or identifying his or her feelings with those of the character in a bibliotherapy book, he or she is more likely to be responsive to a media-directed approach to counseling. Professionals must be open to learning about and utilizing various media-directed approaches to intervention to accommodate the diverse and creative interests of each child they serve.

## STRENGTHS STORY: HELEN McGUIRE

Helen McGuire, the only child of Richard and Lori McGuire, was a joy to her parents who had her relatively late in their lives (Richard at forty and Lori at thirty-nine). Richard and Lori were both elementary school teachers, and they took advantage of summer vacation and other semester breaks to take their daughter to Disney World, national parks, and other historic places. Helen learned her alphabet and numbers at age four. Her parents thought she might be a genius. But when Helen was ten years old, Lori noticed that her daughter spent a great deal of time alone, looking sad on the swing hanging from a tall oak in the backyard. One evening, Helen's teacher called Lori to tell her that Helen was not doing well in class. She said she spent most of her time staring out the window. Lori and the teacher agreed that Helen should be referred to the school psychologist for counseling. The school psychologist informed Lori that Helen should be sent to child psychiatry clinic because Helen had told her in counseling that she did not deserve to live. Helen was diagnosed with bipolar disorder. Because of her emotional instability, despite the prescribed medication, Helen trailed behind in her schoolwork.

Helen continued her visits for outpatient services at the clinic. A social worker at the clinic, Ms. Jones, noticed that Helen's eyes would brighten up when the children were told to draw what they thought. She used bright and unusual colors to tell the stories she created in her mind. Ms. Jones called her uncle, who was an Oriental art curator at the art museum in the city, and asked him what she might do to help Helen enter the world of art. He suggested the art classes that the museum sponsored every Sunday afternoon. Children had to be accompanied by an adult for those classes. When Ms. Jones spoke about the art class to Helen's mother, Lori told Ms. Jones she would be tied up with activities at her church. Lori was spending more and more time at church outside her teaching assignments. Ms. Jones asked if she could take Helen to the museum instead. Lori replied, "Well, it is better than her sitting in the house alone, waiting for us to come home for supper." Ms. Jones picked Helen up every Sunday afternoon for art class. After the class they stopped at an ice cream parlor to talk. Helen shared with Ms. Jones her inner thoughts, which were not happy. By then end of the sixth month of their commute to art class, one art teacher form the School of Fine Arts, part of the school district, insisted that Helen attend his school. Although Helen's mother, Lori, was not really excited about her daughter attending a school where boys were involved in dance class and where girls had their noses pierced, Helen's father thought it was a good idea.

Helen thrived in the high school and had many friends, both girls and boys. She developed a close friendship with Pearl, a fellow art student, and they always spent Saturday afternoons together at the movies or the art museum. Helen also dated one boy seriously for a while in her sophomore year of high school, but his family moved to New York at the end of the year. They continued to keep in touch and she even visited him and his family in New York during her junior year. Helen dated off and on throughout the remainder of high school, but her first love was her art. Helen continued to expand her interest in art techniques, experimenting with collage and heavy acrylics to provide more texture to her work. Her love for artistic expression also provided an outlet for her emotions, and she remained motivated to stay healthy and take her medications.

Helen continued to see Ms. Jones at the clinic every week and told her how exciting it was to be at the School of Fine Arts. Helen won first prize for her senior project that included unusually bright abstract paintings. The Institute of Art, located next door to the art museum, admitted Helen on a full scholarship. Although Helen had to take time off now and then for her psychiatric problems, she managed to complete her required courses. When Helen won another prize for her painting, she asked Ms. Jones to keep it in her office. After the award ceremony, Helen and Ms. Jones went to their favorite ice cream parlor to talk more about her college experiences and her future dreams.

## QUESTIONS FOR DISCUSSION

1. Discuss several types of media-directed therapies and how they may benefit children of different ages.
2. How can a social worker or counselor approach a child by using puppets or a family of dolls?
3. What is bibliotherapy and why is it appropriate as a counseling tool for children of all ages?
4. Discuss the role of the parents in play therapy.
5. How can play therapy help children to overcome traumatic events and foster a sense of well-being?

## REFERENCES

Adams, P. (1998). *House calls: How we can all heal the world with one visit at a time.* San Francisco: Robert D. Reed Publishers.

American Psychiatric Association (1994). *Diagnostic and statistical manual of mental disorders,* Fourth edition. Washington, DC: American Psychiatric Association.

Axline, V. M. (1967). *Dibs: In search of self.* New York: Ballantine Books.

Barrera, M. E., Rykov, M. H., and Doyle, S. L. (2002). The effects of interactive music therapy on hospitalized children with cancer: A pilot study. *Psycho-Oncology* 11: 379-388.

Big Apple Circus Clown Care Unit (1996). *The Reporter* 7(1): 1-2.

Buscaglia, L. (1982). *The fall of Freddie the leaf.* Thorofare, NJ: Slack Incorporated.

Carp, C. E. (1998). Clown therapy: The creation of a clown character as a treatment intervention. *The Arts in Psychotherapy* 25(4): 245-255.

Carroll, J. (2002). Play therapy: The children's views. *Child and Family Social Work* 4: 177-187.

Carter, S. (1987). Use of puppets to treat traumatic grief: A case study. *Elementary School Guidance and Counseling* 21: 210-245.

Cobla, D. C. and Brazelton, E. W. (1994). The application of family drawing tests with children in remarriage families. *Elementary School Guidance and Counseling* 29(2): 129-136.

Dayton, L. (1997). Clowns on call bring hugs and happiness. *Michigan Health and Hospitals* (9): 3.

Doherty, J. M. and Phillips, R. D. (2001). Reading on the "porch swing." In Kaduson, H. G. and Schaefer, C. E. (Eds.), *101 more favorite play therapy techniques* (pp. 41-45). Northvale, NJ: Jason Aronson, Inc.

Gilliland, B. E. and James, R. K. (1997). *Crisis intervention strategies,* Third edition. Pacific Grove, CA: Brooks/Cole Publishing Co.

Howard, E. F. (1991). *Aunt Flossie's hats (and crab cakes later).* New York: Clarion Books.

Hutchison, E. D. (1999). *Dimensions of human behavior: The changing life course.* Thousand Oaks, CA: Pine Forge Press.

Irwin, E. C. (2000). The use of a puppet interview to understand children. In Gitlin-Weiner, K. and Sandgrund, A. (Eds.), *Play diagnosis and assessment,* Second edition (pp. 682-703). New York: John Wiley and Sons.

Kaduson, H. G. and Schaefer, C. E. (Eds.). (2002). *101 more favorite play therapy techniques* (pp. 412-416). Northvale, NJ: Jason Aronson, Inc.

Machler, T. (1965). Pinocchio in the treatment of school phobia. *Bulletin of the Menninger Clinic* 29: 212-219.

McDougall Herl, T. K. (1992). Finding light at the end of the funnel: Working with child survivors of the Andover tornado. *Art Therapy Journal* 9(1): 42-47.

Opie, J. and Opie, P. (1974) *The classic fairy tales.* Oxford, UK: Oxford University Press.

Pardeck, J. T. (1998). *Using books in clinical social work practice: A guide to bibliotherapy.* Binghamton, NY: The Haworth Press.

Pardeck, J. T. and Pardeck, J. A. (1998a). *Children in foster care and adoption: A guide to bibliotherapy.* Westport, CT: Greenwood Press.

Pardeck, J. T. and Pardeck, J. A. (1998b). An exploration of the uses of children's books as an approach for enhancing cultural diversity. *Early Child Development and Care* 147: 25-31.

Petr, P. G. (1998). *Social work with children and their families: Pragmatic foundations.* New York: Oxford University Press.

Sabo, G. and Platzer, K. (2000). "Laughter therapy with Dr. Troot!, please": Professional hospital-clowns brighten everyday life for hospitalized children. *Kinderkrankenschwester* 19(9): 55-9.

Sever, J. A. (1961). *Johnny goes to the hospital.* Boston: Houghton.

Sheafor, B. W. and Horejsi, C. R. (2003). *Techniques and guidelines for social work practice,* Sixth edition. Boston: Allyn and Bacon.

Sontag, M. A. and Graham, M. (2001). Art as an evaluative tool: A pilot study. *Art Therapy: Journal of the American Art Therapy Association* 18(1): 37-43.

Timberlake, E. M. and Cutler, M. M. (2001). *Developmental play therapy in clinical social work.* Boston: Allyn and Bacon.

Tolin, D. F. (2001). Case study: Bibliotherapy and extinction treatment of obsessive-compulsive disorder in a 5-year-old boy. *Journal of American Academy of Child and Adolescent Psychiatry* 40(9): 1111-1114.

Tussing, H. L. and Valentine, D. P. (2001). Helping adolescents cope with the mental illness of a parent through bibliotherapy. *Child and Adolescent Social Work Journal* 18(6): 455-469.

Tyndall-Lind, A., Landreth, G. L., and Giordano, M. A. (2001). Intensive group play therapy with child witnesses of domestic violence. *International Journal of Play Therapy* 10(1): 53-83.

Weisner, D. (2002). *The three little pigs.* Boston: Clarion.

Chapter 10

# Evidence-Based Practice and Research for Promoting Children's Strengths

Each of us has a spark of life inside us, and our highest endeavor ought to be to set off that spark in one another.

Kenny Ausubel

## *INTRODUCTION*

Understanding the definite relationship between protective factors and resilience of children, many professionals have developed and evaluated various programs. Those programs have been implemented because they are consistent with theories and research on strength building among children who are surrounded by risk factors in their environment, including poverty, neglect and abuse, and drug addiction among family members. Evaluations of those programs concluded that they are indeed effective in increasing children's social competency and educational performance. All programs listed here involve active participation of parents or other family members.

The premise is that a child's strengths are mostly fostered within the family environment. The child then enhances strengths or resilience throughout his or her life while interacting with peers and the larger community. To design prevention programs that are resilience based for children and their families, practitioners as well as researchers working with children must pay attention to programs that have proven to increase protective mechanisms. Masten (1996) developed basic guidelines for resilience-based programs, including the following:

1. The program should assess strengths and assets as well as deficits and problems.
2. The program's intended outcomes and methods to produce them should be explicit.
3. The program should be designed to integrate protective factors as well as reduce risk factors in the complex world children live in with family, peers, schools and communities.
4. The program should be multifaceted, targeting multiple risks, assets, and protective systems.
5. There is no single or combined strategy that is best for all situations or all children.
6. The program should include evaluation components which contribute to science and collective wisdom.

Bernard (1996) stated that resiliency research has shown that fostering resilience is a process and not a program, and that we must consider not just content but also process. For that reason, evaluation of resilience-based programs must include both outcome and process evaluations. We learn *what* is achieved from the outcome evaluation and *how* it is achieved from the process evaluation.

## RESILIENCE-BASED PROGRAMS

This section discusses nine programs that have proven effective in increasing children's resilience in different settings. Much of the following information is taken from Masten's (1998) paper on research-based programs.

### Health Realization or Psychology of Mind (POM)

Health realization programs are based on resiliency or the strength-based paradigm known as psychology of mind (POM). Roger Mills, a community psychologist, and his colleagues initiated the program, realizing that existing paradigms were inadequate for addressing the multitude of personal and social issues surrounding their clients. POM assumes the following premises: (1) thought is the source of human experience; (2) all people have the same innate capacity for healthy psychological functioning; and (3) people engage in two modes of thought—one related to memory and the other to healthy, commonsense intelligence. Contrary to cognitive therapy in which problems are seen as the result of irrational beliefs, POM focuses on the process of thought. Pransky and colleagues (1997) show that in POM the source of problems in clients is their failure to see what thought is. Therefore, the program focuses on how we think: teaching clients to recognize the role of thought and how that thought creates reality. The POM approach sees all people as doing the best they can and promotes listening to clients with compassion and without blame.

Mills applied the health realization model in his work with residents of housing projects in urban areas such as Miami, the South Bronx, Minneapolis, and Oakland and produced astonishingly positive results (Mills, 1997a,b). For example, the health realization program serving 150 families and 650 youth in two housing projects in Miami showed striking improvements in several risk factors. Within three years: the number of households selling or using drugs decreased from 65 to 20 percent; school dropout rates declined from 60 to 10 percent; school absenteeism or truancy decreased from 65 percent to almost none; and the parental unemployment rate went down from 85 to 35 percent. Similarly, the health realization program was implemented in another 200-unit public housing project that had the highest rates of homicide and drug-related arrests in Oakland, California. It produced impressive improvements in risk factors: homicides dropped by 100 percent; assault with firearms was reduced by 38 percent; and youth attendance in boys and girls clubs increased by 110 percent. At the end of the program, 80 percent of the residents participated in regular meetings with housing management and community police, and sixty-two families had members gainfully employed.

## *Programs for Families*

Previous chapters have shown that the strengths of families directly influences the strengths of children. For that reason, many programs target families, including parents and children. There are hundreds of such programs, and some of them are theoretically solid and well researched. Kumpfer and Adler (1998) lists a number of principles to keep in mind when reviewing and selecting family programs, including the following:

1. Comprehensive interventions are more effective.
2. Family-focused programs are more effective than child-focused only or parent-focused only.

3. Sufficient dosage or intensity is critical.
4. Tailoring the parent or family intervention to the cultural traditions of the families improves its effectiveness.
5. The program should address both developmentally appropriate risk and protective factors.
6. Family programs targeting changes in the ongoing family dynamics and environment have the most enduring effects.
7. Parent and family programs should include components addressing improvement in family relations, communication, and parental monitoring.
8. Transportation, meals or snacks, and child care are critical in maximizing recruitment and retention rates.

Among exemplary programs targeting families are the Strengthening Families Program, Families and Schools Together (FAST), and the Nurturing Parenting Program. Those programs have been replicated for families from different cultural backgrounds and empirically proven to be effective.

*Strengthening Families Program*

The Strengthening Families Program (SFP) was developed by Karol Kumpfer and associates at the University of Utah in 1983 as a four-year prevention research project funded by the National Institute on Drug Abuse (NIDA). The program was originally designed as a drug abuse prevention program for high-risk abusing parents to help them improve their parenting skills and help their children avoid drug use. The program curriculum is based on modified versions of the TEACH model (Jenson, 1980), Social Skills Training Program (Spivak and Shure, 1979), *Helping the Noncompliant Child* (Forehand and McMahon, 1981), and the Family Relationship Enhancement Program (Guerney Jr., 1977). The SFP is a fourteen session family skills training program designed to increase resilience and reduce risk factors for substance abuse, depression, violence and aggression, delinquency, and school failure in high-risk six- to twelve-year-old children and their parents (Alvarado et al., 2000).

The original program model was the values-attitudes-stressors-coping skills and resources model (VASC) of drug abuse (Kumpfer and DeMarsh, 1985). More recently, the resiliency model (Richardson et al., 1990) was applied to test social ecology model of adolescent substance abuse (Kumpfer and Turner, 1990/1991). This model suggests that a positive family climate significantly affects self-esteem and school bonding. Findings of these studies suggest that the three most powerful protective factors in keeping youth from becoming drug involved are (1) a warm and loving parent-child relationship; (2) family or parental supervision, monitoring, and discipline; and (3) prosocial family norms, including drug nonuse behavior and high expectations for drug nonuse. Ultimately, program participants are expected to display increased positive attention toward the child, an improved parent-child relationship, and strong attachment to the child on the part of parents. The program should also lead to increased peer resistance skills, improved academic performance, reduction in problem behaviors, and increased prosocial skills on the part of children. These outcomes should improve family communication and decrease family conflict and social isolation.

SFP has been tested, evaluated, and replicated in a variety of settings. For example, the SFP implemented in Selma, Alabama, yielded results showing significant reductions in family conflict in high drug use families and increased organization in low drug use families (Kumpfer, 1990). By the end of the program, the children of high drug use mothers were rated as significantly improved in internalized and externalized behavior. Another example of the program's use is the Denver Area Youth Services (DAYS). In this Strengthening La Familia Program, the SFP program was modified for greater effectiveness with Hispanic families. A pretest and posttest completed by 311 participants and six-month and one-year follow-ups showed that families improved in family communication and organization as measured by the Moos Family Environment Scale (Moos, 1994). In addition, children completing the SFP saw themselves as significantly improving their adjustment in the areas of family, self, parents, school, and community. SFP was also implemented with consistently positive outcomes for inner-city African-American families in Detroit (Atkan, 1995), for Asian/Pacific Islanders in Hawaii (Kameoke, 1996), and for rural families in Iowa (Molgaard, Kumpfer, and Spoth, 1994). An estimated cost for one cohort, including dinner, child care, incentives, manuals, supplies, and staff time, is approximately $600 per family. For more information, one can contact Connie Tait, PhD, or Karol Kumpfer, PhD, of the University of Utah, Department of Health Promotion and Education, Salt Lake City, UT 84112-0920.

*Families and Schools Together (FAST)*

Families and Schools Together (FAST) was developed in 1988 at a family service agency in Madison, Wisconsin. Lynn McDonald envisioned collaborating with the schools and asking teachers to identify children with problem behaviors and to intervene earlier than when adolescents were ordered to in-home counseling for their problem behaviors. The United Way of Dane County and the state of Wisconsin first funded FAST as a new approach to reaching at-risk youth. In 1990, the U.S. Office of Substance Abuse Prevention (OSAP) awarded FAST national recognition. In the same year, the Wisconsin state legislature passed the Anti-Drug Bill (WI AB 122), which included $1 million a year to disseminate FAST statewide. FAST has been replicated in 110 Wisconsin school districts, 480 schools total in thirty-four states, and five countries.

FAST has three parts: outreach, engagement, and ongoing multifamily group meetings run by the parents. Desired outcomes are stronger families, indicated by increased family cohesiveness, increased expressed emotions, and decreased conflict. Participation in FAST must be voluntary, and it should be offered at transition points in schooling, including entrance to preschool, kindergarten, middle school, and high school. The program is recommended for disengaged, noninvolved families because an average of 80 percent eventually complete the eight-to-ten-week program if a family attends one FAST session.

Evaluations of FAST implemented in various locations for diverse populations have shown positive outcomes. Using standardized mental health instruments, classroom behaviors and at-home behaviors improved after eight to ten weeks. Participants have also shown increased family closeness and communication and reduced family conflict. After six months these gains were maintained, with parents increasing their involvement in school and self-sufficiency. In addition, FAST improved student behavior (Alvarado et al., 2000). The program's unit cost is about $1,200, including child care, family meals, transportation, and the lottery baskets. More information is available from Lynn McDonald, PhD, FAST program founder, Wisconsin Center for Education Research, University of Wisconsin-Madison, 1025 W. Johnson, Madison, WI 53706.

*Nurturing Parenting Program*

In 1979, Stephen Bavolek, PhD, then of the University of Wisconsin–Eau Clair, sought to create an effective intervention to break the cycle of child abuse and neglect by building nurturing parenting skills. The Nurturing Parenting Program was born. This program is developed to reverse the following continued trends that threaten children's well-being:

1. Reported cases of child abuse and neglect have been on a steady incline in recent decades.
2. Annually 1,095 children or three children daily die from abuse or neglect.
3. Substantial empirical data exist to support the relationship between abuse of children and alcohol use and abuse among the children in later years, delinquent behavior in adolescence, and criminal behavior in adulthood.
4. Parenting and child-rearing attitudes of abusive and neglecting families were significantly more abusive than families not identified as abusive (Bavolek, Kline, and McLaughlin, 1979).

The theoretical assumption of the Nurturing Parenting Program is that parenting is learned behavior; that is, the way parents raise their children is directly influenced by the way they were raised. Therefore, if parents learn new ways of raising their own children that are different from what they experienced, they will break the cycle of negative parenting behaviors.

Parenting behavior is measured by the Adult-Adolescent Parenting Inventory (AAPI) which measures five constructs, including inappropriate parental expectations, the inability of the parents to be empathically aware of their children's needs and emotions, a strong belief in the use of corporal punishment, reversing parent-child family roles, and oppressing children's power and independence (Bavolek and Keene, 1999). The major focus of the nurturing programs is to build empathy among all family members. Parents learn experientially to challenge existing thoughts and feelings. Learning takes place on both cognitive and affective levels through activities engaging parents and children. Developing a positive self-worth is a necessary component of nurturing parenting behavior. Thus, the intermediate objectives of the program include the following:

1. To develop positive self-concept and self-esteem in all family members
2. To build an empathic awareness of the needs of oneself and of others
3. To increase awareness of self-needs, strengths, and weaknesses
4. To increase awareness of the developmental needs of other family members
5. To promote healthy physical and emotional development of self and others
6. To learn to have fun as a family

The nurturing programs have been adapted for different cultural groups, including Hmong, Hispanic, African-American families, and families in substance abuse treatment and recovery.

The initial Nurturing Parenting Program for Parents and Children ages four to twelve years funded by the National Institute of Mental Health included 121 abusive adults and 150 abused children. Of these 121 adults, ninety-five (79 percent) completed the program. Trainers rated eighty-eight (93 percent) of the adults completing the program as having successfully modified their parent-child interactions toward nurturing practices. In addition, pretest and posttest data on the AAPI indicated that significant positive changes occurred in the parenting and child-rearing attitudes of the parents. The one-year follow-up data showed that parents retained empathic attitudes toward children's needs and appropriate parent-child roles (Bavolek, 2000).

Program costs of the Nurturing Parenting Program include the following expenses: a complete program, including manuals, videos, instructional aids, and assessment inventories ($875 to $1,800); staff time; materials (approximately $300), including paper, crayons, etc.; snacks ($20 to $40) per session; and transportation expenses. More information is available from the Family Development Resources, Inc., 3160 Pinebrook Road, Park City, UT 84098.

### Family Therapy Programs

There are several behavioral family therapy programs, including structural family therapy (Szapocznik et al., 1988, 1989), functional family therapy (Alexander and Parson, 1982), parenting adolescents wisely, an interactive computer program (Gordon et al., 1998), and family therapy (Liddle, 1995).

*Functional Family Therapy*

Functional family therapy (FFT) is an empirically grounded, family-based intervention program for acting-out youth. The goal of FFT is to improve family communication and supportiveness and decrease the intense negativity. Other goals include helping family members adopt positive solutions to family problems, and developing positive behavior and parenting strategies. FFT focuses on youth between the ages of eleven and eighteen from diverse ethnic and cultural groups (Saxton and Alexander, 2000). FFT is a short-term intervention extending eight to twelve sessions. Difficult cases may require up to thirty hours of clinical sessions, telephone calls, and meetings involving community resources.

Data from studies of FFT suggest that FFT reduces recidivism and the onset of offending 25 to 60 percent more effectively than other programs (Alexander et al., 2000). FFT also significantly reduces potential offending of siblings of treated adolescents (Klein, Alexander, and Parson, 1977). Implementation costs for FFT are estimated as $2,000 per family. More information on the program is available from James. F. Alexander, PhD, 1329 Behavioral Science, University of Utah, Salt City, UT 84112 (Alvarado et al., 2000).

**Early Childhood Programs**

In addition to programs for families, early childhood programs focusing on parent-child attachment and preacademic and social skill development of children can help children's resiliency. Karoly et al. (1998) found that fostering mother-infant attachment and developing children's social skills increase the children's success in elementary and high school. Again, all successful programs involve extensive parental involvement. For example, in a project with low-income, unmarried, white women in the semirural community of Elmira, New York, families received an average of nine home visits during pregnancy and twenty-three visits from the child's birth through the second birthday. Nurses helped women in three aspects of maternal functioning: health-related behaviors during pregnancy and the early years of motherhood; care for their children; and maternal, personal life-course development. The young mothers learned how to give effective physical and emotional care to their children and how to meet challenges of education, work, and family planning. As compared to the control group, women in the project produced the following positive outcomes: reduced smoking, improved diet, fewer kidney infections, increased social support, increased use of formal services, 75 percent reduction in preterm deliveries, and increased birth weights (Hill, 1998). A fifteen-year follow-up of the participants showed a significant impact on adolescent behaviors, including lower cigarette and alcohol use, lower runaway rates, and lower arrests and convictions (Hill, 1998).

*Dare to Be You*

Dare to Be You (DTBY) is another early childhood program that increases resilience among children. DTBY has focused on children ages five to eighteen, their parents, and community professionals. The program was developed by Jan Miller-Heyl at Colorado State University. The program's "core assumption is that improved perceptions of parental self-efficacy result in family system interactions that foster resiliency in youth, in part because a strong sense of parental competence promotes consistent and supportive child-rearing practices" (Miller-Heyl, MacPhee, and Fritz, 1998, p. 258). Miller-Heyl, MacPhee, and Fritz (1998) found that "preadolescents increased significantly in resiliency factors such as internal locus of control, resistance to peer pressure, and decision making skills" (p. 259). The researchers agreed with other scholars that early family intervention is essential to prevent problems (Smith, 1998; Carpenter, 1997; Reynolds, 1998; Berlin et al., 1998; Block and Block, 2002), and that prevention programs are most effective when they work with multiple contexts, e.g., child, parents, and community (Bronfenbrenner, 1992; Kumpfer, 1999).

The program was tested in different types of sites (urban, town, and rural) with different ethnic compositions. Families were randomly assigned to an experimental (N = 496) and control (N = 301) group. Experimental families received a minimum of twenty-four hours of training with follow-up support. Major findings included the following:

1. Families who received interventions increased in self-efficacy and self-esteem, which were sustained through the two-year follow-up.
2. In the intervention families, harsh punishment decreased, and effective discipline and limit setting increased through the follow-up.
3. Parents in the intervention group increased on scores in parenting ability and decreased their tendency to blame their children, enhancing children's developmental levels and decreasing oppositional behavior.
4. Parents' social networks did not change significantly, suggesting that structural changes occur slowly.
5. Parents in both groups reported an increased level of stress over time, slowing their efforts for additional education and income (Miller-Heyl, MacPhee, and Fritz, 1998).

The program costs include trainer ($3,000 plus travel and per diem) and $150 to $200 for complete sets of protocol manuals for program and evaluation replication. For more information, contact Jan Miller-Heyl, MS, Dare to Be You Program (DTBY), Colorado State University, Cooperative Extension, Fort Collins, CO 81321.

## Programs for Preschoolers: Ages Four and Five

### High/Scope Educational Research Foundation's Perry Preschool Project

The High/Scope Educational Research Foundation's Perry Preschool Project is one of the programs proven to be effective for preschoolers. A longitudinal study of children from African-American families with lower socioeconomic status and who attended a preschool program focused on cognitive, language, social, and behavioral development. The program emphasized child-centered active learning in problem solving, decision making, and planning, as well as interactions among children and adults. Teachers visited parents weekly and encouraged them to be involved in the classroom (Berruta-

Clement et al., 1984). Children who participated in the program showed superior outcomes at age nineteen compared to a control group, including higher cognitive gains, higher scholastic achievement, lower delinquency, lower rates of teen pregnancy, higher rates of college entrance, and better high school graduation rate. Cost-benefit analysis of the program showed that benefits of participating in the program were sevenfold. Participants also made more successful transitions to adulthood, engaging in fewer crimes, earning higher wages, and indicating a greater commitment to marriage (Schweinhart and Weikart, 1986, 1997). Barnett and Escobar (1990) reported that the Perry Preschool Project has reduced the cost of delinquency and crime by approximately $2,400 per child.

## Programs for Kindergarten or Elementary School Children

### Be a Star

The Be a Star program was initially implemented in 1992 in St. Louis, Missouri, building on the existing infrastructure of the United Church Neighborhood Houses' community-based after-school program which provided various activities for young children in areas afflicted with gang activities and child abuse and neglect. Research was conducted on this program for five- to twelve-year-old children, the majority of whom were African American. There were 386 children in seventeen treatment groups and 397 children in twenty-one comparison groups. The groups met once a week for ninety minutes from September through May while school was in session. The treatment groups were provided with a special curriculum, focusing on decision-making skills, interpersonal competence, cultural awareness, self-esteem, and avoidance of alcohol and drug use. Their parents participated in support groups. The comparison groups received more traditional programs centering on holidays and games. The centers worked closely with community residents to create a safe environment for the children.

The results for the 1994-1995 project year yielded significant differences between the intervention and comparison groups: Children ages eight to twelve in the intervention groups showed significantly higher scores on family bonding, prosocial behavior, self-concept, self-control, decision making, emotional awareness, assertiveness, confidence, cooperation, negative attitudes about drugs and alcohol, self-efficacy, African-American culture, and school bonding (Pierce and Shields, 1998). These positive traits lasted long enough to create changes in the community (Garmezy, 1985).

## Programs for Middle and High Schoolers

Masten (1998) listed four research-based programs for middle and high school students: Learn and Service America; Say It Straight; Big Brothers/Big Sisters of America; and Adventure Education and Outward Bound.

### Big Brothers/Big Sisters of America

The Big Brothers/Big Sisters of America (BB/BS) is the oldest and most carefully structured mentoring program in the United States. Among 400 matches, more than 70 percent met three times a month for an average of three to four hours per meeting. A three-year evaluation of BB/BS presented encouraging evidence that caring relationships between adults and youth can be created and supported by programs (Public/Private Venture, 1995). The same study found that compared to the controls, these children were 70 percent less likely to initiate drug use and 33 percent less likely to hit someone, skipped fewer classes and half as many days of school, felt more competent about doing schoolwork, showed modest gains in their grade point averages, and improved their relationships with both their parents and their peers. These findings were particularly noteworthy as the participating youths were considered high risk. For example, "90 percent lived with one parent, more than 40 percent received either food stamps or cash public assistance, and nearly 30 percent came from families with a record of domestic violence" (Masten, 1998, p. 65). Successful volunteers made these meetings enjoyable and fun for both partners, listened to the young person nonjudgmentally, and looked for the youth's interests and strengths. In contrast, unsuccessful volunteers were reluctant to adjust their expectations of the youth, instead trying to "fix" kids whom they considered somewhat deficient. In such matches, both volunteers and youths found their experience frustrating and nonsupportive (Masten, 1998).

## CONCLUSION

As Masten (1998) states, resilience researchers need to come to a consensus about the definition of resilience operationally and about how we study the resilience process. To design and implement effective interventions, we need to know what causes desired outcomes. For optimal effectiveness, practitioners should replicate evidence-based practice with proven outcomes with adaptations to local needs. Researchers need to continue controlled study of programs to examine their efficacy in enhancing the strengths of families and children. Such programs tend to cost more, dissuading policymakers from investing up front to save money in the long run. One word of caution for practitioners and researchers is that programs lacking cultural competency would be a waste of resources, even if the program replicates an evidence-based practice. A true replication includes adaptations of the program on all levels so that the program is compatible with a community's culture.

### STRENGTHS STORY: CHARLES ELLIOTT MAPLES

Charles, an African American, was born in a small West Virginia town to Sally Faye Maples, a sixteen-year-old unmarried girl. Charles' father, Glenn Lee Jackson, was twenty-four and a coal miner at the time of Charles' birth. Glenn Lee took an interest in his son and brought Sally Faye and the baby to live with him and his parents, Johnnie Ray and Alice Marie Jackson. Glenn Lee had three younger siblings who still lived at home and two older brothers who had moved to Detroit to work in automotive factories.

Charles' mother and father never married, and when Charles was a toddler his father was killed in a mine cave-in. He always asks his mother about that day as he believes that his father might have been saved if only the mine had had better safety precautions. Charles and his mother continued to live with the Jacksons although finances were tight. Cooper Ray Jackson, Charles' grandfather, had worked in the mines for thirty years and was ailing from black lung disease. His grandmother, Alice Marie, was a kind and loving woman who loved to sit with the children around her and tell stories of her early years in eastern Kentucky. She also sang mountain songs and played the banjo, just as her father had taught her. Charles and his aunts and uncles loved to sit for hours on a cold winter's evening and listen to Alice Marie's songs. Sometimes she would play church hymns on her dulcimer, which Charles decided as a young boy he must learn to play.

When Charles was six years old his mother married a man named Hobart Wayne Jenkins, who lived in a nearby town. He too worked in the mines and had two sons from a previous marriage who lived with him. Charles was close to his mom but he did not want to leave his grandparents' home when she moved out. So he remained in the home where he had grown up and saw his mother on weekends at the Missionary Baptist Church where the family were members. He also would go over sometimes and help his stepbrothers with the garden they planted each year.

Charles attended the local elementary school and made above-average grades. When he was fourteen, he sneaked away from home on a Saturday night and drank some "home brew" beer which two of his friends had made. He came in at 3 a.m. and was chastised by his grandparents for not telling them of his whereabouts and for getting drunk. He went to bed and slept off his inebriation, but he decided that he liked beer a lot. This incident led to his drinking more, as during high school he hung out with an older group of boys who had cars and would get beer illegally in an adjacent county's supermarket. Charles' grades began to slip and his grandparents were worried about him. They did not know how to handle his sometimes defiant and boisterous behavior. When Charles was sixteen his grandfather passed away and he grieved inwardly without showing much emotion. However, he started using marijuana, which a friend grew on a local farm, and once gave some to his nephew who was only eleven years old.

Charles' grandmother was devastated by his behavior although she loved her grandson dearly. She called the family together, including Charles' mother and stepfather, and came up with a plan to help her grandson. The family decided to send Charles to live with his Aunt Ellie Sue who had lived in Detroit since her late teens. Ellie Sue and her husband Noah both worked at an automotive parts plant and had two daughters who were attending a local college. At first, Charles was resistant but he felt he wanted to get away from all the nagging of the family. In Detroit, he did well for a while and was making good grades. But his bad habits returned and he once again began abusing alcohol and marijuana.

The family was supportive of Charles and let him know they were committed to helping him succeed and make something out of himself. Charles' aunt and uncle did not see sending him home to West Virginia as an option. They had enrolled their daughter, Jenny, in a family therapy program offered through the local mental health center when she had used drugs and been incarcerated in juvenile detention. Now Jenny was a sophomore in college studying elementary education. Ellie Sue and Noah went with Charles to therapy each week and also joined a parent support group offered as an adjunct to the family therapy intervention. Charles learned that he was not alone in his problems. Other adolescents were also dealing with grief, self-esteem issues, and drug use. After the eight-week program, Charles was communicating more openly with his family and had stopped abusing substances. He joined an Alateen group as well and kept closer contact with the family back in West Virginia. He was homesick, but his aunt and uncle always managed to take him back home every few months. Charles said he loved Detroit but he someday wanted to go back to the mountains.

Charles worked hard in school. Not only did he finish high school but also completed a degree in engineering. He married a young woman from Toledo and they moved back to West Virginia, where Charles is now working with a coal mine and has developed a protocol for mine safety. He and his wife, Delilah, have a two-year-old son and a baby on the way. They often go over to Alice Marie's house to hear her songs and stories. They take her to church with them, as she no longer is able to drive her car due to failing vision. Charles has learned to play the mandolin and impressed the whole church recently with a mesmerizing rendition of "Blessed Be the Tie That Binds." Charles tells everyone who will listen that his family saved his life and he will never let them down again.

## QUESTIONS FOR DISCUSSION

1. Select one of the programs evaluated and state why you think the model has proven effective in increasing resilience in children and adolescents.
2. Discuss why cultural competence is such an important element of evidenced-based practice and research for promoting children's strengths.

3. Discuss several research programs in this chapter which demonstrate the collaboration of families, schools, and communities in strengthening resilience in children and adolescents.
4. Discuss how professionals can make early interventions for children and their families possible.

## REFERENCES

Alexander, J., Oygh, C., Parsons, B.V., and Sexton, T. L. (2000). Funtional family therapy. In Elliott, D. S. (Ed.), *Blueprints for violence prevention,* Book 3, Second edition (pp. 3-56). Boulder, CO: Center for the Study and Prevention of Violence, Institute of Behavioral Science, University of Colorado.

Alexander, J. and Parson, B. (1982). *Functional family therapy: Principles and procedures.* Carmel, CA: Brooks/Cole.

Alvarado, R., Kendall, K., Beesley, S., and Lee-Cavaness, C. (Eds.) (2000). *Strengthening America's families.* Washington, DC: The U.S. Office of Justice and Center for Substance Abuse Prevention of the Substance Abuse and Mental Health Services Administration.

Atkan, G. (1995). Organizational framework for a substance use prevention program. *International Journal of Addictions* 30: 185-201.

Barnett, W. S. and Escobar, C. M. (1990). Economic costs and benefits of early intervention. In Meisels, S. J. and Shonkoff, J. P. (Eds.), *Handbook of early childhood intervention* (pp. 560-582). New York: Cambridge University Press.

Bavolek, S. J. (2000). The Nurturing Parenting Programs. *Juvenile Justice Bulletin,* November. Available at <www.ncjrs.org/html/ojjdp/2000_11_1/contents>.

Bavolek, S. J. and Keene, G. R. (1999). *Adult-Adolescent Parenting Inventory-2 (AAPI-2).* Park City, UT: Family Development Resources, Inc.

Bavolek, S. J., Kline, D. F., and McLaughlin, J. A. (1979). Primary prevention of child abuse: Identification of high risk adolescents. *Child Abuse and Neglect: The International Journal* 3: 1071-1080.

Berlin, L. J., Brooks-Gunn, J., McCarton, C., and McCormick, M.C. (1998). The effectiveness of early intervention: Examining risk factors and pathways to enhanced development. *Preventative Medicine* 27(2): 238-245.

Bernard, B. (1996). Creating resiliency-enhancing schools: Relationships, motivating beliefs, and schoolwide reform. *Resiliency in Action,* Spring, pp. 5-8.

Berruta-Clement, J., Schweinhar, L., Barnett, W., Epstein, A., and Weikart, D. (1984). *Changed lives: The effects of the Perry Preschool Program on youth age 19.* Ypsilanti, MI: High/Scope Press.

Block, A. W. and Block, S. R. (2002). Strengthening social work approaches through advancing knowledge of early childhood intervention. *Child and Adolescent Social Work Journal* 19(3): 191-208.

Bronfenbrenner, U. (1992). The process-person-context model in developmental research principles, application, and implications. Unpublished manuscript. Ithaca, NY: Cornell University.

Carpenter, B. (1997). Early intervention and identification: Finding the family. *Children and Society* 11(3): 173-182.

Forehand, R. L. and McMahon, R. J. (1981). *Helping the noncompliant child: A clinician's guide to parent training.* New York: Guilford Press.

Garmezy, N. (1985). Stress-resistant children: The search for protective factors. In Stevenson, J. E. (Ed.), Recent research in developmental psychopathology. *Journal of Child Psychology and Psychiatry,* book supplement No. 4 (pp. 213-233). Oxford: Pergamon.

Gordon, D. A., Arbruthnot, J., Gustafson, K. A., and McGreen, P. (1998). Home based behavioral-systems family therapy with disadvantaged juvenile delinquents. *American Journal of Family Therapy* 16(3): 243-255.

Guerney, B. G. Jr. (1977). *Relationship enhancement skills training program for therapy: Problem prevention and enrichment.* San Francisco: Jossey-Bass.

Hill, P. (1998). The state of knowledge: Family in-home support in pregrancy and early childhood. Presentation at Center for Substance Abuse Prevention conference, Washington, DC, October 5-6.

Jenson, W. R. (1980). *CBTU Parenting Program.* Salt Lake City, UT: Children's Behavior Therapy Unit, Salt Lake County Mental Health.

Kameoke, V. A. (1996). The effects of a family-focused intervention on reducing risk for substance abuse among Asian and Pacific-Island youths and families: Evaluation of the Strengthening Hawaii's Families Project. Honolulu: University of Hawaii, Social Welfare Evaluation and Research Unit.

Karoly, A. A., Greenwood, P. W., Everingham, S. S., Hoube, J., Kilburn, M. R., Rydell, C. P., Sanders, M., and Chiesa, J. (1998). *Investing in our children: What we know and don't know about the cost and benefits of early childhood interventions.* Santa Monica, CA: Rand Corporation.

Klein, N. C., Alexander, J. F., and Parsons, B. V. (1977). Impact of family systems intervention on recidivism and sibling delinquency: A model of primary prevention and program evaluation. *Journal of Consulting and Clinical Psychology* 45(3): 469-474.

Kumpfer, K. L. (1990). Services and programs for children and families. Paper presented at the National Forum of the Future of Children and Families: Workshop on Children and Parental Illicit Drug Use. National Academy of Sciences, Washington, DC.

Kumpfer, K. L. (1999). Factors and processes contributing to resilience: The resilience framework. In Glantz, M. D. and Johnson, J. L. (Eds.), *Resilience and development: Positive life adaptations* (pp. 179-224). New York: Kluwer Academic/Plenum Publishers.

Kumpfer, K. L. and Alder, S. (1998). Family interventions for the prevention of drug abuse: The need to disseminate research based programs with effective results. Draft, October 5.

Kumpfer, K. L. and DeMarsh, J. P. (1985). Prevention of chemical dependency in children of alcohol and drug abusers. *NIDA Notes* 5: 2-3.

Kumpfer, K. L. and Turner, C. W. (1990/1991). The social ecology model of adolescent substance abuse: Implications for prevention. *The International Journal of the Addictions* 25(4A): 435-463.

Liddle, H. A. and Dakof, G. A. (1995). Efficacy of family therapy for drug abuse: Promising but not definitive. (Special issue on the state of the art of family therapy research). *Journal of Marital and Family Therapy* 21(4): 511-543.

Masten, A. S. (1996). Fostering resiliency in kids: Overcoming adversity. Transcript of proceedings of a Congressional Breakfast Seminar, March 29, 1996, sponsored by the Consortium of Social Science Associations, pp. 19-24.

Masten, A. S. (1998). Research-based programs. Available at <http://www.mentalhealth.org/specials/schoolviolence/5-28Resilience.htm>.

Miller-Heyl, J., MacPhee, D., and Fritz, J. J. (1998). Dare to Be You: A family-support, early intervention program. *Journal of Primary Prevention* 18(3): 257-285.

Mills, R. (1997a). Comprehensive health realization community empowerment projects: List of completed and current projects. Unpublished paper.

Mills, R. (1997b). Psychology of mind-health realization: Summary of clinical prevention, and community empowerment applications documented outcomes. Unpublished paper.

Molgaard, V., Kumpfer, K. L., and Spoth, R. (1994). *The Iowa Strengthening Families Program for Pre and Early Teens.* Ames: Iowa State University.

Moos, R. H. (1994). *Family environmental scale manual,* Third edition. Palo Alto, CA: Consulting Psychologists Press.

Pierce, L. H. and Shields, N. (1998). The Be a Star community-based after-school program: Developing resiliency factors in high-risk preadolescent youth. *Journal of Community Psychology* 26(2): 175-183.

Pransky, G. S., Mills, R. C., Sedgeman, J.A., and Blevens, K. (1997). An emerging paradigm for brief treatment and prevention. In Vandecreek, L., Knapp, S., and Jackson, T. L. (Eds.), *Innovations in clinical practice: A source book,* Volume 15 (pp. 401-421). Sarasota, FL: Professional Resource Press.

Public/Private Ventures (1995). *Making a difference: An impact study of Big Brothers/Big Sisters.* Philadelphia: Public/Private Ventures. November.

Reynolds, A. J. (1998). Developing early childhood programs for children and families at risk: Research-based principles to promote long-term effectiveness. *Children and Youth Services Review* 20(6): 503-523.

Richardson, G. E., Neiger, B. L., Jensen, S., and Kumpfer, K. L. (1990). The resiliency model. *Health Education* 21(6): 33-39.

Saxton, T. L. and Alexander, J. F. (2000). Functional family therapy. *Juvenile Justice Bulletin,* December. Available at <www.ncjrs.org/html/ojjdp/jjbu/2000_12_4/contents/>.

Schweinhart, L. and Weikart, D. (1986). Consequences of three preschool curriculum models through age 15. *Early Childhood Research Quarterly* 1(1): 15-45.

Schweinhart, L. and Weikart, D. (1997). *Lasting differences: The High/Scope Preschool Curriculum Comparison Study through age 23*. Ypsilanti, MI: High/Scope Press.

Smith, M. K. (1998). *Adolescents with severe emotional and behavioral disabilities: Transition to adulthood*. Lewiston, NY: Mellen Press.

Spivak, G. and Shure, M. (1979). Interpersonal cognitive problem solving and primary prevention: Programming for preschool and kindergarten children. *Journal of Clinical and Child Psychology* 9(2): 89-94.

Szapocznik, J., Perez-Vidal, A., Brickman, A., Foote, F. H., Santisteban, D., Hervis, O., and Kurtines, W. H. (1988). Engaging adolescent drug abusers and their families into treatment: A strategic structural systems approach. *Journal of Consulting and Clinical Psychology* 56(4): 552-557.

Szapocznik, J., Rio, A., Murray, E., Cohen, R., Scopetta, M. A., Rivas-Vasquez, A., Hervis, O. E., and Poseda, V. (1989). Structural family versus psychodynamic child therapy for problematic Hispanic boys. *Journal of Consulting and Clinical Psychology* 57(5): 571-578.

# Chapter 11

# Empowerment of Children in the Global Arena

Love is a fruit in season at all times, and within reach of every hand.

Mother Teresa

Children in the twenty-first century will have more opportunities for growth, development, and well-being than in previous decades. The twentieth century was called the Century of the Child and many advancements helped children thrive, receive proper health care, and be protected from their own families as well as from threats from society at large. Landmark legislation was passed to protect children's rights at home, at school, and within society. The twentieth century saw the birth of the Social Security Act and other life-changing pieces of legislation such as child labor laws, child protection laws, education for the handicapped laws, and family preservation laws, just to mention a few.

In the United States since 1973 the Children's Defense Fund, founded by Marian Wright Edelman, has followed the mission to "Leave No Child Behind" (Children's Defense Fund, 2002b). The Children's Defense Fund has, for three decades, attempted to ensure that all children transition to adulthood with the support of nurturing and supportive families and communities. The Children's Defense Fund reminds us that every forty-four seconds a baby is born into poverty, every minute a baby is born without health insurance, every minute a baby is born to a teen mother, and every two hours a child or youth under twenty is killed by a firearm. Moreover, it is estimated that 9 million children under nineteen have no health insurance and that 90 percent of these children live in working families (Children's Defense Fund, 2002a). Through programs such as Healthy Start and Head Start, the Children's Defense Fund continues to work for the safety and security of all children and to promote their well-being in all aspects of daily life.

Internationally, the United Nations International Children's Emergency Fund (UNICEF), through its unfailing commitment to the rights and well-being of children around the globe, passed a Rights of the Child treatise, which is far-reaching in its commitment to protecting all children's rights to be safe, healthy, educated, and happy. The Convention on the Rights of the Child (CRC) was initiated in 1989 and marked the thirtieth anniversary of the Declaration of Children's Rights and the tenth anniversary of International Year of the Child (United Nations General Assembly, 1989). The most recent Convention on the Rights of the Child, held in 2002, proclaims the CRC to be the first legally binding international instrument to incorporate the full range of human rights— civil, political, economic, and cultural. One hundred ninety-one countries ratified the document, a greater number than has supported any other human rights document. The CRC is composed of fifty-four articles, which define principles, different types of rights, and mechanisms for monitoring and implementation. UNICEF's executive director proclaimed that the twentieth century began with children having virtually no rights and ended with children having the most powerful legal instrument that not only recognizes but also protects their human rights. The Convention on the Rights of the Child sets forth a collection of standards and obligations that are universally agreed upon and nonnegotiable. The children's rights set forth by UNICEF may be categorized into four major areas:

1. The right to survival
2. The right to develop to the fullest
3. The right to protection from harmful influences, abuse, and exploitation
4. The right to participate fully in family, cultural, and social life (UNICEF, 2002)

Alderson (1993) states that the CRC rights may be divided into three distinct categories:

1. Rights to resources and care—good hospital care, food, warmth, safety, and parents' loving care
2. Rights to protection from harm—from neglect and abuse, fear, pain, and loneliness, and too many medical interventions or the neglect of being denied necessary treatment
3. Rights to self-determination—dignity, respect, integrity, non-interference, and the right to make personal informed decisions (p. 13)

The U.N. Convention on the Rights of the Child exemplifies the social work definition of empowerment, which Barbara Solomon (1976) defines as facilitating clients' connection with their own power and, in turn, being empowered by the very act of reaching across cultural barriers. Empowerment is a vital process for children so that they are able to benefit from innate resources that buffer them against multiple risks and strengthen their resilience for overcoming adversity. Some critics of the Rights of the Child movement fear that, if given the choice, children will deny services basic to their survival, such as health care. In looking at the care of children in hospitals, Alderson (1993) states that in many European countries children are still held in hospitals and residential facilities for the treatment of problems that could be handled at home. In the United Kingdom, children form the only group that is not protected from assault. However, Austria is one of the few countries to ban all physical punishment by law and has a children's ombudsman.

The NASW International Policy Statement on Human Rights includes a commentary on human rights that emphasizes the human dignity, social justice, and worth of all persons. The National Association of Social Workers acknowledges the human rights declarations and treaties, all of which support the NASW Code of Ethics. NASW perceives the United Nations as providing a human rights template for enhancing the quality of life of all persons around the world. The NASW endorses the life-giving work of the United Nations and endorses its Universal Declaration of Rights, as well as the Convention on the Rights of the Child. Social workers are charged with the responsibility to address the human rights violations of child labor, child prostitution, and crimes of abuse, and are advised to be take leadership in developing public and professional awareness regarding these issues (Mayden and Nieves, 2000).

The Save the Children organization, which was founded over seventy-five years ago, reiterates the Rights of the Child Convention and states specifically why children should have rights separate from those of adults. Save the Children acknowledges that although children are referred to in human rights documents, these references are scattered and run the risk of being de-emphasized or overlooked. Save the Children advocates that children are a special case, with needs and entitlements that are different from those of adults. Therefore, their rights deserve particular attention and recognition. Save the Children states that each individual child must be protected and that conditions must be created for all children to develop their full potential. Children's rights must, therefore, reflect the special status of childhood, a time of quick change and development during which children experience different vulnerabilities. Save the Children believes that physical weakness and a lack of knowledge render most children dependent or semidependent on adults for long periods. The survival and development of children hinge on the commitment and quality of care provided to them by responsible adults (Save the Children, 2003).

## UNITED NATIONS CONVENTION
## ON THE RIGHTS OF THE CHILD

These authors have chosen not to analyze each of the forty-two articles on children's rights constituting the Convention on the Rights of the Child (CRC) but will summarize further some of the key mandates that call for a child's right to safety, personal choice, nationality, identity, cultural heritage, religious freedom, and family ties. Professionals who take the Convention on the Rights of the Child seriously will inform children of rights and procedures, listen to their views and opinions, and actively involve them in any decision making about their care (Alderson, 1992). Article 12 of the CRC addresses the rights of children as citizens and how children may contribute to any decisions on their behalf, in both administrative and judicial matters concerning their well-being. De Winter (1997) emphasizes that this proclamation comes down to our viewing children as fellow citizens who share in society and are not only appreciated but also recognized as stimulating because of the constructive contributions they are able to make. De Winter (1997) notes further that this participation, as outlined by the CRC, can be provisionally defined as opportunities for children and young people to become actively involved in decisions made about their own living arrangements.

One of the authors of this book is reminded of his involvement with a therapeutic foster care case wherein an eight-year-old African-American boy told the worker to make sure that she found a good home for his brother and him. She knelt down on the floor where he and his seven-year-old brother were playing a game and asked him to tell her what he thought a good home would be like. She listened intently as he told her he wanted loving parents who had lots of toys and had birthday parties, and would let him and his brother sit on their laps. The foster care worker told the boys that she would do her very best. The worker had taken the time to listen to this little boy who also felt that he must look out for his younger brother.

Article 19 proclaims that all states shall take appropriate legislative, administrative, social, and educational measures to protect and care for children who have been abused or neglected. Article 18 states that both parents have responsibility for the upbringing and development of a child, and that the states shall make appropriate services available to parents and legal guardians. Article 23 points out that children with mental and physical disabilities have a right to a full and decent life and that states must recognize and respond to the child's right to resources and services that will facilitate the child's participation in the community. Article 14 states that a child has the right to freedom of thought, conscience, and religion, and that the states should respect the rights of parents and legal guardians to direct the child in fulfilling these rights. Article 17 recognizes the significant role of the media, both national and international, in ensuring that the child has access to information which will promote his or her spiritual and moral well-being, as well as physical and mental health. This would also include dissemination of age-appropriate literature and information, such as children's books, which would benefit the child linguistically, socially, and culturally.

Article 21 addresses the best interests of the child in adoption and specifies that the appropriate legal and ethical measures be followed, including informed consent from all parties involved. The convention acknowledges international adoption as an alternative form of child care, if a child cannot be cared for suitably in his or her own country of origin. International adoptions must follow standards that are equivalent to those pertaining to national adoption and not bring about financial gain for those involved in the adoption process.

Forrester and Harwin (2000) have addressed UNICEF's initiatives in developing indicators to measure the compliance of countries who ratified the first United Nations Convention on the Rights of the Child. Although these countries are mandated to submit reports on the measures they have developed to implement the convention, there is no standardization. Much concern is given to the fact that there is no standardized tool to measure the maltreatment of children globally. However, progress is being made to enhance awareness of child abuse and neglect and the efforts to measure child maltreatment on an international scale.

## INTERNATIONAL ADOPTIONS

International adoptions bring millions of children to the United States from countries where they might otherwise receive less than optimal care or even remain in a residential institution until they are able to fend for themselves. Since 1989, the number of children in institutional care has risen by 45 percent in Romania and Russia, and by as much as 75 percent in Latvia (Harper, 1997). Due to poverty and the lack of government support, most of these children are being denied basic rights to proper nutrition, education, health services, shelter, and protection. In the People's Republic of China, estimates are that more than 100,000 homeless children, 98 percent of them girls, are available for adoption. The largest country in the world by population, China has 1.2 billion people, which prompted the nation to impose a one-child policy in 1979. Almost all Chinese families, especially in rural areas, will keep a son and cast aside a daughter, who generally ends up in an orphanage (Miller-Loessi and Zeynep, 2001). China has a strict licensing requirement for international adoption and has bilateral adoption agreements with fourteen countries: Australia, Belgium, Canada, Denmark, Finland, France, Ireland, the Netherlands, New Zealand, Norway, Spain, Sweden, the United Kingdom, and the United States. By the year 2000, China had become the largest source of foreign adoptions in the United States, with Russia following closely. Many view this mass adoption of Chinese girls as a victim diaspora, but others perceive China's adoption agreements with other countries as a humane effort to empower these children with freedom and opportunities unavailable in their native land (Miller-Loessi and Zeynep, 2001).

When these children are adopted to families outside their native land, they must be given ample opportunities to know about, interact with, and identify with their culture of origin. Article 30 of the CRC specifically relates to the maintenance of a child's native culture by stating that a child must not be denied the right to enjoy his or her own culture, to profess and practice his or her own religion, or to use his or her own language. Since most Chinese-American adoptions involve a cross-racial configuration, families and professionals must be prepared to address complex questions which the child will eventually ask. In the case of Chinese girls who are adopted by Caucasian families, the parents must be prepared to explain to their daughters the circumstances of their birth and banishment from their homeland. Most of these girls are born into rural, poverty-stricken families and then later placed with middle- or upper-middle-class white families for adoption. These girls look physically different than their adoptive parents, and therefore the racial differences may not be as covert as in adoptions involving Caucasian parents and Romanian or Russian children (Miller-Loessi and Zeynep, 2001). These children may remember abandonment and other manifestations of abuse perpetrated by their families of origin. Moreover, families may need professional counseling on an ongoing basis to help them respond to their Chinese daughters' inquiries about the Chinese government's one-child policy and, even more challenging, the reasons why they were singled out for institutionalization or expulsion because of their gender.

Parents who adopt these Chinese girls have a range of options for creating a culturally competent home and community environment for them. Baden (2002) proposes a cultural-racial identity model, which addresses the multiple racial, ethnic, and cultural identity issues that often arise in transracial adoptions. Identities are based on the degrees to which persons are knowledgeable of, aware of, and competent in dealing with their own racial group's culture, as well as their parents' racial group and other racial groups. In the case of Chinese children who are adopted into Caucasian families, the parents may be able to locate both local and national resources to help them place their children closer to their culture as they grow and develop. Some families have joined a group called Families with Children from China that provides social and emotional support from other families with similar circumstances. This group, and others similar to it, may develop play groups, organize charities for children in Chinese orphanages, plan trips to mainland China, and campaign for human rights in China. Other advantages include access to language, native- speaking baby-sitters, Chinese goods (e.g., food, books, and toys), as well as celebrations of Chinese holidays, such as the Lunar New Year, the Moon Festival, and the Dragon Boat Festival. Although new to understanding Chinese culture and worldviews, these families make a strong effort to authenticate Chinese culture for their daughters by emulating Chinese traditions and activities. In essence, these adoptive parents have socially constructed a community of Chinese and American identities which hopefully will lead to a sense of cultural identity for the girls when they grow older (Miller-Loessi and Zeynep, 2001).

## *A CASE SCENARIO OF INTERNATIONAL ADOPTION*

The following case scenario of an international adoption of a Chinese girl by an American family exemplifies how these issues have been addressed.

Fong Li, age five, was adopted by a Caucasian couple, Roger and Emma Saddler, who live in a midwestern city. The Saddlers found out about Fong Li through an international adoption agency run by their church denomination. The social worker at International Child and Family Match (ICFM) was a specialist in international adoptions and had worked with multiple Asian and European countries in the adoption of children by American families. She was eager to meet with the Saddlers and set out to find out as much as possible about the couple and their reasons for wanting to be parents.

They had not been able to have children of their own because Roger had a childhood illness that caused sterility. They had wanted an infant but after waiting for over two years, they decided to try international adoption. Roger Saddler works with a local marketing firm and travels approximately one week out of each month. Emma Saddler is a pediatric nurse who plans to give up her job and stay at home once the adoption takes place. The couple was highly motivated and stated that they preferred to adopt an older child, between the ages of three and six, citing the success of Mrs. Saddler's brother who adopted a child from the Ukraine. After completing the necessary forms and approving the couple, the social worker, Laura Barnes, told the couple about a little girl, Fong Li, age five, who was born in the Hunan province to a father who worked in a paper mill and a mother who was a laundry worker. The parents already had two sons so they took Fong Li to an orphanage and abandoned her. The couple listened carefully as Ms. Barnes described the sociocultural oppression in China that has led to a high percentage of Chinese girls being placed in orphanages.

After a few months, the time arrived for the Saddlers to go to China to pick up their daughter. They had already prepared her room with every amenity a little girl might enjoy—toys, dolls, storybooks, and a stack of Disney movies. Ms. Barnes had made arrangements with the Saddlers to meet with an international adoption worker in Hong Kong, along with other American parents adopting Chinese girls. They flew to Hong Kong and met with Lee Chan, who spoke several provicincial languages and would serve as interpreter and liaison for the orphanage. The Saddlers met four other families who were adopting infants or preschoolers from the same province of China. They all met with Lee Chan, who provided information about the itinerary of the next few days and gave the families time to get acquainted to discuss their expectations and anxiety about the adoption process. The Saddlers were surprised to meet a couple, the Liddys, who were adopting an infant. Mr. Liddy was Caucasian and his wife was a biracial Chinese American whose mother also grew up in the Hunan province before she immigrated to the United States with her family in the early 1960s.

The next day the families traveled to the Hunan province where the social welfare center (the orphanage) was located. They were accompanied by Mr. Chan who made the introductions and spoke with the staff about this initial meeting. All of the parents were to meet their children that day, but then they would have to go to the U.S. Consulate to complete the necessary paperwork to obtain visas for each child. The families were then given four additional days to explore the area before going back to Hong Kong for the flight home. The older children were placed in a playroom near the main entrance and the infants were all brought to the front of the nursery to meet their new parents. The Saddlers were introduced to Fong Li by a caregiver, who obviously had bonded with the little girl but was happy to see her find a home. Mr. and Mrs. Saddler were overjoyed to finally meet their daughter and played several games with her. The caregiver interpreted for the Saddlers who had already mastered several Chinese phrases they had been studying. Fong Li smiled and was at first somewhat shy and clung to the caregiver. When she was told that she was going to have a home and a new family, she finally embraced her new parents with open arms. The next few days went fast but were filled with meals, marketplace visits, and bus tours around the region so that the Saddlers could spend time with their daughter and acquire some perspective on the culture which had given birth to their precious daughter.

The Saddlers gave Fong Li an American name, Christine Marie, after Mr. Saddler's widowed mother who lives in the same neighborhood. Christine Marie is especially fond of her daddy, and he cherishes her. He always brings her fruit, gum, or candy, which he hides in his coat pocket for her to find. Emma Saddler resigned her position as a pediatric nurse to care for

Christine Marie. The Saddlers are much attuned to cultural diversity and want their daughter to become knowledgeable of and appreciate her Chinese culture. They plan to raise their daughter in a home environment that will encourage her to understand and accept diversity and be open to new ideas. Emma Saddler's older brother, Lucian, and his wife, Stella, have four sons, but four years ago they decided to adopt an infant from the Ukraine. They had been on a waiting list for several years but finally were able to receive a baby girl, whom they named Ekaterina (a.k.a. Katya). Christine Marie has met most of her cousins, and she and Katya have become close. They enjoy spending time together, though Christine Marie sometimes gets frustrated with Katya who still gravitates toward parallel play (i.e., playing side by side without interacting with each other).

The Saddlers live in a community that is somewhat racially and ethnically diverse, but there is only a small Asian community. However, they live fifty miles from a large city which has a Chinatown area and a growing Asian-American population. The parents are determined to learn as much about Chinese culture as possible. Mr. and Mrs. Saddler have met a Chinese couple, the Chins, who have two children and live in a nearby city. The couple has taught the Saddlers to play mah-jongg, which they refer to as Chinese dominoes. Moreover, the Chins have talked to the Saddlers and introduced them to several other Chinese families who live in Chinatown, including a restaurant owner and a Chinese herbalist. They took Christine Marie to a Chinese New Year's celebration in Chinatown and she was fascinated with the silk dragons that floated above her in the parade. Consequently, her parents got her a mobile with little colorful dragons to hang in her room. The Saddlers are comfortable with their decision to immerse themselves in Chinese cultural traditions, but at the same time they want Christine Marie to appreciate her American lifestyle and traditions. As the mother said, "I want her to be truly bicultural and appreciate the best of both worlds."

The International Child and Family Match adoption agency has continued to be involved with several families in the midwestern area who have adopted Chinese girls, and Laura Barnes is leading a parent group that meets monthly to provide support and information for the families. The Saddlers were pleased to find out that the Liddys also attend this group and the two families have become close and visit socially every few weeks. Christine Marie is fascinated with the Liddys' baby, Angie, whom she adores and cannot wait to see each time the families get together. The Saddlers want to take Christine Marie back to China when she is ten years old and have considered adopting another Chinese daughter within the next few years.

## CONCLUSION

Children must be seen as competent human beings who have as much a right as anyone else in society to fulfill their basic needs, and they must not be blocked from moving toward the attainment of self-actualization. When children are perceived from the standpoint of their strengths, they are more likely to develop a positive self-image and increase their motivation to achieve. Children around the world have something in common: the right to live a safe and dignified life that allows them equal opportunities and social justice. The United Nations Convention on the Rights of the Child, Save the Children, and the Children's Defense Fund join countless other human rights and professional child care organizations in calling for rights of children and assurance that these rights will be respected and legally sanctioned. Treating children with respect not only will increase their self-confidence and belief in themselves but also will help them to be trusting of others. Alderson (1992) reports that a research study on hundreds of twelve-year-olds found that when parents expected them to be responsible, children responded in ways such that they were given even more responsibility and handled it well.

Depriving children of their basic rights and a sense of well-being not only robs them of their dignity but also reflects on the moral conscience of society at large. Robert Coles (1997) indicated that the reasoning abilities and moral capacities of many nine-year-olds are as sophisticated as those of some adults:

> We grow morally as a consequence of learning how to be with others, how to behave in this world, a learning prompted by taking to heart what we have seen and heard. The child is a witness; the child is an ever-attentive witness of grown-up morality—or lack thereof. (p. 5)

Treating our children well is a reflection of how we perceive ourselves and humankind in general. An individual's sense of what is just and right for a child will inevitably make a statement about who that individual is. Goldstein (2002) states: "We get a better understanding of what the elusive ideas of strength and resilience mean when we have a sense of the inner invincible moral voice that insists on a moral bearing" (pp. 45-46).

Each child in the twenty-first century has a right to maximize his or her strengths, skills, and hopes so that the world of tomorrow will evolve from the fulfillment of dreams that children have today.

## *STRENGTHS STORY: ANTUN (TONY) BOSKOVICH*

Antun (a.k.a. Tony) Boskovich, age seven, was born in a small Croatian village near Dubrovnik, where he lived with his older brother, Ivo, and his younger sister, Luce. His parents worked in a factory and struggled to take care of the family. When the war began, the family went into hiding in a small village where Antun's aunt, uncle, and cousins lived. Antun was always a brave little boy who tried to help his family out as much as he could, especially during difficult times. He would help his older brother, whom he adored, chop wood and pump water from the well in the village. However, during the war Antun's life changed drastically and would never be the same. His parents, his brother, and his other relatives all died in a shelling of the village. Antun was not harmed but was frightened and tried to protect his four-year-old sister, Luce.

The children wandered for days between villages in hopes of finding food and shelter. They had only two stale pieces of bread, a raw potato, and a bottle of water, which Antun carried in his father's old knapsack. The children were terrified of the night but found a place to sleep on a pile of straw in a dilapidated shed. After two days of wandering and dodging the tanks and other war artillery vehicles, they saw an American Red Cross station across a wide field. Antun took his little sister, still crying and begging for food, by the hand and headed for the safe haven of the Red Cross. About two-thirds of the way across the field, Antun stepped on a land mine, which severely injured his foot and leg. He was bleeding profusely, and he started screaming out loud for help. His little sister lay by him as he went into shock. An American soldier rescued Antun and Luce, taking them to a hospital that was staffed by American doctors. Unfortunately, Antun's leg was too badly injured to save and had to be amputated at the knee.

Antun Boskovich and his sister were then placed in an orphanage where they remained for another year. Antun walked on braces provided by the hospital and looked out for his younger sister. She did not talk for three months after his injury and seemed to be suffering from PTSD. Antun sometimes saved part of his food at dinner and took it to Luce as he feared she was not getting enough to eat. The children did well and their grief began to subside despite the multiple traumas they had experienced. Antun's leg healed enough for him to be fitted with a prosthetic leg, although a crude one. Eventually, the children were separated for international adoptive placement, which was excruciatingly painful for both of them. Antun would lie awake at night and cry when he thought of losing his whole family.

Antun was adopted by a Canadian family when he was eight years old. He joined a family of five, a mother and father with three daughters who were all younger than he. He started school in Newfoundland and his new parents, both schoolteachers, were able to have Antun fitted for an artificial leg with a fleshlike covering that looked almost like real skin. Antun was happy and convinced his parents to let him play Little League baseball. He amazed the family and his coach with his ability to catch the ball with precision and make it to a base each time he was up to bat. Antun had largely overcome the adversity of his physical disability, but he missed his sister Luce. He loved his new little sisters, ages six, four, and three, but he wanted to locate Luce. After about a year, his adoptive family was able to locate Luce, who had been adopted by a family in Maine who had no other children. Antun and Luce have visited with each other twice and keep in touch by phone on a regular basis.

Antun is now fifteen years old and a high school sophomore. He tried out for track but did not make it. However, he continues to overcome his disability in many ways and amazes his family and friends with his motivation and high self-esteem. He is studying now to get a driver's permit, and last spring he ran in a local marathon, which he managed to finish. Despite his new life in Canada, Antun never forgot his roots and his family. He tells his parents regularly: "I just kept on going; otherwise I might not have been able to save Luce and myself." And that has become Antun's motto for life.

## QUESTIONS FOR DISCUSSION

1. Discuss the United Nations Convention on the Rights of The Child and how it protects the rights of children worldwide.
2. What are some efforts that Save the Children and the Children's Bureau have made to ensure the safety and well-being of children in the United States?
3. What are several factors that should be considered for international adoptions?
4. Discuss the ethical dilemmas endemic in the diaspora affecting Chinese girls.

# REFERENCES

Alderson, P. (1992). The rights of children and young people. In Coote, A. (Ed.), *The welfare of citizens developing new social rights.* London: Institute for Policy and Research/Rivers Oram Press.

Alderson, P. (1993). European charter of children's rights. *Bulletin of Medical Ethics* October: 13-15.

Baden, A. (2002). The psychological adjustment of transracial adoptees: An application of the cultural-racial identity model. *Journal of Social Distress and the Homeless* 11(2): 167-191.

Children's Defense Fund (2002a). CHIP, Medicaid, and Uninsured children. Available at <www.childrensdefense.org/childhealth/chip/>.

Children's Defense Fund (2002b). Marian Wright Edelman. Available at <www.childrensdefense.org/about/mwe.asp>.

Coles, R. (1997). *The moral intelligence of children.* New York: Random House.

De Winter, M. (1997). *Children as fellow citizens: Participation and commitment.* Abingdon, United Kingdom: Radcliffe Medical Press.

Forrester, D. and Harwin, J. (2000). Monitoring children's rights globally: Can child abuse be measured internationally? *Child Abuse Review* 9(6): 427-438.

Goldstein, H. (2002). The literary and moral foundations of the strengths perspective. In Saleebey, D. (Ed.), *The strengths perspective in social work practice,* Third edition (pp. 23-47). Boston: Allyn and Bacon.

Harper, C. (1997). Their future, our future. People's Recovery, Empowerment, and Development Assistance Foundation, Inc. Available at <www.preda.org/archives/research/r01110601.html>.

Mayden, R. W. and Nieves, J. (2000). *Social work speaks: National Association of Social Workers policy statements 2000-2003,* Fifth edition. Washington, DC: NASW.

Miller-Loessi, K. and Zeynep, K. (2001). A unique diaspora: The case of adopted girls from the People's Republic of China. *Diaspora* 10(2): 243-260.

Save the Children (2003). Welcome to savethechildren.org.uk. Available at <www.savethechildren.org.uk/scuk/>.

Solomon, B. (1976). *Black empowerment.* New York: Columbia University Press.

UNICEF (2002). Convention on the Rights of the Child. Available at <www.unicef.org/crc/crc.htm>.

United Nations General Assembly (1989). U.N. Convention on the Rights of the Child. U.N. General Assembly Document A/RES/44/25. Available at <www.cirp.org/library/ethics/UN-convention>.

# Epilogue

Children survive circumstances each day that many could not even imagine. Their strengths and resilience provide them with the ability to overcome risk factors that have the power to destroy their will and motivation to succeed. Children and adolescents in the twenty-first century will face new challenges and crises that will test their fortitude and their capacity to achieve in the midst of uncertain conditions. Families must realize the powerful, ongoing effect they have on their children's lives, the choices they make, and the contributions they make to the world around them. Children are vulnerable to what those around them think and often look to others for some validation of their worth. However, key individuals in children's lives can serve as role models and help them to realize their strengths and assets. As children interact with peers and are socialized to societal institutions, they will not only test their competencies and skills but also search for ways to improve their quality of life. Families, school personnel, and community professionals have many avenues for extending their time and energy to help a child with the process of self-awareness and self-discovery. A little praise goes a long way in helping children develop a sense of well-being and pride in what they do well.

Children will almost always tell you what they need, and this should be the central focus of any child-centered intervention. For over a century professionals in the helping disciplines have evaluated and intervened with children from a problem-focused perspective, rather than looking at the child as a total human being. This rather linear approach to assessment and treatment can easily lead to labeling and stereotyping children. Moreover, problem-focused approaches to understanding children tend to target only those children whose problems have been brought to the attention of professionals. By focusing on a child's strengths and resilience, professionals in the primary child care fields may take a closer look at the total child in reference to how the child copes with life in general. Intervention models that take into consideration the internal makeup of the child are more likely to recognize and support strengths and assets, as well as the child's limitations. Considering internal protective factors in children, along with those in the social environment, will help children to counteract and overcome those risk factors that can hinder growth and development and lead to maladaptation.

Considering the strengths and well-being of children provides a proactive and holistic approach to helping children develop a strong sense of self in an ever-changing world. Professionals working in a world that is becoming more culturally diverse and has limited resources must not forget or minimize the power and resilience within children to bring about changes in the future. Children learn quickly how those around them affect the fulfillment of their wants and needs and are insightful about their world. Professionals, as well as all other influential adults, should intently listen to the voice of the child.

# Index

## Order a copy of this book with this form or online at:
*http://www.haworthpress.com/store/product.asp?sku=5078*

# MENTAL HEALTH PRACTICE WITH CHILDREN AND YOUTH
# A Strengths and Well-Being Model

_____in hardbound at $39.95 (ISBN: 0-7890-1574-9)

_____in softbound at $24.95 (ISBN: 0-7890-1575-7)

Or order online and use special offer code HEC25 in the shopping cart.

COST OF BOOKS_____

POSTAGE & HANDLING_____
*(US: $4.00 for first book & $1.50*
*for each additional book)*
*(Outside US: $5.00 for first book*
*& $2.00 for each additional book)*

SUBTOTAL_____

IN CANADA: ADD 7% GST_____

STATE TAX_____
*(NY, OH, MN, CA, IL, IN, & SD residents,*
*add appropriate local sales tax)*

**FINAL TOTAL_____**
*(If paying in Canadian funds,*
*convert using the current*
*exchange rate, UNESCO*
*coupons welcome)*

☐ **BILL ME LATER:** (Bill-me option is good on
US/Canada/Mexico orders only; not good to
jobbers, wholesalers, or subscription agencies.)
☐ Check here if billing address is different from
shipping address and attach purchase order and
billing address information.

Signature_____

☐ **PAYMENT ENCLOSED: $**_____

☐ **PLEASE CHARGE TO MY CREDIT CARD.**

☐ Visa ☐ MasterCard ☐ AmEx ☐ Discover
☐ Diner's Club ☐ Eurocard ☐ JCB
Account # _____

Exp. Date_____

Signature_____

Prices in US dollars and subject to change without notice.

NAME_____

INSTITUTION_____

ADDRESS_____

CITY_____

STATE/ZIP_____

COUNTRY_____ COUNTY (NY residents only)_____

TEL_____ FAX_____

E-MAIL_____

May we use your e-mail address for confirmations and other types of information? ☐ Yes ☐ No
We appreciate receiving your e-mail address and fax number. Haworth would like to e-mail or fax special
discount offers to you, as a preferred customer. **We will never share, rent, or exchange your e-mail address
or fax number.** We regard such actions as an invasion of your privacy.

*Order From Your Local Bookstore or Directly From*
**The Haworth Press, Inc.**
10 Alice Street, Binghamton, New York 13904-1580 • USA
TELEPHONE: 1-800-HAWORTH (1-800-429-6784) / Outside US/Canada: (607) 722-5857
FAX: 1-800-895-0582 / Outside US/Canada: (607) 771-0012
E-mailto: orders@haworthpress.com

**For orders outside US and Canada,** you may wish to order through your local
sales representative, distributor, or bookseller.
For information, see http://haworthpress.com/distributors

*(Discounts are available for individual orders in US and Canada only, not booksellers/distributors.)*
PLEASE PHOTOCOPY THIS FORM FOR YOUR PERSONAL USE.
http://www.HaworthPress.com                                          BOF04